# Understand
# Patterns of

## George Pan Kouloukis

*Take Charge of Your Destiny!*

**RED**Feather

MIND | BODY | SPIRIT

An Imprint of Schiffer Publishing

Published by Red Feather Mind Body Spirit
An Imprint of Schiffer Publishing, Ltd.
4880 Lower Valley Road
Atglen, PA 19310
Phone: (610) 593-1777; Fax: (610) 593-2002
E-mail: Info@schifferbooks.com
Web: www.schifferbooks.com

For our complete selection of fine books on this and related subjects, please visit our website at www.schifferbooks.com. You may also write for a free catalog.

Schiffer Publishing's titles are available at special discounts for bulk purchases for sales promotions or premiums. Special editions, including personalized covers, corporate imprints, and excerpts, can be created in large quantities for special needs. For more information, contact the publisher.

We are always looking for people to write books on new and related subjects. If you have an idea for a book, please contact us at proposals@schifferbooks.com.

# CONTENTS

Introduction .................................................................4
Chapter 1. The Alternations of Seasons ...............................6
Chapter 2. The Advantages ...........................................15
Chapter 3. Ludwig van Beethoven....................................20
Chapter 4. Giuseppe Verdi ............................................27
Chapter 5. Pablo Picasso................................................34
Chapter 6. Mikhail Gorbachev ........................................43
Chapter 7. The Dalai Lama of Tibet ..................................48
Chapter 8. Margaret Thatcher ........................................55
Chapter 9. Elizabeth Taylor ...........................................61
Chapter 10. Jackie Kennedy Onassis ................................67
Chapter 11. Christopher Columbus...................................73
Chapter 12. Queen Elizabeth I of England ..........................79
Chapter 13. Napoleon I..................................................86
Chapter 14. Victor Hugo ................................................93
Chapter 15. August Rodin.............................................100
Chapter 16. Winston Churchill .......................................106
Chapter 17. Aristotle Onassis.........................................117
Chapter 18. Nelson Mandela .........................................129
Chapter 19. Maria Callas..............................................137
Chapter 20. Sarah Bernhardt ........................................146
Chapter 21. Josephine, Napoleon's wife ...........................153
Chapter 22. King Henry VIII of England .............................160
Chapter 23. Jimmy Carter ............................................167
Chapter 24. John Glenn................................................173
Epilogue ..................................................................178
Endnotes .................................................................180
Bibliography ............................................................192

# INTRODUCTION

Great German composer Ludwig van Beethoven went through a bad period of his life around the age of thirty-two because he had become totally deaf. Contemplating suicide, he wrote his will. But later, he overcame his hearing problem, was recognized as one of the greatest composers of all time—he wrote nine insuperable symphonies—and became a celebrated member of Viennese society.

Napoleon provides another such an example. During the years 1792 to 1809, he conquered almost all of Europe, was crowned Emperor of France, and lived a life full of grandeur, triumph, and success. But then things reversed: Napoleon lost all he had achieved, he was defeated at the Battle of Waterloo, and he was exiled ultimately to the remote island of St. Helena.

All of us have had alternations of good and bad seasons in our lives; great men are no exception. These seasons of our lives alternate from good to bad and vice versa according to a certain pattern. A good season gives its place to a bad, and a bad season gives its place to a good one—and so on. In this book, I explain in detail that pattern, based on the way the good and bad seasons have alternated in the lives of lots of famous men and women.

The existence of that pattern confirms, of course, that all of us are in a position to *foresee* how our own good and bad seasons will alternate *in the future*. The moment you've finished reading this book, you'll be able to learn whether the years just ahead are good or bad for you, and how long this season will last. You'll be able thus to act accordingly: if there is a storm on the horizon, you'll take shelter in time; if sunny days loom ahead, you'll take advantage of it before the opportunity passes. In short, you'll be able to make crucial decisions regarding your career, marriage, family, relationships, and all of life's other issues.

This knowledge radically transforms the way we all live today, and helps us to live a much better life. I explain first in this book how our seasons alternate from good to bad ones and vice versa and how you can foresee how your seasons will alternate in the future. Then, I cite all the advantages and benefits derived from this ability.

The results are astonishing, all helping us to live a much better life. You will see among other things, why you mustn't be seized by despair and pessimism when you are in a bad season—fearing that this season will never end. Winston Churchill, for example, failed his exams in school again and again when he was in a bad season of his life, and at a moment of another of his bad seasons he said: "I am done; I am finished." But, later, he became prime minister of his country.

You will also see why you can dare when you are in a good season—fate is with you. Christopher Columbus, for example, succeeded in discovering the New World since he was in a good season of his life, despite the fact that almost everybody—the Spanish royal council included—was skeptical and had rejected his idea. There are many other benefits deriving from our lives' alternations of seasons, as you will see in detail.

Some of you may not have noticed that there are good and bad seasons in your life, so you might have a hard time believing these seasons exist. To be convinced, you only have to look back over your life using the methods I explain in this book. Before continuing, however, we will see, in Chapter 1, that follows what derives *in brief* from those people's lives.

# Chapter 1
# THE ALTERNATIONS OF SEASONS

From the alternations of the good and bad seasons in the lives of famous people, very important observations are extracted. We start with Beethoven's alternations of good and bad seasons. As we'll see in Chapter 3, his good and bad seasons alternated in 1776, 1792, 1809, and 1825. Between each of these dates there are 16–17 years. Between 1776 and 1792 there are 16 years, while between 1792 and 1809 there are 17 years. The same also happens in the following two dates: between 1809 and 1825, there are again 16 years.

However, this alternation of seasons every 16–17 years happens in the lives of *all* people. Great Italian composer Verdi's, for example, good and bad seasons in his life alternated in 1842, 1859, 1875, and 1892 (as we will see in Chapter 4). Again, between each of these dates there are constantly 16–17 years. Between 1842 and 1859 there are 17 years, while between 1859 and 1875 there are 16 years. The same also happens in the following two dates: between 1875 and 1892, there are again 17 years.

Famous Spanish painter Pablo Picasso's good and bad seasons alternated in 1892, 1908, 1925, 1941, and 1957, and between each one of these dates there are constantly 16–17 years. The same happens with the Dalai Lama of Tibet, former US President Jimmy Carter, and America's national hero John Glenn. The dates of seasonal alternations (1941, 1957, 1974, 1990) each show 16–17 years between them. The dates of seasonal alternation for Napoleon (1776, 1792, 1809), Winston Churchill (1875, 1892, 1908, 1924, 1941), King Henry VIII of England (1496, 1512, 1529, 1545), or Christopher Columbus (1479, 1496) have a constant distance between each one of 16–17 years.

This observation creates the first base of our discovery. We proceed with our second observation.

# Alternations According to a Certain Pattern

From the alternations of good and bad seasons in the lives of the people that we'll consider in this book, it can also be derived that the alternations of their seasons did not happen irregularly or at random but according to a certain pattern. As we'll see in Chapter 3, Beethoven's seasons alternated in 1776, 1792, 1809, 1825, while we'll see that Chapter 4 Verdi's seasons alternated in 1842, 1859, 1875, 1892. Connecting the dates of these two men we see that their seasons alternated in a continuous row of dates, this: 1776, 1792, 1809, 1825, 1842, 1859, 1875, 1892—every 16–17 years.

An alternation of seasons according to a certain pattern is also observed in the seasons of Verdi (1825, 1842, 1859, 1875) and of Pablo Picasso. As we'll see later, Picasso's seasons alternated in 1892, 1908, 1925, 1941, 1957. Connecting the dates of these two men, we see that their seasons alternated at a continuous row of dates: 1825, 1842, 1859, 1875, 1892, 1908, 1925, 1941, 1957—every 16–17 years. We continue combining the dates of seasons of Picasso (1892, 1908, 1925, 1941, 1957) and of the Dalai Lama (1941, 1957, 1974, 1990). Their lives' seasons also alternated in a continuous row of dates— every 16–17 years: 1892, 1908, 1925, 1941, 1957, 1974, 1990.

If we put in a row the dates of the seasonal alternations in the lives of all the above four men (Beethoven, Verdi, Picasso, Dalai Lama) we now find that their seasons' alternations happened in a continuous row of dates—covering a period of more than 220 years—specifically this: 1776, 1792, 1809, 1825, 1842, 1859, 1875, 1892, 1908, 1925, 1941, 1957, 1974, 1990—every 16–17 years.

The same phenomenon is also observed in the lives of the other six men researched in this book: Napoleon the great, great French poet and playwright Victor Hugo, famous French sculptor August Rodin, famous British politician Winston Churchill, Greek tycoon shipowner Aristotle Onassis, and South Africa's national hero Nelson Mandela. If we put in a row the dates of the seasonal alternations in the lives of these six men, we find that their seasons' alternations also happened in a continuous row of dates, again covering a period of more than 220 years: 1776, 1792, 1809, 1825, 1842, 1859, 1875, 1892, 1908, 1925, 1941, 1957, 1974, 1990—every 16–17 years.

As mentioned, the same phenomenon is observed in the lives of *all* other people. We'll see the dates of the seasonal alternations in the lives of Margaret Thatcher, Elizabeth Taylor, Jacqueline Kennedy Onassis, Napoleon's I wife Josephine, famous French actress Sarah Bernhardt, Jimmy Carter, astronaut John Glenn, and famous Greek opera singer Maria Callas.

The conclusion is, therefore, that the alternations of seasons in the lives of all people we'll see in this book did not happen irregularly or at random but according to a certain pattern in a continuous row of certain dates—covering a period of more than 220 years—specifically: 1776, 1792, 1809, 1825, 1842, 1859, 1875, 1892, 1908, 1925, 1941, 1957, 1974, 1990—every 16–17 years. This observation creates the second base of our discovery. We continue with our next observation.

# A Period of More than 500 Years

Our next observation is this: the alternations of seasons started more than 500 years ago. As you will see in the life of Christopher Columbus, who lived more than 500 years ago, the seasons of his life alternated in 1479, 1496. If we extend these dates every 16–17 years, we arrive at the year 1990—this way: 1496, 1512, 1529, 1545, 1562, 1578, 1595, 1611, 1628, 1644, 1661, 1677, 1694, 1710, 1727, 1744, 1760, 1776, 1792, 1809, 1825, 1842, 1859, 1875, 1892, 1908, 1925, 1941, 1957, 1974, 1990. This is a period of more than 500 years.

The same observation also comes from the life of King Henry VIII of England, who also lived more than 500 years ago. His life shows that his seasons alternated in 1496, 1512, 1529, and 1545. If we again extend these dates every 16–17 years, we also arrive at the year 1990—exactly as above again. Also from Queen Elizabeth's I of England life—who lived more than 450 years ago—the same phenomenon is observed. Her life's good and bad seasons alternated in 1545, 1562, 1578, 1595, as we'll see in her biography. If we again extend these dates every 16–17 years, we also arrive at the year 1990—exactly as above.

The conclusion is, therefore, that the alternations of seasons we'll see in this book start more than 500 years ago, and they continue until 1990 and beyond.

# Two Courses of Seasons

As you will see later, Napoleon's alternations of seasons in his life happened *at the same dates* as those of Beethoven (1776, 1792, and 1809). But there is a significant difference in their seasonal alternations: While in 1776 a *good* season started for Beethoven, on the contrary, a *bad* season started for Napoleon that same year. Similarly, while in the next date 1792, a bad season started for Beethoven; on the contrary, a good season started for Napoleon that same year. Also, in the next date, 1809, a good season started for Beethoven, while a bad season started for Napoleon the same year.

The same phenomenon is also observed in the lives of other men, too. Victor Hugo's dates of his seasonal alternations (1825, 1842, 1859, 1875) are the same as Verdi's, but their seasons are opposite: when a good season for Hugo begins, a bad one starts for Verdi and vice versa; when a bad season starts for Hugo, a good one begins for Verdi. The same also happens with the dates of the Dalai Lama of Tibet and Nelson Mandela (1941, 1957, 1974, 1990).

The same phenomena are also observed in the lives of *all* people featured in this book. The conclusion we will derive is that there are *two opposite* courses of seasons in the lives of the people we'll see. The seasons of people belonging to one course are opposite to those of the people belonging to the other course. One course starts with Beethoven and continues with Verdi, Picasso, Gorbachev, the Dalai Lama, Thatcher, Taylor, Kennedy Onassis, Columbus, and Queen Elizabeth I. The other course starts with Napoleon and continues with Hugo, Rodin, Churchill, Onassis, Mandela, Josephine, Bernhardt, Carter, Glenn, Callas, and King Henry VIII.

The reversal of seasons is analogous to the climatic seasons on our earth. When there is winter in the Northern Hemisphere, there is summer in the Southern Hemisphere. And vice versa: when there is winter in Australia, South America, and South Africa, there is summer in Europe, North America, and Asia. For convenience, we'll call the pattern that starts with Beethoven, the first course; we'll call the opposite pattern, which starts with Napoleon, the second course.

# Men and Women, Equally

Our next observation is this: the conclusions we have arrived at up to now are valid not only for men, but also for women. The seasons in the lives of women alternated every 16–17 years at the same dates as those of the men, and also in two opposite courses. The seasons of the women Thatcher, Taylor, and Kennedy, for example, alternated at the dates 1941, 1957, 1974, 1990, exactly as the seasons of two of the men, the Dalai Lama and Gorbachev. These three women and two men belong to the first course of seasons as we have seen before.

The same similarity is also observed in the lives of women and men who belong to the second course of seasons. Josephine's seasons alternated in the same dates as those of Napoleon (1776, 1792, 1809). Sarah Bernhardt's seasons alternated in the same dates as those of August Rodin (1859, 1875, 1892, 1909). Maria Callas' dates of her seasonal alternations (1941, 1957, 1974) are the same as these of Onassis, Mandela, Carter, and Glenn.

All the findings we have seen, therefore, in this chapter are valid for both men and women.

# The Seasons of Ordinary People

But the prior findings are not valid only for famous people—they are also valid for "ordinary people" like you and me. Indeed, there is no indication or any reason to assume that the alternations of the seasons in the lives of an ordinary person must be *different* than those of the famous people researched here.

A first confirmation of this comes from the life of Josephine, Napoleon's wife. Some people might not consider her an ordinary person. But as you will see in her biography, Josephine was an insignificant woman in the early periods of her life, reduced to the role of courtesan, until the age of thirty-eight. Although her husband, Napoleon, later named her an empress for five years, she didn't become a *ruling empress*, and she remained in his shadow and at his mercy. When Napoleon divorced her at age forty-six, she continued being an insignificant person until her death. However, her life's good and bad seasons alternated exactly the same way as those of famous people, though she was an ordinary person.

From my own life I derive that the alternations of seasons in the lives of ordinary people are not different than those of famous people. I will report in detail how I arrived at this conclusion. Like most of us, I too, observed in my life that a certain obvious alternation of my seasons from good to bad and vice versa had occurred. Later, I asked myself whether these alternations happened according to a certain pattern—and thus could we foresee how long each season would last—or irregularly, without any pattern. But since it appeared to me too difficult to find the answer to this question, I abandoned every such idea.

Suddenly, however, a book arrived in my hands (*The Universe*, published by Time-Life Books), which gave me the first impulse to continue trying to find whether our seasons alternate according to a certain pattern or irregularly. The book mentioned that the magnetic poles of the sun reverse themselves every 11 years: the North Pole becomes the South Pole and vice versa every 11 years. That reversal always occurs on certain dates: somewhere in 1957, in 1968, in 1979, and so on every 11 years. These solar alternations led me to a spontaneous thought: Do the alternations of the sun's poles influence human behavior? Are the alternations of the good and bad seasons of life synchronized with the patterns of solar activity?

To test this hypothesis, I reflected on my own life. But my hypothesis proved to be wrong: my life's good and bad seasons hadn't alternated the way the sun's poles reverse —every 11 years. All I could come up with, however, was a turning point in 1957: a bad season had ended for me then, and a good one had started. But 11 years later—in 1968—there was no reversal. On the contrary, my good season continued to be even better. I, therefore, realized that my idea was groundless, and I abandoned it.

Later, a new book caught my attention. It was its title that aroused my interest: *The Seasons of a Man's Life*. Its author, Daniel J. Levinson, a professor of psychology at Yale University, carried out a study showing that everyone's life has four seasons, each lasting 20–22 years. But he did not distinguish which of those seasons were good and which were bad. That book, however, brought me back to the question of the alternations of the good and bad seasons in our lives. Do those alternations, I wondered, happen not on certain dates—say, with the movement of the sun—but at certain *points in* our lives, such as the intervals of 20–22 years suggested by Levinson?

With that possibility in mind, I decided to look back over my life again. But the outcome was again negative: my life's good and bad seasons hadn't alternated every 20–22 years. The only finding was that my life had taken a second turn around 1974: my previous good season then gave way to a bad season. However, between those two "turns" (1957 and around 1974) there wasn't a period of 20–22 years, as I expected to find, influenced by Levinson's study. On the contrary, it was only a period of 16–17 years. I abandoned the effort once more.

Some years later, though, a new element appeared. A new turn had occurred in my life around 1990: the bad season I'd been previously experiencing had ended and a new good one had started. I observed thus that my life's seasons have alternated around the years 1957, 1974, and 1990—every 16–17 years. The above observation was, of course, a starting point. So, I decided to explore the subject further. I ought, I said, to examine what happens in the lives of other people. Have their lives alternated the same way as in my own life?

To find out what was happening in the lives of others, I decided to examine some biographies. But since biographies on ordinary people usually don't exist, or there are very few, I realized that only biographies of famous people could be examined. That work took me many years of research. Finally, the outcome was unbelievable. The results derived from the biographies all confirmed that the alternations of good and bad seasons in my own life—the life of an ordinary person—always occurred exactly as in the lives of the famous people I studied: at the certain dates 1957, 1974, and 1990—every 16–17 years.

The final conclusion up to now is, therefore, that the alternations of the good and bad seasons in our lives at certain dates is valid not only for famous people but also for ordinary persons. These alternations happen every 16–17 years in two opposite courses and at the certain dates we have seen: 1776, 1792, 1809, 1825, 1842, 1859, 1875, 1892, 1908, 1925, 1941, 1957, 1974, 1990.

# A Universal Phenomenon

Furthermore, from the biographies in this book you will also observe that the phenomenon of the alternations of seasons is *universal* and happening all over the world. Napoleon for example, was born and brought up in Europe, as well as Beethoven, Columbus, Verdi, and others. On the other hand, John Glenn and Jackie Kennedy were born and brought up in the United States of America, while Gorbachev was born and brought up in Russia, and Mandela in South Africa (in the southern hemisphere of the earth). Also, the Dalai Lama was born and raised in Asia. However, the Dalai Lama belongs to the Asian human race, while Mandela to the black one and all the others belong to the white human race. This reveals, therefore, that the phenomenon of the alternations of seasons happens all over the world and in all kinds of human races.

# Foreseeing Our Seasons

Based on our earlier discovery, it is obvious now that we can foresee how the good and bad seasons will alternate in the future in the life of every one of us.

If the alternating 16–17 year cycles extend back 500 years into the past—from 1479 to 1990, as we've seen—there is, of course, no reason to think they will not continue 500 years into the future. That means, therefore, we can foresee how our own seasons will alternate in the future. Since the *last* alternation of seasons happened in 1990 (as you will see in the biographies of Gorbachev, Mandela, Thatcher, Glenn, Taylor, Kennedy Onassis, the Dalai Lama, and Carter), that means the next turning point of seasons in our lives lies 16–17 years after 1990—around 2007. A new season starts then that lasts 16–17 years—and continues until 2024. The next alternations of our seasons after 2024 will happen at the dates 2040, 2056, 2073, and so on—every 16–17 years.

Recall, however, that our seasons alternate in two opposite courses, the first course and the second course. To find how your own seasons will be in the future, you first have to find which course of seasons you belong: the first course or the second. You can follow this way: examine whether in 2007 a good or bad season started in your life. In doing this, you have to see your life "from above" like a helicopter pilot, in large periods, not day by day. See whether the years after 2007—compared with the years before 2007—were a good season, or a bad season.

We also have to clarify that a "good" season tends to include both inner satisfaction and outer success, while a "bad" season is a season of anxiety, with failure and disappointment. But a good season is not always like a paradise without any concerns or difficulties. Life is never like this. Similarly, a bad season is not necessarily a hell; it may contain moments of satisfaction. Conditions are especially mixed at the beginning of each season, which could be seen as a transitional period. The first part of each good season resembles spring, and the first part of each bad season resembles fall. So there can be "storms" in spring and "Indian summers" in fall. That means your first years after 2007 may not seem clearly good or bad, but something like springtime or autumn.

Also, we have to clarify that the specific criteria that characterizes a good or bad season usually include factors like money, fame, love, and health. These criteria differ from person to person and can change over time. But usually there is only one main factor at a given moment that shapes the good and bad seasons of a person. For famous Greek shipowner Aristotle Onassis, for example, only money had any meaning throughout most of his life, as you'll see later. But at the end of his life, when he fell seriously ill from an incurable disease, only his health counted—though he was the wealthiest person on earth, money meant nothing for him any more.

Also for Beethoven, health—his hearing problem—was of utmost importance during one of his early bad seasons, but later—when he overcame that problem—his recognition as a composer became the main factor shaping his seasons. For Napoleon, on the other hand, fame was the only main factor shaping his seasons throughout his life.

So, for finding whether your years after 2007 were a good or bad season you have to see what big events good or bad regarding your studies, health, business, career, love, family, etc., happened—and continued—in your life during 2007, 2008, 2009 and so on up to now. For example, does a period of failures and disappointments or a period of successes and satisfactions characterize your studies, business, family, or love during the above years?

If you find that a good season started in your life in 2007, that means you belong to the first course of seasons; if you find that a bad season started, you belong to the second course of seasons. Then you will be able to foresee how your life's good and bad seasons will be in the future. If you belong to the first course of seasons, the years from 2007 to 2024 will be good, while the years from 2024 to 2040 will be bad—and so on every 16–17 years. If you belong to the second course, the years from 2007 to 2024 will be bad, while the years from 2024 to 2040 will be good—and so on every 16–17 years.

I have to also clarify, however, that in finding whether the years after 2007 were a good or a bad season for you, you will be decidedly helped after finishing this book and understanding the good and bad seasons in the lives of the famous people cited. You will see clearly in these chapters how our good and bad seasons exactly alternate in our lives and so you will more easily find whether your life after 2007 was good or bad for you.

Meanwhile, we'll see in the next chapter what benefits and advantages derive from our ability to foresee our life's good and bad seasons. The benefits are many, and most are astonishing.

## Chapter 2
# THE ADVANTAGES

The ability to foresee our life's good and bad seasons changes profoundly the way we cope with our life today. Besides *being itself* a great advantage, it has also a lot of other advantages, all helping us live a much better life. We begin with the benefits derived when we are in a *good season* of our life. If you find as explained in the previous chapter that you are in a good season of your life, you can benefit enormously from this knowledge.

First, you can dare when you know you are in a good season—fate is with you. As noted earlier and we'll also see later, for example, in Christopher Columbus's biography, he succeeded in discovering the New World only because he was in a good season of his life, despite of the fact that almost everybody—the Spanish royal council included—was skeptical and had rejected his idea.

Second, as we'll see later in former British prime minister Margaret Thatcher's biography, though the majority of the British cabinet members were against fighting the Falklands war, Thatcher disagreed, and her good season helped her to succeed: Argentina surrendered immediately. Her risky action had ended in triumph. Don't hesitate, therefore, to risk bold actions when you are in a good season of your life—and take advantage of your good season before the opportunity passes.

Furthermore, when you are in a good season, you should not behave as if you assume that this season will never end. On the contrary, you have to take into consideration the measures necessary to face successfully the problems that may occur in the bad season that will follow. You must not be spendthrift, for example, but you have to save money for facing possible financial problems that will appear during the bad season. Also, you have to take care of your health, so that you can successfully face serious illnesses that may appear in your bad seasons. In short, you have to make provisions for the winter that will come, so that you can effectively diminish its chilliness. Take shelter for your bad season in time.

# Benefits in our Bad Seasons

There are also many other advantages when you are in a *bad* season of your life. First of all, you mustn't be seized by despair and pessimism when you are in a bad season—fearing that this season will never end. Instead, you have to anticipate the arrival of the good season, knowing that this will surely come. Verdi, Picasso, and many others often didn't even have enough money for food, as we'll see in their biographies. But later they became very rich. Also, Onassis arrived at bankruptcy at the age of fifty, but later became the world's wealthiest person.

If your problem lies within your career in your bad season, wait to see it solved. Winston Churchill said at a moment of one of his bad seasons as noted earlier: "I am done; I am finished." But later, he became prime minister of his country. If on the other hand, the difficulties are with your wife, husband, loved one, or children, you must be tolerant with all and don't despair. Things will be cured later. The same outcome will also come in case you have divorced, for example, after a long or short period of happy marriage. When the woman Beethoven loved abandoned him, he contemplated suicide, but later she came back, while lots of other women filled his life.

Also, if you have health problems in your bad season, remember that they can be cured, or faced, successfully. The doctors had said that famous French theater actress Sarah Bernhardt and the Dalai Lama of Tibet would die soon, but both survived for many more years. Similarly, if your health problem is psychological, don't despair: It will pass. Picasso was given to bouts of anger during one of his bad seasons; he isolated himself in his house, refused to see anybody, and he didn't complete any of the paintings that he'd been commissioned to do. But later he became the famous Picasso.

If you are a talented artist (painter, sculptor, writer, or composer), but your works are rejected in your bad season, don't despair: You will be recognized some time later. Picasso, great French sculptor August Rodin, and many others saw their works rejected during their bad seasons, but later they were considered masterpieces. Also, if you have difficulties with your studies in school or university in your bad season, don't worry: This will not have an influence in your future. Churchill failed his exams in school again and again, and when Verdi applied to the Milan Conservatory, the school rejected his application.

The ability to foresee our seasons shows that a bad season is also a great advantage, and it should not lead readers to feel that this knowledge may cause them unbearable disappointment, and it would be better for them—a kind of consolation—assuming, though, wrongly, that the bad season may end soon. If you are in a bad season and you don't know how long it will last, you may participate in some actions that will end, with certainty—because of the bad season—in failure. This would, of course, worsen your bad situation even more or lead sometimes even to catastrophe.

Keep in mind the case of Napoleon. If he knew that in 1812 he was in a bad season of his life that would last more years, he wouldn't have attacked Russia at that time, an action that lead to his humiliating defeat, marking the beginning of his end. Also, he wouldn't have, for the same reason, in 1815, attacked the English and Germans in Waterloo, where he suffered total destruction that led him to death. Things may have thus taken another course for Napoleon, and though his bad season couldn't have been avoided, it might have been less tragic: maybe he wouldn't have had such a sad end or may not have died at such an early age—and who knows, a *new good season* of 16–17 years, a glorious one again, may have started for him. Napoleon's example shows with clarity, therefore, that it is a great advantage knowing that you are in a bad season of your life, which will not end soon but will last more years—up to 16–17.

Of course, people who are over 60 or 70 and in a bad season that they know will last many years (up to 16–17) may feel there isn't enough time for a new good season to come for them. However, these people can find ways to ameliorate that fact. They can adjust their lives to the reality and pass their bad years in a much better way, free from any unattainable expectations that frustration can cause. They must also remember that a bad season isn't necessarily a hell, while knowing they are in a bad season may be proved a great advantage, as explained earlier.

Finally, don't blame yourself—and have no remorse—for the fact that you are in a bad season of your life. You haven't made any mistake to cause the arrival of this season, and you couldn't have done anything to avoid it; the bad season would have been inevitable in any case.

# Other Advantages

The knowledge of how your life's seasons alternate can help you to take *further* advantage of it. First, this ability can help you take advantage of *other people's* seasons. You can, for example, entrust an employee or colleague with the solution of a difficult problem—or a politician to govern your country, or even a coach of a football team—only if you know they are in a good season of their life, thus operating from a position of strength. If the members of the French Parliament, for example, had known that Napoleon was to enter a bad season in 1809—as he did—they probably wouldn't have named him the leader of their country *for life*. They might have avoided the destruction of France during Napoleon's bad season.

Also, the ability to know how our seasons alternate in life can help you to foresee the life evolution of other people—of your friends and relatives, famous people (artists, singers, and songstresses, actors and actresses, etc.), or even the politicians that govern you. For example, will the leader of your country or the president of a foreign power win the next election? The answer depends, of course, on the season these persons are in at a given moment: If they are in a good season, they have many chances to win. But if they are in a bad season when the election day comes, they will probably lose. You can also predict, for example, how long a political leader will stay in power after his election or for how long a famous singer will continue his successful career.

Finally, this discovery will radically change the mentality and character of all people in the future. People will become more philosophized, realists, and peaceful. They will know that a good season doesn't last forever. On the contrary, a bad season awaits; it hasn't any meaning, therefore, being quarrelsome or aggressive is nonproductive. Man will become tolerant and merciful and have more understanding towards the others. Superficiality and imprudence, even if they don't disappear completely, will drastically be reduced.

# Questions for the Future

The theory explained in this book is, of course, a fresh piece of knowledge—and we could say that maybe something like a kind of science can be born from it. In the light of our findings, therefore, new studies by other persons (scientists or scholars) are absolutely necessary in the future, so that they can enable us to take more advantage of this method. Among other things, these studies must answer the following questions deriving from what we've seen so far.

What is this that causes the alternations of seasons in our lives? And why there are two opposite courses of seasons? Do astronomical influences—such as unknown magnetic fields around the earth that come from the sun, other planets, or even other galaxies—cause the alternations of our seasons? Finding the answers to these questions may help us avoid or ameliorate in the future the bad seasons in our lives, perhaps the way migratory birds leave one hemisphere during the winter and fly to the other, so that they can continually experience summer. Future generations of scientists and scholars, therefore, may come up with a similar answer. Ancient peoples didn't know what caused the alternations of the four seasons in the earth—fall, winter, spring, and summer—though they didn't deny these seasons' existence. Only thousands of years later, we learned that the main cause of the four seasons for our earth is the shifting distance between the earth and the sun.

How does that unknown cause influence the alternations of the seasons? Is it influencing the function of our minds? As an example of this possibility, consider the case of Winston Churchill. As you'll see in his biography, when World War I began in 1914, Churchill, as first lord of the admiralty, thought the only salvation for England was to land at Antwerp, Belgium. But no one agreed with him. Then he went alone to Antwerp, assumed leadership of a small body of sailors, and ordered two divisions of inexperienced recruits to be transferred from England to Antwerp. What followed was a catastrophe. Had Churchill's state of mind been influenced by what causes the alternations of seasons in our life? The answer can, of course, help us to more benefit from our discovery.

There are other questions to be answered. For example, should we marry a person belonging to the same course of seasons or to the opposite? Onassis and the woman he loved, Maria Callas, belonged to the same course of seasons, and their relation was extremely satisfactory, as we'll see later. But Onassis and his second wife, Jackie Kennedy, belonged to opposite courses, and their marriage was a failure.

# The Confirmation

As confirmation for what we have seen so far, I cite in the next chapters the good and bad seasons of the famous people mentioned in Chapters 1 and 2. You will see how their seasons alternated according to the certain patterns described. Based on the findings, you will be able to foresee how your own seasons will alternate in the future. Also, you will find confirmation that the advantages exhibited in this chapter are based on the real lives of the famous people studied.

We start with the good and bad seasons in the life of great German composer Ludwig van Beethoven.

## Chapter 3
# LUDWIG VAN BEETHOVEN

Beethoven was born in 1770. We don't know enough about the first five years of his life to know whether it was a good or bad season. But from 1776 on, we know he had a pleasant childhood. Though his family was poor and his father was strict and severe, he was lucky enough to have a devoted mother, and he spent happy hours in her presence. He also had many friends and many opportunities to have fun.

In 1778, little Beethoven was recognized as "a child prodigy": He gave his first public concert in Bonn where he was born. The following year, he began to study with a well-known musician, a director of the National Theater, who immediately recognized his talent and took him under his wing. After two years of instruction, in 1781, when Beethoven was only eleven, he composed three sonatas and one concert for the piano, all of which were published immediately. The same year, he had another reason to be very happy: He became acquainted with a family in Bonn that offered a supportive environment and nurtured his musical talent. Their home was a "refuge for happiness,"[1] as he put it.

In 1784, Beethoven became financially independent, while only fourteen years old. That year he was appointed deputy organist in Bonn's court with an excellent salary. Thus he could support his whole family. His father had become an alcoholic, his mother was seriously ill, and there were two younger brothers to care for.

Three years later, in 1787, Beethoven's big dream came true: He was able to leave Bonn for Vienna. Vienna was a cultural magnet at the time where all the arts, and especially music, flourished. Bands "played in the streets and the whole city was awash in music,"[2] while "the theaters and the academies were always overflowing."[3] There, the young Beethoven met Mozart for the first time and received the first major encouragement of his life from him. He improvised a composition on the piano, but Mozart was skeptical, because he believed that the young man had previously memorized the composition. Beethoven then asked Mozart to choose the theme himself—and he improvised again. When Beethoven finished, Mozart said, "This young man will surprise the world someday."[4]

But Beethoven's first stay in Vienna lasted only a few months, since he became the head of his family and had to return to Bonn. That year his mother died, while his father was still an alcoholic. That bad event didn't change Beethoven's good season, however: He soon managed to be granted a substantial allowance by the state with which to take care of his father as well as his two younger brothers.

In 1789, Beethoven met Prince Maximilian, who held him in high esteem and received him under his protection. With the prince's help, Beethoven enrolled that year, at the age of 19, in the university where he had an opportunity to study the works of the philosophers and writers of his era: Kant, Schiller, Goethe, and others. The next year, Beethoven's first important musical compositions were published, and he began to be recognized as a composer.

At the age of twenty-one, in 1791, he entered high society. He was received at the most exclusive salons, where he taught music and moved in fashionable court circles. A year later, he met the great composer Haydn who heard him playing a serenade on the piano. Enthusiastic, Haydn invited Beethoven to Vienna. A jubilant Beethoven again left Bonn for Vienna—this time as Haydn's student. Another dream had become a reality. He was now twenty-two years old.

# The Bad Season from 1792 On

In Vienna, however, Beethoven's experiences did not meet his expectations. Haydn, no longer young, had too many other preoccupations and turned out to be indifferent to his gifted student. Disappointed, Beethoven had to start studying with other, lesser-known musicians in 1793. The next year he was able to accept the hospitality of a prince, but even that was short-lived, because Beethoven found the atmosphere in the prince's palace uncongenial. To support himself, he was now obliged to give music lessons to a diverse array of students.

The big shock, in 1794, was more personal: Beethoven began to realize he had a hearing problem. He was only twenty-four. In 1795, another cause of worry was added: Beethoven gave his first major concert in Vienna, performing his Concerto No. 2 for piano and orchestra. It was a novel, stunning piece that made people think. Beethoven was bringing a more philosophical perspective to music. But the Viennese, accustomed to joyful music and entertainment, had serious reservations.

Beethoven continued giving concerts in other cities: Nuremberg, Berlin, Dresden, Prague. But though he had great success, at the end of one of those concerts he realized with terror that his hearing had become worse. He began experiencing an incessant buzzing in his ears that sounded like a waterfall, and he couldn't always understand speech clearly.

At first he kept quite about his problem. But over the next several years (1797–1800), the situation became catastrophic: Beethoven became almost totally deaf. The "winter" had entered Beethoven's life. While the previous bad years can be described as "autumn," the years that followed are real "winter."

In 1801, Beethoven decided to confide in a close friend: "I am extremely distressed," he wrote to him, "the most vital part of myself—my hearing—has become impaired and is steadily worsening. And I do not know whether I will ever be cured."[5]

To his doctor he also wrote: "For the last two years I have avoided any social interaction—I cannot tell people that I am deaf. It is terrible."[6] In 1802, his doctor advised him to spend the summer recuperating in the countryside. But "it was a summer full of despair."[7] Beethoven composed a letter to his brothers that was meant to serve as a kind of will, with the proviso that it be read after his death. He was only thirty-two years old. The document said, among other things: "I want to end my life, but the music prevents me from doing so. For so long, I have never felt any real happiness. I live as if I am in exile, since it is impossible for me to participate in the company of others, to talk with friends, to hear and be heard. I feel I am indeed a miserable creature."[8]

The same year, a new reason for despair was added to Beethoven's life. The woman he loved, Giulietta Guicciardi—said to have been "frivolous and self centered"[9]—abandoned him after a two-year relationship. His despair over the lost relationship, combined with his illness, created the worst crisis of his life so far. Beethoven was on the brink of suicide. He didn't know his bad season would be followed by a good one in time.

Things were not much better in the musical arena, normally his only consolation. In 1805, Beethoven's melodrama *Fidelio* was performed—the only opera he wrote. Though it would later be considered a masterpiece, the initial production was a total failure; it closed after only three days. This failure was repeated the following year. *Fidelio* was presented again, in a new form, but only for two performances. The theater was almost empty, the earnings insignificant.

Things only got worse between 1807 and 1809. Beethoven experienced another disappointment in love. He fell in love with a young, aristocratic Hungarian woman, Theresa von Brunschwick. Though they became engaged, her mother disapproved, and did not allow them to see each other. Finally they broke off the engagement.

Beethoven was also beset by financial problems. In 1808, he decided to leave Vienna to accept a position as a choir director in Kassel. But some of his friends interceded and helped him get a state allowance so he could stay in Vienna. In 1809, however, the situation worsened: Napoleon's army seized Vienna after a violent attack that convulsed the city. The "royal court and all the nobility abandoned the city, while in the streets and homes chaos prevailed."[10]

Beethoven "found shelter in a pub, covering his aching ears with pillows to avoid the deafening report of the cannons."[11] Ordinary life in Vienna came to a standstill. The currency "became worthless, prices soared, and inflation loomed."[12] Beethoven's state allowance almost evaporated, and he often didn't even have enough money for food. At the same time, he suffered "from excruciating abdominal pain."[13] Shabbily dressed, "ill, and stooped over, he attended the funeral of his former teacher Haydn, under the menacing guard of armed French soldiers."[14]

But at some point, in 1809, this bad season finally ended for Beethoven.

# The New Good Season from 1809 On

Just after this season began, in 1810, Beethoven finally achieved a major goal: He became acquainted with a charming, clever woman, Bettina Brentano, who would devote herself to him and would make up for all the failed relationships he had experienced with other women. "Being close to Beethoven," she wrote in a letter to Goethe, "causes me to forget the world."[15]

The most important fact, however, is that in this favorable season Beethoven managed to triumph over his cruel fate—the problem of his deafness. This problem stopped bothering him because he found a solution: He would hold with his teeth a wooden hearing aid—basically a long, slim piece of wood—and touch it to the piano; this allowed him to perceive the sound of the music through the mouth to the inner ear.

In other ways, too, the good days returned: In 1812, Beethoven became acquainted with Goethe, and a comfortable friendship evolved between them despite their age difference (Beethoven was forty-two, Goethe sixty-two). When they strolled through the streets of Vienna, people would bow, something that annoyed Goethe, but for Beethoven it was heaven sent: "Don't worry, Your Excellency," he once said to Goethe jokingly, "maybe the bows are only for me."[16]

In 1813, Napoleon began to lose power, and Beethoven, full of enthusiasm, started to compose the *Victory of Wellington*—an immediate success. The following year, Beethoven performed that work at the congress that took place in Vienna after Napoleon's downfall. The czar of Russia, the emperor of Austria, the kings of Denmark, Prussia, and Bavaria, "princes, ministers, diplomats, and other statesmen"[17] were all present, and they paid homage to Beethoven. It was a concert triumph.

From then on, Beethoven's life was glorious. The years that followed can be described as "summer" in his life compared with the previous good years, which were rather "springtime." In 1814, Beethoven's melodrama *Fidelio*—a failure a few years earlier—was performed again in Vienna, this time in a revised and better form. The good season he was in helped very much, and the melodrama was a tremendous success. Repeat performances of *Fidelio* were held in other European cities, including Prague, Leipzig, and Berlin, always to great acclaim.

As Beethoven's reputation reached its apogee, he began to earn a great deal of money. His performances attracted audiences of thousands, among them many celebrities. The Austrian government offered state-owned halls for his performances, and friends began to surround him and draw him into an active social life. He frequented the various cafés and restaurants of Vienna, where the previously gloomy Beethoven became unrecognizably gregarious, telling jokes and drinking champagne. He walked the streets of Vienna, stopping in shops to browse or buy things and talk with ordinary people.

In Vienna's central park, the Pratter, children would offer him flowers. After his walk, Beethoven would meet his friends in the park's noisy cafés, where "amidst cigarette smoke and the smell of alcohol, all the artistic and intellectual problems of the times were solved."[18] To communicate, he would hand a notebook to his companions and have them write down their questions or comments. He would respond orally with ease and humor.

In this good season, too, the women who had previously ignored him began to fill his life. They were young, beautiful, and from the upper social echelons. His biographers report that there were at least fifteen of them: Besides Bettina Brentano, they included Dorothy von Ertmann, Marianne von Wester-holt, Eleonore von Breunig, Rachel von Ense, and Josephine von Brunschwick (the sister of Theresa von Brunschwick, to whom Beethoven had been engaged in 1807, until her mother cut it off). Giulietta Guicciardi, the Italian woman who had abandoned him in 1802, leading him to contemplate suicide, also returned, but Beethoven was no longer interested.

In the professional arena, Beethoven had a prodigious musical output: he finished his thirty-two sonatas for the piano, composed his famous oratorio *Missa Solemnis*, and finished part of the *Ninth Symphony*. The oratorio *Missa Solemnis*—"Beethoven's hymn to God"[19]—was completed in 1820. From then on, Beethoven had a deeply spiritual outlook.

The same year (1820), the city of Vienna proclaimed Beethoven an honorary citizen of the city, an honor that thrilled him. In 1825—at the age of 55—Beethoven arrived at the high point of his life: His *Ninth Symphony* was performed in Vienna and was an unprecedented triumph. The audience went wild, and Beethoven was profoundly moved. When the concert was over, several theater workers "had to carry him out: he had fainted!"[20]

# The New Bad Season after 1825

Starting in 1825, Beethoven began facing serious health problems: arthritis and eye ailments. He remained at home, often in bed. He was forced to ask his brother for help and retreated to his brother's home in the countryside, staying in a small room and subsisting on an inadequate diet. The next year (1826), things got worse. Beethoven's friends abandoned him, he gave up composing, and his works stopped being performed. After the *Ninth Symphony's* success in 1825, no other concerts featured his works. Deeply disappointed, he complained in his diary: "Vienna's high society seems interested only in dancing, horseback riding, and attending the ballet."[21]

Beethoven tried to get all of his works published, but without success—his bad season didn't allow it. The royal court that previously supported him now ignored him. Late in 1826, on a chilly December day, he abandoned his brother's "lukewarm hospitality"[22] in the countryside and returned to Vienna . . . on the "milkman's cart,"[23] because his brother, despite having his own coach, had not made it available to him. As a result, Beethoven arrived in Vienna seriously ill with pneumonia.

After a few days, his health took a turn for the worse: His feet became swollen and he suffered from abdominal pain. On January 3, 1827, he wrote his will. Bedridden, he complained to two friends visiting him that he had been left alone in life, without family members to care for him. Beside him was a portrait of Theresa von Brunschwick, the woman he had been engaged to two decades earlier.

On March 24, 1827, the end came. Beethoven asked the two friends attending him for Rhein wine. But it was too late. Two days later, on March 26, 1827, the great Beethoven died—at the age of 57—while a violent storm battered Vienna.

# Conclusion

By analyzing Beethoven's good and bad seasons, we can derive that in 1776 a good season began in his life. Then, a bad season started in 1792. A new good season began in 1809 while another bad season started in 1825. Between one of these dates there are 16–17 years. We have confirmation that Beethoven's good and bad seasons alternated, indeed, every 16–17 years.

But there is also another confirmation derived from Beethoven's life. As we've seen in this chapter, because Beethoven had become totally deaf and the woman he loved abandoned him, he contemplated suicide and wrote his will. But he didn't know that a good season would soon return, he would overcome his hearing problem, and lots of women would fill his life. We are confirmed so that we mustn't be seized by despair and pessimism when we are in a bad season, fearing that this season will never end. Instead we have to anticipate the arrival of the good season, knowing that this will surely come.

In the next chapter we'll continue and extend our confirmation by seeing how the good and bad seasons alternated in the life of great Italian composer Giuseppe Verdi.

# Chapter 4
# GIUSEPPE VERDI

Giuseppe Verdi was born in 1813—that is fourteen years before Beethoven died. We do not know much about his childhood and youth before age of eighteen to say whether these years were good or bad. We only know that he was born in a small village near Parma, Italy, his father was a grocer, when he was eight his father bought him a piano, and at the age of twelve, he was appointed an organist in the village church.

But we do know that from 1832 on, when Verdi was nineteen, he was in a bad season of his life. A wealthy merchant friend of Verdi's father was aware of his great talent and offered him a music scholarship in Milan. Accompanied by his father and his teacher, Verdi arrived in Milan in May 1832. A great letdown, however, awaited him there: He applied to the Milan Conservatory, but after hearing him playing the piano, the school rejected his application.

He was a "foreigner," they said; he was above the age of fourteen and he had a "rural look."[24] He also seemed inadequately trained. Deeply disappointed, the young Verdi "felt uprooted and lost in the big city."[25] Finally, he enrolled in a different private school. The same year (1832), he experienced another blow: His beloved sister, Josephine, died. It was the first great sorrow of his life.

The following year, 1833, Verdi encountered one more injustice. The Philharmonic Orchestra of Busseto, a small town near his village, was without a conductor and invited Verdi to take that position. The church authorities rejected him, however, and "appointed a candidate of their own choice."[26] The scandal even attracted the attention of the local government, and a major uproar ensued. Though finally Verdi got the job in 1835, the incident wounded him deeply.

After two years a great misfortune found Verdi in 1837. From his marriage to Margherita Barezzi in 1836, he had a daughter, Virginia, whom he adored. But Virginia died in 1837 when she was only a few months old. In a dispirited condition, Verdi isolated himself in his home. He resigned from his position with the Philharmonic Orchestra of Busseto—a position he had fought so hard for—and, in 1838, he left for Milan.

In Milan, Verdi faced tremendous difficulties: He was jobless, had no money, and often could "only eat once a day in miserable inns."[27] As if all that were not enough, in 1839, his second child, a young son, died. Verdi's life became unbearable. Despite all that sorrow, he had to compose lighthearted music to earn a living. He was commissioned, in 1840, to write *Un Giorno di Regno (King for a Day)* for the impresario Merelli, a famous Italian manager.

The bad season hadn't yet finished for Verdi. In 1840, he received the most tragic blow of all: His beloved wife, Margherita Barezzi, died. Grief stricken, Verdi fled Milan for Busseto so that he could find solace. But impresario Merelli reminded him of his obligation to complete *King for a Day*, so Verdi had to return to Milan.

He would have been better off not returning. *King for a Day* was performed in La Scala on September 5, 1840, but it was a catastrophe. After pandemonium broke out, with the audience whistling and shouting its disapproval, the opera ceased being performed the same day. Verdi was devastated. He became reclusive and lost his desire to compose music.

In late 1840, Merelli, who never lost faith in Verdi, asked him whether he would like to compose the music for a work titled *Nabuchodonosor*. Verdi refused. But Merelli insisted, putting the libretto for that work in Verdi's pocket. Halfheartedly, he tried to start composing. But "the notes weren't appearing"[28]—or if they were, they were full of sorrow, like the composer's soul. However, he finished it in 1841.

# The Good Season from 1842 On

Rehearsals on the opera *Nabuchodonosor*—or *Nabucco* as it was named in the meantime—started early in 1842. But immediately it became clear that Verdi had composed a masterpiece. *Nabucco* was performed for the first time in La Scala in Milan on March 9, 1842. What followed was an unprecedented triumph. The enraptured audience responded with a standing ovation, "demanding—with a frenzy of applause—repeated encores of the moving chorus song 'Va, pensiero, sull' ali dorate' "[29] that still causes shivers of emotion.

Verdi, now twenty-nine, had suddenly become famous. People were singing the chorus song from *Nabucco* in the streets, while "hats and neckties with Verdi's name inscribed on them"[30] were sold everywhere. Milan's wealthiest families opened their homes to him. The same year (1842), the composer became acquainted with a famous soprano, Josephina Strepponi, and developed a lasting relationship with her that persisted until her death in 1897.

During the next nine years, between 1843 and 1851, Verdi composed thirteen operas, which were performed in all the big cities of Italy—Milan, Rome, Venice, Naples, Trieste—as well as in London, and all had great success. The first of those operas was *I Lombardi*, which was performed at La Scala on February 11, 1843. The day of its premiere, enthusiastic crowds mobbed the theater, and the success of that opera was similar to *Nabucco*.

*Ernani* followed in 1844, based on Victor Hugo's work of the same name. It premiered in Venice on March 9, 1844, to great acclaim. Exuberant Venetians "lifted Verdi to their shoulders and carried him triumphantly around Saint Mark's square."[31] With the money he earned from *Ernani*, Verdi was able to buy a small farm near his village.

*Jeanne d' Arc (Giovanna d' Arco)* followed in 1845, with equally great success. Verdi now had so much money that he acquired a mansion in Busseto. Other accomplishments included *Attila* in 1846, and *I Masnadieri (The Bandits)* in 1847. The *Bandits'* premiere was held in London with a particular fanfare: Queen Victoria and almost all the members of Parliament were present. The opera was a big hit, and Verdi made staggering amounts of money. He bought a large farm with woods and vineyards near Busseto and an apartment in Paris, where he retreated from time to time to relax with his companion, Josephina Strepponi.

Tension between Italy and Austria was mounting in this period, and to stir up patriotic sentiments, Verdi composed *La Battaglia di Legnano (The Battle of Legnano)*. That opera was first performed in Rome in 1849. Tickets for the premiere were sold out. It was another smash hit. Ecstatic, the audience demanded as an encore "the repetition of the entire fourth act."[32] Verdi had become a national hero. At the end of the same year, a Verdi opera was performed in Naples, too: *Luisa Miller*, based on Schiller's tragedy of the same name.

At this point, the "summer" entered Verdi's life. While the previous good years can be described as "springtime," the years that followed are like "summer." During the next eight years (1851–1859), Verdi composed his extraordinary masterpieces *Rigoletto, Il Trovatore, La Traviata, Les Vêpres Siciliennes, Simon Boccanegra, Un Ballo in Maschera*, and others, and he arrived at the culmination of his glory. He finished the first of those masterpieces, *Rigoletto*, early in 1851, and its premiere was staged in Venice on March 11 of the same year. All night, Venice's canals resounded with the voices of gondoliers' singing "Feather in the Wind,"[33] a song well-known even now. After twenty-one performances in Venice, *Rigoletto* began to be performed all over the world.

In 1851, Verdi also began to compose his next masterpiece *Il Trovatore*, which he completed the following year. The premiere was held in Rome in January 1853, again to great acclaim. Two months later, his third masterpiece, *La Traviata*, premiered in Venice. It was again an instant hit and was even performed in America.

In 1855, Verdi finished *Les Vêpres Siciliennes*. Its premiere was held in L' Opera de Paris; in 1856, it was performed in La Scala in Milan with tremendous success. Its ardent patriotism stirred the souls of Italians. In 1857, *Simon Boccanegra* was performed in Venice, and the same year, Verdi composed *Un Ballo in Maschera*. The latter opera was performed in Rome in February 1859 with great success—"the ticket prices were seven times normal."[34]

Verdi had arrived at the pinnacle of his career; at the age of forty-six, he was considered Europe's greatest composer. To make his success complete, in early 1859 he married the woman with whom he had lived for the last 17 years, Josephina Strepponi.

# The New Bad Season from 1859 On

From 1859, however, Verdi began to be shaken by a profound moral crisis—a crisis that lasted for a number of years. He isolated himself on his farm in Busseto and became preoccupied with ordinary farm chores. He rose "at daybreak, took care of the farm animals (horses, dogs, and so on), bought cows and other animals at the local market, and looked after the harvest."[35]

"There is not a place uglier than this one," he complained in a letter, "but where else can I find solitude for thinking?"[36] Especially during the winter, time stood still, and the tediousness was unbearable. Verdi's connection with the larger world was through the mail. To alleviate his boredom, he took interminable walks in the area around his farm accompanied only by his dogs—his precious assistants, as he called them.

Verdi also spent quite a bit of time composing music during that season. Still, he managed to compose one work every four or five years in contrast to his previous output of one work a year. For a while, he was distracted by politics, because he was elected to the Parliament of Turin in 1861. But he didn't know he was in a bad season of his life: political wrangling left him disillusioned, and so he stopped attending the sessions.

The next year, Verdi finished his work *La Forza del Destino (The Power of Destiny)*, which the Russian Theater of Petrograd had commissioned. But when the opera was performed, after many obstacles and delays, in November 1862 in Petrograd, it had little success. More than five years passed before Verdi finished another work. In March 1867, *Don Carlos* was performed for the first time in Paris. What followed, however, was a major disappointment for the composer: The critics accused him—unjustifiably—of borrowing from Wagner's music. Deeply wounded, he closeted himself in a hotel before he could face the public again.

The same year, Verdi suffered two more blows. First, his father died, which had a devastating effect on the composer. Soon afterward, his father-in-law (his first wife's father), his benefactor Antonio Barezzi to whom Verdi owed so much, also died. At the funeral, the eulogy was extraordinarily moving: "My second father, who loved me so much and whom I loved dearly, is gone,"[37] Verdi lamented.

Now the "winter" entered Verdi's life. Four more years would pass before he was able to finish another work. At the end of 1871, after numerous delays, his opera *Aïda* was performed in Cairo. The performance lasted more than eight hours—from 7:00 p.m. to 3.00 a.m.—and was attended "by odd and variegated audience members ranging from Christian Coptics and Jews to many women from the harem."[38] But the composer wasn't satisfied with his work. For the first time in his life, he had decided not to be present to conduct the performance himself.

The same year, the great conductor and Verdi's close friend, Angelus Mariani, who had conducted many of Verdi's operas, abandoned him and joined the ranks of Wagner's supporters. The Wagner camp was extremely antagonistic toward Verdi. Mariani's decision to conduct Wagner's opera *Lohengrin* in Bologna was a blow to Verdi. He now felt an immense loneliness and sorrow. He expressed these feelings in his next work, the mournful *Messa da Requiem*, performed in May 1874, in the church of St. Mark in Milan.

But finally, this bad season for Verdi ended.

# The New Good Season from 1875 On

In 1875, Verdi's sorrowful *Requiem* suddenly realized enormous success. After having conquered all of Italy, it did the same in the rest of Europe, while in London an "unbelievable chorus of 1,200 voices"[39] would participate in the performance, a fact that moved the critics to write rave reviews.

Verdi had shaken his loneliness, and—now aged sixty-two—again began to enjoy the delights of life. He became acquainted with a young intellectual, Arrigo Boito, who shared the pleasures of culture with him, exposing him to the new intellectual currents and fashions. Verdi acquired a new lease on life, and a prolific new period began for him.

In 1876, Verdi conducted, personally this time, his *Aïda* in Paris, and soon the opera was performed triumphantly all over Europe. From now on, the composer began writing new works, though each now took him many years to complete because of his advancing age. In 1881, he rewrote *Simon Boccanegra*, which was performed that same year in its new form with great success.

From 1879 on, he had started setting the music for Shakespeare's *Otello*, which he finally finished in 1886. The premiere took place at La Scala in 1887. Celebrities from all over Europe arrived for the performance, and tickets prices reached unprecedented heights. At the end of the performance, the audience's cries of joy could be heard blocks away. When Verdi came out of the theater overcome with emotion, the people "unhitched the horses of his carriage and drew it themselves to his hotel."[40]

Between 1888 and 1892, Verdi composed another masterpiece, *Falstaff*, again based on Shakespeare. But now, he worked only a few hours a week. It was "as if he was in a long summer vacation,"[41] his biographers say.

# The New Bad Season after 1892

In 1892, Verdi was seventy-nine years old. The idea of death, therefore, was often on his mind. Two years later, when *Falstaff* was performed in La Scala, he reiterated Shakespeare's words: "Everything has finished, old John. Go away now."[42] More disturbing was the fact that Verdi's romanticism was losing its luster in Italy. Verdi found himself increasingly dismissed as old-fashioned. He began to question the quality of his early works and discouraged their revival. Many of his works had virtually vanished from the stage; many of his greatest achievements were unknown.

In 1897, Verdi was left alone in life: His beloved companion, his wife Josephina Strepponi, the "divine gift"[43] as he called her, died. From then on, his health crumbled, and the year 1900 found him confined to a wheelchair. In 1901, the great composer—one of the greatest in the world—departed from this life, at the age of eighty-eight.

# Conclusion

Verdi's alternations of seasons show that his seasons alternated in the dates 1842, 1859, 1875, and 1892. As you can recall, Beethoven's dates alternated in 1776, 1792, 1809, 1825, as we've seen in Chapter 3. Connecting Beethoven's dates to those of Verdi, we find this continuous row of dates: 1776, 1792, 1809, 1825, 1842, 1859, 1875, and 1892. This confirms that the seasons of these two men alternated in the continuous row of dates indicated in Chapter 1. We also see and confirm that their seasons alternated every 16–17 years, also indicated in Chapter 1.

But there is another confirmation deriving from Verdi's life. As we've seen in this chapter, when Verdi applied to enter the Milan Conservatory, the school rejected his application—because he had a "rural look," they said. But later Verdi became the greatest composer, that confirms what we've seen in Chapter 2: If you have difficulties with your studies in school or university in your bad season, don't worry: This will have not any influence in your future. The good season will come in any case.

In the next chapter we'll continue and extend our confirmation by seeing how the good and bad seasons alternated in the turbulent life of Pablo Picasso, the famous Spanish painter.

# Chapter 5
# PABLO PICASSO

Pablo Picasso was born in Malaga, Spain, in 1881—that is, sixty-eight years after Verdi. When he was eleven years old, in 1892, a bad season was underway for him. Picasso's family moved to La Coruna, a town on the Atlantic Ocean, where they lived for about four years. There, rain and fog prevailed almost every day, in contrast to sunny and hot Malaga. "The rain . . . and the wind," Picasso wrote in a melancholy tone as a young child, "have begun, and will continue until Coruna is no more."[44]

After 1895, Picasso's family moved to Barcelona. There, Picasso, now fourteen, entered art school and started producing his first drawings. Almost immediately, conflict with his father arose. The father, also an amateur painter, felt his son's drawings were not up to par. Not surprisingly, Picasso wanted to get away from his father's influence. In 1897, he left for Madrid with financial help from one of his uncles. There he enrolled in the School of Fine Arts, but almost immediately he dropped out. His uncle then stopped supporting him, and Picasso became penniless. He didn't have enough money for food, and, in 1898, he became seriously ill from scarlet fever.

A year later, Picasso was forced to return to Barcelona. His moods alternated between joy and despair. In 1900, he resumed wandering and left Barcelona for London. But he didn't get farther than Paris, which he decided to explore for a few months. In the Christmas season of 1900, he returned to Barcelona. It was a disastrous homecoming. Picasso's unkempt hair, his "bohemian" attire, and especially his paintings, aroused his father's ire. To escape his father's wrath, he fled to his uncle's home in Malaga again.

But the situation there was equally bad: His uncle demanded that Picasso cut his hair and begin painting "naturally." Not able to find peace anywhere, Picasso went back to Madrid. There, he found a friend from Barcelona—an anarchist named Francisco de Asis Soler—and they both decided to publish a magazine for which Picasso would provide the illustrations. But after a few issues, the magazine folded.

Picasso again left Madrid in the spring of 1901, heading for Paris. On the way, he stopped in Barcelona to say goodbye to his family. But his father had become extremely hostile; the rift between them would never be bridged. Not long after that, the son stopped using his father's name—Ruiz—and kept only the name of his mother: Picasso.

In Paris Picasso faced extreme hardship. He was unable to sell any of his paintings, and he became more desperate from day to day. At the end of 1901, the prodigal son's life continued and he was forced to go back to his family in Barcelona again so he would at least have something to eat.

Picasso stayed in Barcelona for three years. Those years were full of depression, which was reflected in his work. He painted beggars, prostitutes, and other lonely and dejected street people. These paintings were dominated by the color blue, which suited their themes and Picasso's mood.

In the spring of 1904, Picasso became restless again, so he returned to Paris. He stayed in a miserable ground-floor room with a rotten floor, without ventilation and without heat. He was as poor as many of the "bleu people" he was painting. He tried to sell some of his works, but the results were disappointing. He made contact with an agent who handled artworks, an unscrupulous former circus clown named Clovis Sagot, who used him and bought his works for almost nothing. He had another bad experience with the owner of a furniture shop who wanted to sell some of his paintings. This man who had a drinking problem and knew nothing about art, bought Picasso's drawings "wholesale" for a penny.

In the meantime, Picasso got involved with a young woman who lived next door, Fernande Olivier. He now tried to make his works "commercial" in an effort to sell them. Two years after arriving in Paris, in 1906, he produced *Les Demoiselles d' Avignon*, featuring five nude women with deformed bodies and animal-like faces. When he showed the painting to his friends, it caused a stir. No one had a good word to say about it. Matisse, the great French painter, said that this painting "would sink Picasso."[45] Deeply disappointed, he put the painting in a corner so nobody could see it.

But Picasso continued with his bizarre paintings. In the summer of 1908, he went to the countryside near Paris, and on his return he brought some paintings with country scenes. They were, however, all distorted landscapes in which you couldn't tell "where the grass ends and the sky begins."[46]

# The Good Season from 1908 On

From the first year of this season Picasso at last began to earn a good income from his paintings, and he could, in 1909, go for a summer vacation with Fernande to a small village in Spain. In the fall of the same year, he abandoned the miserable room he had lived in for the past five years, and moved with Fernande to "a large apartment ... with a living room, dining room, bedroom, and a separate [room for a] studio"[47]—in one of the best sections of Paris. He furnished this in great luxury and decorated with expensive carpets and statues. He also hired a maid and started receiving wealthy friends and others at receptions on Sunday afternoons.

In 1909, Picasso inaugurated a new kind of painting: cubism. This was a bizarre kind of painting. His works emphasized objects and faces divided into squares and other geometric forms. But he was in a good season of his life. Soon these paintings made him world famous. The following year, he produced a great number of those works, which were snatched up immediately by collectors. In 1911, Picasso's paintings were exhibited in the Salon des Indépendants in Paris. The cubist movement spread rapidly, and collectors from New York, Munich, and London proudly showed off their collections of Picasso's cubist works.

The same year, Picasso ended his relationship with Fernande, after they'd been together for seven years. He immediately became involved with another woman, Marcelle Humbert (or Eva, as he called her). At the same time that he was beginning a new life with her, he moved his studio to a more exclusive section of Paris: Montparnasse.

In 1914, World War I began. Though the wartime situation was very difficult for many people, for Picasso it was not. Most of his friends went to the army—and he never saw many of them again—but because he had Spanish citizenship, he was not required to serve in the military. On the contrary, he spent the summer of 1914 with Eva at Avignon, where he continued with his cubist paintings—usually with vivid colors now.

At the end of 1915, Eva became seriously ill (probably with cancer) and died the following year. Picasso soon found a substitute: Olga Khokhlova, a Russian ballet dancer and a general's daughter whom he had met while doing the costumes and set design for a ballet performance. In July 1918, Olga and Picasso were married.

From now on, a "summer" entered Picasso's life compared with the previous good years that can be described as "springtime." The ballet not only brought Olga to Picasso, it also brought him huge profits and fame. His works were now eagerly bought up, and his income was so substantial that he and Olga could move to a luxurious apartment in the fashionable Champs Élysées area. Their apartment was decorated according to the latest fashion, and paintings by Renoir, Cézanne, and other famous artists hung on the walls. Picasso rented another similar apartment upstairs for his studio.

He could no longer be described as a bohemian; by the age of thirty-seven, he had become bourgeois. He wore tailored suits, had a handkerchief tucked into his breast pocket, sported a gold watch with a chain attached to his buttonhole, and had meticulously groomed hair. He could often be seen walking his wife's Russian wolfhounds, while she spent freely on whatever pleased her.

World War I ended in 1918. The next year, Picasso accompanied the ballet to London. London was a triumph for him: the English were fascinated by his decorations for the ballet, and he was invited to receptions everywhere. With his morale at a high point in 1920, Picasso depicted whatever pleased him: He painted his old love and his new one, the clowns, the dancers, as well as the bathers by the sea and the peasants in the countryside. He employed a variety of styles ranging from realism to cubism.

For Picasso, the next five years, between 1921 and 1925, were full of money, comfort, and pleasure. He was deprived of nothing during those years, while he was constantly invited to the receptions and dances of the Parisian nobility. He spent the summers in the most expensive French resorts—for example, at Cannes on the Riviera.

# The New Bad Season from 1925 On

Beginning in 1925, Picasso became, according to his biographers, "possessed by some great inner rage."[48] He began painting nightmarish works, depicting figures with the faces of monsters, rotten teeth, naked human bones, and twisted limbs—all for no apparent reason. The first of those works was done in 1925. It was *The Three Dancers*, showing figures with dislocated bodies and displaced noses, mouths, hands, and breasts, a work that revealed his own fragmented mental state, a state of perpetual nightmare.

That situation continued into the next years. In 1927, he painted the *Seated Woman*, depicting another disconnected, menacing figure, while in 1929, he produced the *Woman in an Armchair*, having only a "suspicion" of a human head, with displaced breasts, a gaping jaw, jagged teeth like a shark's, and a confusion of limbs that made it impossible to tell "which of these limbs are arms, [and] which are legs."[49] In 1930, he painted another seated woman (seated women were the subjects of most of his works in this period). Called the *Seated Bather*, this painting again shows a nightmarish, distorted figure, with pincer-like jaws and sharp teeth. In short, the theme is pure brutality.

That violent treatment of women, Picasso's biographers say, was not unrelated to his own family life. In those years, his relationship with his wife, Olga, had become very difficult, and, in 1931, their marriage began deteriorating. She was a strong woman, and they argued constantly. As their marriage fell apart, the fifty-year-old Picasso became involved with a German woman in her early twenties, Marie-Thérése Walter.

Despite this new relationship, however, his works continued to emphasize violent images of women. In 1932, he painted the *Girl before a Mirror*, with Marie-Thérése as his model; this was another dislocated and inconceivable figure. The other two works he painted the same year—the *Figure in a Red Chair* and the *Yellow Belt*—were even more disturbing. Their subject was again seated women, always fragmented and dislocated.

In 1933, the "winter" of this season definitely entered Picasso's life: The great painter ceased painting. In 1935, he produced some portraits of Marie-Thérése, but he would not show them to anyone for many years. The summer of that year was the first summer of his life—in about 30 years—in which he didn't go away on vacation but stayed in Paris. "I am alone in the house," he wrote a friend, "[and] you can imagine what has happened and what is waiting for me."[50] His marriage to Olga had ended definitively that year; She had left, taking their fourteen-year-old son, Paulo, with her.

Marie-Thérése was living in an apartment elsewhere in Paris, with their daughter Maya, who was a few months old. Picasso visited them regularly and sometimes also helped with the care of the baby by washing diapers and performing other tasks. But though he wanted to marry Marie-Thérése, he couldn't do that: His Spanish citizenship did not permit a divorce from Olga.

Picasso was at a complete loss. He was given to bouts of anger, isolated himself in his house, and refused to see anybody. He became lethargic. He didn't get any of the paintings done that he'd been commissioned to do; instead, he started writing surrealistic poems, without rules of grammar or form, which "he tried to keep . . . secret."[51]

That situation persisted in 1936 and 1937. In 1937, new problems emerged when Spain began to be torn apart by the civil war. Picasso was deeply afflicted and he did what he could, offering financial support to those who were loyal to the Spanish government, the Loyalists. To express his personal feelings, he painted a huge work, *Guernica*, that movingly depicted the horrors of fascism and of war.

When that work was shown at the Paris World Exhibition, in 1937, it provoked a terrible reaction. Critics called it "vulgar," "debasing," and the like. It was indeed another of Picasso's nightmarish works, again with dislocated bodies, distorted eyes, noses, and ears, twisted feet and hands, menacing teeth, and with faces that were a cross between those of bulls, dogs, and humans. The French patriots reacted cruelly: Instead of wasting his energy on that work, they said, Picasso would have been better off going home and serving in the army. (Guernica was a small Spanish town bombed by Hitler's planes in 1937. The town was leveled and most of its inhabitants—men, women, and children—were killed. Picasso's *Guernica* is now considered one of his masterpieces.)

Picasso didn't want to give up his surrealistic works. Another young woman, Dora Maar from Yugoslavia, had replaced Marie-Thérése in his life, and he began to use her as his model. In 1938 and 1939, he produced more ghoulish paintings, including one of a woman who had the head of both a person and a dog, and another of a menacing cat with huge sharp teeth devouring a bird.

In September 1939, World War II broke out. Frightened, Picasso abandoned Paris and went with Dora to a small town on the Atlantic coast, Royan. He wasn't able to bring most of his art supplies with him and had to use whatever was available. He even made his own brushes. Picasso stayed in Royan until August 1940—when the Germans arrived. Unable to do anything else, he was forced to return to Paris, where the German troops were already in complete control.

In that disturbing atmosphere, 1941 began.

# The New Good Season from 1941 On

To Picasso's surprise, the Germans treated him with great politeness and respect. Officers frequently visited him at his home, admiring his works—including *Guernica*— and sometimes offered him coal for fuel during the chilly 1941 winter. But he refused with grace and humor. In 1942, a new Picasso was born: His anger dissipated, giving way to a calm and joyful disposition that was reflected in his works.

The first of those works was a statue (the first time that Picasso was involved with sculpture), called the *Man with a Sheep*. This was a serene, natural work like those of the great Italian Renaissance painters. Picasso started the statue in 1942 and finished it in 1943. Also in 1943, he painted another joyful and calm work, the *First Steps*, in which a mother with a radiant expression guides her small child as he takes his first steps.

In June 1944, the course of the war changed after the Allies landed at Normandy. A new spirit of hope spread through Paris, and Picasso began to paint Paris scenes. These are beautiful and romantic scenes from the Seine bridges, showing Notre Dame, Montmartre, Sacré Coeur, and other landmarks. In August 1944, sharp, vivid colors returned to the painter's palette for the first time in many years.

The same month, the Allies triumphantly entered Paris. Filled with joy, the crowd ran through the streets. Picasso's old friends and acquaintances, together with soldiers and others, flocked to his studio—a celebration that lasted for days. Picasso had suddenly become a new kind of hero, a symbol of passive resistance to the enemy during the oppressive days of the occupation. In the fall of 1944, it seemed that "Picasso loved everybody and everybody loved him."[52] He was one of the most popular people in France. The only person who could be compared to him was general Charles de Gaulle, the great hero of the war.

Picasso accepted that approbation with warm words and deeds: His house was always open at any time of the day or night. Exhausted soldiers even arrived to sleep during the night; sometimes as many as twenty people were accommodated in his studio. Around that time, the large exhibition, Salon d' Automne, again opened its doors after four years of enforced idleness—an exhibit where Paris's most important paintings were shown every year. Until then no foreign painter had been invited to participate; now Picasso was the honored guest. A whole gallery was made available to him, and he sent seventy of his paintings and five of his sculptures, all made after 1940 and unknown to the public.

But there was a "spring rain shower." On the third day of the exhibition, an infuriated crowd of young men invaded the gallery screaming: "Take his paintings down." They tore Picasso's pictures from the walls until the officials squelched the riot. It was a reaction against Picasso's affiliation with the Communist Party, which he quit a little later. The next day, however, a group of pro-Picasso students and friends moved in to guard the gallery.

From 1945, Picasso's "storm and fury" evaporated forever. He turned to cheerful and vivid subjects, and to a new art form: lithography. The same year, another woman entered his life: Françoise Gilot, twenty-one years old and beautiful, clever, and vivacious. (Picasso was sixty-four.) He painted his new model in a deft, cheerful manner: like "a flower with . . . a face surrounded by leaves or petals."[53]

He continued with the same style in 1946. On the Riviera, where he again spent the summer, he painted more than thirty lighthearted works—all multicolored with delicate rosy, blue, and green hues. One was *Joie de Vivre*, again depicting Françoise as a dancing flower. When he returned to Paris in the fall of 1946, he suddenly faced a tremendous demand for his works: All the museums wanted to acquire them.

The next year Picasso and Françoise had a child, a son named Claude, and settled in a village on the Riviera. They acquired a house there, and Picasso got involved with a new art medium: ceramics. From then on a period of unprecedented calmness and happiness began for him. He produced some clay masterpieces, like the *Pregnant Woman* (1950) and others, with Françoise as his model.

In the summer of 1953, his relationship with Françoise ended and another woman, number six, came into his life. She was Jacqueline Roque, a beautiful and self-possessed young woman—he was seventy-two years old now—who would later become his second wife and would be with him until the end. The following year Picasso painted her and created a picture of insuperable beauty and grace.

Invigorated by his new life, Picasso left the village on the Riviera in 1955 and bought a villa in Cannes, where he created some of the most beautiful portraits of Jacqueline. In 1957, he arrived at the distillation of his life's work: He painted a series of variants on his compatriot Velazquez's works titled *Las Meninas*, which remain unsurpassed.

But this good season finally ended here.

# The New Bad Season from 1957 On

From the very beginning of this season, Picasso felt old. He was seventy-six. His main concern at that age was, of course, his health. But he wasn't feeling good; he also felt disappointed, and his mental condition was bad. So, he soon withdrew from the world's stage. In 1961, he bought a villa on the Riviera surrounded by lush trees that screened the house from the outer world. Frustrated, he isolated himself there for the rest of his life. His days of innovation and of surprising the public with his works were over. In 1973, he left this life at the age of ninety-two.

# Conclusion

Picasso's alternations of seasons show that his life's good and bad seasons alternated every 16–17 years in the dates 1892, 1908, 1925, 1941, 1957. Adding these date of Picasso's to Beethoven and Verdi's row of dates we've seen in the previous chapter, we find this continuous row of dates: 1776, 1792, 1809, 1825, 1842, 1859, 1875, 1892, 1908, 1925, 1941, and 1957. We have confirmation that the seasons of these three men alternated every 16–17 years in the continuous row of dates indicated in Chapter 1.

Another confirmation derives from Picasso's life. As we've seen in this chapter, Picasso often didn't even have enough money for food. But later, he became very rich. When he was in one of his bad seasons, he was given to bouts of anger, isolated himself in his house, refused to see anybody, and he didn't complete any of the paintings that he'd been commissioned to do. But later, he became the famous Picasso. That confirms what we've seen in Chapter 2: If you have financial or even psychological problems in your bad season, don't despair, the good season will come in any case.

In the next chapter we'll continue and extend our confirmation by seeing how the good and bad seasons alternated in the life of Mikhail Gorbachev, last president of the Soviet Union.

# Chapter 6
# MIKHAIL GORBACHEV

Mikhail Gorbachev was born in Privolnoye, a small village near Stavropol, in 1931—that is, 50 years after Picasso. The people in his village "lived in wretched poverty,"[54] as he says in his memoirs. When he was six or seven years old (1937–1938), Gorbachev experienced the first real trauma of his life: his grandfather, with whom he was living, was arrested and taken away by the police as an "enemy of people." Neighbors "began shunning [their] house as if it were plague-stricken,"[55] and the boys from the neighborhood avoided him. This shock remained engraved in his memory for the rest of his life.

Three years later, in 1941, there was another shock. The Germans invaded Russia and his father left for the front. Town after town fell to the enemy, and by fall, the Germans were approaching Moscow.

## The Good Season from 1941 to 1957

At the end of 1941, however, the situation changed, and a good season was initiated for the young Mikhail: Moscow thwarted the enemy attacks, and next year, 1942, the Germans were driven back. In 1943, the total defeat of the German troops at Stalingrad came. When the war ended in 1945, Mikhail was again a happy young man: He went to school again, and by 1946, he was operating a combine harvester with his father on the farm. His father treated him with respect and they became true friends.

In 1947, the Gorbachev family was "better off than the others"[56] in their village, and the next year they produced such a bumper crop that his father received the Order of Lenin and young Gorbachev the Order of the Red Banner of Labor. It was, as he says, "a lucky year."[57]

In 1950, "the summer" of this good season entered Gorbachev's life: He graduated from school with a silver medal and applied for admission to the Faculty of Law at the University of Moscow. To his great surprise, despite being a "worker and peasant," he was admitted as a top student. He left his village and went to Moscow—with the Red Square, the Kremlin, the Bolshoi Theater. At the Law Faculty he was exposed to a wide-ranging curriculum: political history, economics, the history of philosophy, Latin and German, and so on.

The university was "a temple of learning,"[58] as he says, revealing a whole new world to him. During his years at the university (1950–1955), other important things happened to him as well. In 1952, he joined the Communist Party. The same year he met Raisa Titorenko, a philosophy student, and fell in love with her. The following year they were married, when he was twenty-two and she was twenty-one.

After graduating from the university in 1955, Gorbachev returned to Stavropol, where he joined the Communist Party's local youth organization (Komsomol) as deputy head of the propaganda department. He was soon promoted—without expecting it—to first secretary of the Komsomol's city committee for Stavropol.

# The Bad Season from 1957 to 1974

On January 6, 1957, a heavy burden was added to Gorbachev's life. His wife, Raisa, gave birth to their daughter, Irina, and soon their life became complicated. They "could not exist on one salary, and Raisa had to go back to work"[59] despite having difficulties working and being a mother at the same time. They "lacked everything and led a frugal life … [they] were still wearing the clothes … [their] parents had bought for … [them in their] student days."[60] Conditions in Stavropol were in a miserable state: The city lacked both a central water supply and central sewage; sewage often poured into drainage ditches lining the streets.

Things were not much better in Gorbachev's career. As he says in his memoirs, the years from 1958 to 1961 were packed with bureaucratic routine. Innumerable instructions kept arriving from the Central Committee, as if without these directives "no grass would grow and no cow would calve."[61] That situation prevailed until 1968.

In 1962, Gorbachev was transferred from the Komsomol to Party work at the agricultural department, and he was spending days and often nights traveling around the district and visiting farms. In 1964, he found himself in the "eye of the storm"[62] of a rivalry between two local Party organizations, while in 1966–1967 he was confronted with "scores of problems to worry about."[63]

Despite Gorbachev's efforts, he was unable to significantly improve the quality of life in Stavropol. He was so disappointed that he decided to leave the Party and turn to academic work.

He stayed, however. But the problems still remained unresolved, and in 1969, a "period of stagnation" started, as he says, that lasted until 1974.

# The New Good Season from 1974 to 1990

The year 1974 marked the end of Gorbachev's bad season. That year the Great Stavropol Canal was almost completed. In 1976, Gorbachev proposed a plan to save the farms from droughts. Although his plan was met with great skepticism from his superiors, he flew to Moscow and succeeded in seeing General Secretary Brezhnev. There, Gorbachev's new good season enormously helped him. Soon the big news arrived; Brezhnev telephoned him and said, "Go ahead."[64] He had won. In 1977, they had "a bumper crop"[65] as a result of Gorbachev's plan, while in 1978, there was an unheard of yield. Gorbachev's fame had already started to spread.

At the end of 1978, a crucial moment arrived. Without expecting it, Gorbachev was unanimously elected Secretary of the Soviet Union's "all powerful" Central Committee. He left Stavropol for Moscow. "Colleagues, ministers and acquaintances surrounded … [him] to congratulate … [him],"[66] while a limousine was placed at his disposal and bodyguards escorted him everywhere. He was forty-seven years old.

From this point on, Gorbachev's march to power would continue uninterrupted. In 1979, he was elected a candidate member of the Politburo, a decision-making government board consisting mainly of ministers and other high-ranking party officials, and in 1980, he was elected a full member of the Politburo. In 1982, when General Secretary Andropov became seriously ill, Gorbachev chaired the Politburo meetings, and continued doing so during 1983 as well as 1984, when the new General Secretary Chernenko also became ill.

In 1985, the "summer" of this good season entered Gorbachev's life: He was elected General Secretary of the Soviet Union. A new era thus began that would radically transform the picture of world politics. Early the next year at the Party Congress, Gorbachev called for radical economic reform in his country, and in October of the same year, he met President Ronald Reagan to discuss extensive arms cuts.

In 1987, Gorbachev proposed political reforms in the Soviet Union (including multi-candidate elections), and the Supreme Soviet adopted his proposal to give more independence to business enterprises. In 1988, he emphasized the need for glasnost (transparency) in the work of Party organizations and proposed a new presidential system and a new parliament. He also argued for perestroika (restructuring of the system). Simultaneously, in addressing the United Nations in New York, he called for a new world order and renounced the use of force.

The transformations continued. In 1989, the first free elections were held in the USSR and a new parliament, the Congress of People's Deputies, was convened. Gorbachev was elected chairman of the Congress. In the summer of the same year, Gorbachev astonished the world by declaring that Warsaw Pact nations were free to choose their own path. The Berlin Wall came down by the end of the year. (For his efforts to improve East-West relations, Gorbachev was honored later with the Nobel Peace Prize).

In 1990, Gorbachev proposed that the Soviet Communist Party abandon its leading role in the USSR's political and economic life, and the proposal was accepted by the Congress. Thus the Party's monopolization of power for more than seventy years ended. At the same time, the Congress elected Gorbachev as the first Soviet president.

But somewhere in 1990, Gorbachev's good season came to an abrupt end.

# The New Bad Season from 1990 On

In the middle of 1990, alarming signs of the breakup of the Soviet Union suddenly appeared. In July 1990, Ukraine declared its sovereignty; in August, Armenia, Turkmenistan, and Tajikistan followed, and in October, Boris Yeltsin's Russia declared its laws sovereign over the laws of the Soviet Union. In 1991, the situation worsened: Estonia, Latvia, Belorussia, Moldavia, Georgia, Azerbaijan, and other republics declared their independence. Yeltsin ordered the Communist Party of the Soviet Union to suspend its activities in the territory of the Russian Federation.

Gorbachev's bad season that had just begun didn't allow him to reverse the situation. By the end of 1991, the Soviet Union no longer existed. Under these circumstances, he appeared to have only one alternative: He resigned as president of the Soviet Union on August 24, 1991, and advised the Central Committee to dissolve. In his address to the Soviet citizens on December 25, 1991, Gorbachev said: "Given the current situation . . . I am ceasing my activities as president of the USSR. . . . Events have taken a different course. A trend toward dismembering the country and the disintegration of the state has prevailed, which I cannot accept."[67]

This bad season for Gorbachev continued uninterrupted. His attempt to be elected president of Russia in 1996 failed. In 1999, he lost his beloved wife, Raisa, his life's companion for more than forty-six years. To survive, he would deliver speeches all over the world.

# Conclusion

Gorbachev's alternations of seasons show that his life's good and bad seasons alternated every 16–17 years in 1941, 1957, 1974, and 1990. Adding these Gorbachev dates to Beethoven, Verdi, and Picasso's row of dates from the previous chapter, we find this continuous row of dates: 1776, 1792, 1809, 1825, 1842, 1859, 1875, 1892, 1908, 1925, 1941, 1957, 1974, and 1990. We are confirmed so that the seasons of these four men alternated every 16–17 years in a continuous row of dates—in a period of more than 220 years: from 1770 (Beethoven) to 1990 and beyond (Gorbachev)—as also indicated in Chapter 1.

But Gorbachev's life also shows how you can benefit knowing that a good season will come at a certain moment later. Recall that in one of his bad seasons, Gorbachev was so disappointed that he had decided to leave the Communist Party and turn to academic work. But finally he stayed, and later, he was elected General Secretary of the Soviet Union. If he had then left the Party, he wouldn't have become the leader of his country. Don't act forcedly, therefore, in your bad seasons; wait for the good season that will come with certainty in the future, and—who knows? It may lead you to unprecedented heights.

In the next chapter we'll continue and extend our confirmation by seeing how the good and bad seasons alternated in the stormy life of the Fourteenth Dalai Lama of Tibet.

Chapter 7
# THE DALAI LAMA OF TIBET

Born in 1935, the Fourteenth Dalai Lama of Tibet is an almost contemporary of Mikhail Gorbachev (born in 1931). He was born in a small rural village 9,000 feet above sea level in northeastern Tibet. His name was Lhamo Thondup. When he was about three, a search party sent by the government decided that he was the reincarnation of the previous religious leader of Tibet, the Thirteenth Dalai Lama, who had died three years earlier. Thus, the little boy was taken from his family and was put in a monastery. It was an "unhappy period of my life,"[68] he says in his autobiography, because he was a small child detached from his parents. When he was transferred to the capital, the Holy City of Lhasa, in 1939, he confesses he suffered from various restrictions put on him—for example, the fact that he was not allowed to eat eggs and pork. He still remembers also how scared he was of his teacher, even of "the sound of . . . [his] footsteps, at which . . . [his] heart missed a beat."[69] That situation prevailed also in 1940, when he was officially installed as spiritual leader of Tibet.

## The Good Season from 1941 On
But in the following year (1941), a new season began for him—not only a good season, but perhaps the best of his life. He soon began to enjoy life as a young boy. He had many toys, among them "a pair of beautiful singing birds and a magnificent gold watch, "[70] as well as a telescope on the roof of the palace with which he had a magnificent view of Lhasa. Another passion for him at that time, especially from about the age of fifteen on, were the three cars his predecessor had imported into Tibet: Once he managed to drive one of them around the garden.

And, in 1950, the "summer" of this good season started for the Dalai Lama: Because Communist China's troops invaded northern Tibet, the people demanded that the young Dalai Lama receive complete power and be enthroned immediately, two years before his majority. Thus, in November 1950, the enthronement ceremony was held. The fifteen-year-old Dalai Lama became now the leader of a country of six million people. Throughout 1951 to 1953, a kind of truce with the Chinese prevailed. In 1954, the big event came: The Dalai Lama was officially invited to visit China. He was not only excited at the prospect of seeing the outside world and that great country at the age of nineteen, but also thought he could help improve Tibetan-Chinese relations. "The prospect of the adventure that lay ahead was very thrilling,"[71] he says in his autobiography.

When they arrived in Beijing—a retinue of 500 people, including his family and many high officials—they were greeted at the railway station by the Chinese prime minister himself, Chou Enlai. The next day, he officially met Chairman Mao Tsetung. They had almost twelve meetings, and Mao treated him exceptionally: He "always made … [the young Dalai Lama] sit next to him, and on one occasion he even served … [him] food."[72] Most important, however, was the fact that during those meetings, Mao assured the Dalai Lama that his desire was to establish a constructive relationship between China and Tibet, whose nature would be directed by the Tibetan people only. Buoyed by those promises, the Dalai Lama left Communist China in the spring of 1955. When he returned to Lhasa, he had every reason to be happy and optimistic.

Early the next year, another invitation came that this time made him feel ecstatic: He was invited to visit India. For Tibetans, India is the Holy Land, and the young Dalai Lama had always wanted to make a pilgrimage there. "It was the place that . . . [he] most wanted to visit,"[73] he says. In November 1956, filled with joy, he left Lhasa for India. When he arrived in the capital, New Delhi, Indian Prime Minister Pandit Nehru was there at the airport to greet him, and there was even more ceremony and pageantry than he had encountered in his previous visit to China.

The general atmosphere in India made the Dalai Lama—now twenty-one—feel that a sincere friendship could be developed between India and Tibet. That would decidedly help Tibet's case with the Chinese, who, despite Mao's assurances, had not shown any sign of peaceful cooperation in the meantime. With this optimism, the Dalai Lama left India in the spring of 1957 and returned to Lhasa, believing that if he would offer the Chinese one more opportunity, they would keep their promises, as Nehru had advised him.

But 1957 was the last year in this good season of the Dalai Lama's life.

# The Bad Season from 1957 On

Soon after his return to Lhasa in the spring of 1957, the Dalai Lama's optimism about his country's peaceful cooperation with the Chinese began weakening dramatically: Widespread fighting had started in the eastern part of the country between the Tibetans and the Chinese, and the situation seemed out of control. "Whole areas were laid waste by artillery barrages . . . while thousands of people . . . had fled to Lhasa. . . . Disaster was [thus] in the offing."[74] The Dalai Lama was powerless, and he felt that soon Tibet would become a subject state of Communist China.

The situation had worsened even more by the summer of 1958, and early in 1959 a terrible crisis was created: The general commanding the Chinese troops in Tibet invited the Dalai Lama to attend festivities to be held at the Chinese military headquarters. The Dalai Lama felt he was obliged to accept the invitation. But the news spread like wildfire with catastrophic results. Thousands of people gathered outside the palace and warned him not to go to the Chinese headquarters. Though he assured them he wouldn't go, they refused to leave the palace.

As soon as the Chinese general learned of the Dalai Lama's decision, he became furious and accused him of arranging opposition against China because he permitted the crowd to stay outside the palace. The Dalai Lama realized then that the Chinese intended to use arms to scatter the people. It was "a horrifying moment,"[75] he says. Should he try to escape, or should he stay? Finally, he decided that leaving was the only way for him; if he was no longer in the palace, the people would have no reason to stay. His bad season couldn't indicate any other solution.

Thus the ordeal began that led the Dalai Lama out of his country. The trip to India, the Dalai Lama's country of exile, lasted three weeks. Escorted by his mother and a party of about a hundred people, he crossed a lot of high mountain passes, one of them 16,000 feet high, in the midst of blizzards. Physically exhausted and mentally distraught from the ordeal, the Dalai Lama and his party crossed the Indian border and then were escorted to the nearest town. The long period of self-exile had started.

The beautiful days of his good season had gone forever: The days when he was "accompanied by a retinue of servants, . . . was surrounded by government ministers and advisors clad in sumptuous silk robes, men drawn from the most aristocratic families in the land . . . [as well as by] brilliant scholars and

. . . religious adepts . . . and was escorted by a procession of hundreds of people"[76] every time he left the palace, as he says in his autobiography.

Soon the Dalai Lama learned the bad news: The Chinese had crushed the rebellion of his countrymen in Lhasa. Even worse was the fact that when he met Nehru a few days later, Nehru denied help to Tibet; he didn't want to destroy the amicable relations between India and China. With that, the Dalai Lama "experienced a profound feeling of disappointment."[77]

In June 1959, another calamity came: The Indian government officially announced that it did not recognize the government the Dalai Lama had established in that country. Soon after, the Dalai Lama was transferred to a new place, in a small house at a remote location near the border with Tibet, at Dharamsala, a twenty-four-hour trip from New Delhi, the capital. It was obvious that they wanted to hide him away, incommunicado, hoping he "would disappear from the view of the outside world,"[78] he says.

Soon, great difficulties appeared with the Tibetan refugees who had left their country and went to India. The majority of the refugees were settled by the Indian government in various locations, but the problems were insurmountable. Hundreds had died from the heat, in part because they had to work as laborers on road building projects. The Dalai Lama was heartbroken at their condition but could do nothing to help, and "one of the greatest difficulties … [he] faced . . . was lack of money,"[79] he says. The Indian government gave him an allowance of about a dollar a day, which was theoretically enough to pay for his food and clothing.

That situation continued from 1960 to 1967. In 1968, the "winter" had already entered the Dalai Lama's life for good: He fell seriously ill of jaundice that year. His skin turned yellow, he was exhausted, and the illness caused permanent liver damage so that the doctors said that he wouldn't live for long. He became so depressed that, in 1973, he had, as he says, "a strong desire to undertake a three-year retreat"[80]—to withdraw himself from the active life. And he did that. He was only thirty-eight.

But in the next year (1974), this bad season of his life finally ended.

# The New Good Season from 1974 on

The Dalai Lama's retreat for rest and meditation that started in 1973, gave him at last, in 1974, the rest he so much needed. At the same time, he also recovered entirely from the jaundice. In 1976, a hopeful turning point arrived: Chinese Chairman Mao Tsetung died in September. The Dalai Lama says that the day after Mao's death, he saw "the most beautiful rainbow he had ever seen. . . . [He] was certain that it must be a good omen . . . [of] the dramatic pace of change [that would soon follow in China]."[81]

And indeed, the next year, that change appeared in fully bloom; the Chinese government announced that they would welcome the Dalai Lama to return to Tibet. At the same time, the Chinese announced that they would permit a restoration in Tibet of the Tibetan customs, the national dress included. That announcement—promising new freedoms—came as a surprise and brought the Dalai Lama enormous joy. Soon after that, also to his great joy, Chinese authorities allowed foreigners access to Tibet, and permitted Tibetans to visit their relatives living in exile in India, and vice versa.

In November 1978, another joy came: Many prisoners in Lhasa, members of the Dalai Lama's administration, were publicly freed. In February 1979, the greatest news he could have heard was added: The Dalai Lama was informed that Deng Xiaoping, the new Chinese prime minister, wished to start direct communications with him. The Dalai Lama asked that first, a fact-finding mission be permitted, to visit Lhasa to see the real situation there. The Chinese agreed to this request and, in August 1979, a delegation of five members of the Dalai Lama's government in exile, his brother included, left New Delhi for Tibet via Beijing.

The welcome they received in Lhasa "was ecstatic...they were greeted by an immense crowd . . . and the streets . . . [were packed] with thousands and thousands of well-wishers,"[82] the Dalai Lama says. The same happened with two other delegations sent in May 1980. So, in April 1982, the Dalai Lama decided to send a team of negotiators to Beijing to discuss the future of his country. There, the Chinese declared that they wanted very much for the Dalai Lama to return to Tibet. They assured him that he would "enjoy the same political status and living conditions as he had before [his exile]."[83]

Soon, however, it became clear that he must not return to Tibet. The Chinese indicated they did not intend to make any changes in the way Tibetans were living. On the contrary, by May 1984, they encouraged a massive immigration of Chinese to Tibet, and a colossal influx of Chinese occurred. In view of that change, the Dalai Lama found a better strategy for solving the Tibetan problem: In 1984, he visited the United States in an effort to convince it to do something for Tibet. Indeed, in July 1985, many members of the American Congress sent a letter to Chinese officials stating their interest. It was the first time that the Dalai Lama had serious political assistance. The justice of his case was finally winning international recognition.

In September 1987, another cause for that recognition was added: The Dalai Lama had the opportunity to address the US Congress. There, he outlined his Five-Point Peace Plan, involving the transformation of Tibet into a zone of peace. (That proposal for peaceful coexistence later gave him the Nobel Prize for Peace). China, however, rejected his plan. As a result, huge demonstrations against the Chinese followed in Lhasa. "For the first time since 1959, Tibet was again headline news [worldwide],"[84] he says.

In 1988, the Dalai Lama had the opportunity to speak before the European Parliament. Again, as a result, several western governments called on the Chinese to respect human rights in Tibet and to open negotiations with the Dalai Lama on the future of Tibet. In the fall of 1988, the big news arrived: The Chinese indicated they would meet the western governments' demands and start discussions with the Dalai Lama. Full of optimism, he thus nominated a team of negotiators to prepare talks with the Chinese.

In the fall of 1989, the greatest moment in the Dalai Lama's life came: He won the Nobel Peace Prize at the age of fifty-four. He couldn't have a greater satisfaction. But this positive season would end in 1990.

# The New Bad Season after 1990

Little progress has been made on the Tibetan problem after 1990—the negotiations with China proposed by the European governments never started. On the contrary, for security purposes China maintains at least a third of its nuclear weapons on Tibetan soil, and the Chinese population in Tibet exceeds that of Tibetans. For this reason, the Dalai Lama had little hope after 1990 that he would be able to return to his country in the next few years. He would have to continue living in the remote Indian town of Dharamsala, near the border of Tibet, looking at his country from afar.

# Conclusion

The Dalai Lama's alternations of seasons show that his life's good and bad seasons alternated every 16–17 years in 1941, 1957, 1974, and 1990. We observe that these are the same dates as those of Gorbachev in the previous chapter. This also confirms further that our seasons alternate every 16–17 years.

Another confirmation derives from the Dalai Lama's life. As we've seen in this chapter, when the Dalai Lama fell seriously ill of jaundice at the age of thirty-three, the doctors said he would die soon, because the illness had caused permanent liver damage. But he survived for many more years; he passed age eighty. That confirms what we've seen in chapter 2: If you have health problems in your bad season, don't despair. Remember that they can be cured.

In the next chapter we'll continue and extend our confirmation by seeing how the good and bad seasons alternated in the life of Margaret Thatcher, ex-British prime minister.

# Chapter 8
# MARGARET THATCHER

Margaret Roberts Thatcher was born in 1925. The few facts available regarding her early years suggest that her childhood was a bad season compared to what followed. Her family's small apartment was furnished with used furniture and lacked conveniences like hot running water. On Sundays the whole family went to church four times: at 10:00 a.m., 11:00 a.m., 2:30 p.m., and 6:00 p.m. Margaret began to dread Sundays, so she finally got the nerve to ask her father "why they couldn't just go to church once or twice [like everyone else] instead of all day."[85] Her father was silent for a while, then gave a reply that worried her very much: "Margaret . . . never do things . . . just because other people do them."[86]

## The Good Season from 1941 On
In 1941, Thatcher decided to go to Oxford University and she applied in 1942. She took the entrance exams for the chemistry school, and some weeks later received a telegram from the university offering her a place and a scholarship. It was a major victory for her; her joy was indescribable.

In October 1943, Thatcher arrived at Oxford as a chemistry student. She was not only caught up in her studies but also became active in campus politics, joining the university's Conservative Association (OUCA), which had 1,750 members. She also found time for a couple of boyfriends and learned ballroom dancing. Chemistry didn't seem to interest her. Her spare time was increasingly devoted to politics, and before long she was elected president of OUCA.

That was the start of her political career. She met the politicians who visited Oxford, and was increasingly in the political spotlight. When a friend asked whether she was interested in becoming a member of Parliament, she didn't conceal her desire and replied: "Yes, but I don't know whether it's possible."[87] In the 1945 general election, Thatcher worked on the campaign of a Conservative candidate and "succeeded in stirring the enthusiasm of the crowds."[88]

In 1946, she received bachelor of science and master of arts degrees from Oxford, but she commented to a friend: "I should have read law. That's what I need for politics."[89] First, however, she had to find a job to support herself. She was able to get a position with a plastics factory, though this was not her real interest. Her life revolved around her political activities. She joined the local Conservative group as well as the Oxford Graduate Association.

In 1948, the big opportunity arrived: The Graduate Association chose Thatcher to represent it at the annual Conservative Party conference. There, an old friend from Oxford encouraged Thatcher to submit her name as a candidate in the next national election. She made a formal application. When she spoke before the selection committee, everybody was amazed. She was selected unanimously to run for Parliament as the Conservative candidate. It was February 28, 1949.

A young man, Dennis Thatcher, had also been invited to attend the conference. He was from a moderately wealthy family and from a socially respectable background. That evening Margaret began a relationship with the man who would become her husband. Within a month, Thatcher began organizing political fund-raisers and campaigning against the Labor candidate. Although Thatcher lost the election of February 1950, the failure didn't discourage her. The same situation arose in October 1951, when another general election was called: Thatcher again decided to be a candidate, but she lost. As she stood before the voters, however, "Dennis jumped onto the platform and announced"[90] their impending marriage. They were married in December 1951.

For the time being, Thatcher "put aside her desire for a parliamentary seat and concentrated on becoming a lawyer"[91]—a barrister specializing in tax law. In 1953, she took the first exam and passed. She already was pregnant. A year later, she passed the final examination. In the meantime, she had given birth to twins, Mark and Carol. Eventually, Thatcher looked for a firm where she could practice law and remained there from 1954 to 1961. At the same time she joined the Society of Conservative Lawyers where she triumphed: She became the first woman member of its executive committee, and she stayed at that position from 1955 to 1957.

## The Bad Season from 1957 On

Though very successful as a lawyer, Thatcher was not satisfied during 1957–1958: Her dream of becoming a Member of Parliament was unfulfilled. So, when a seat became available in 1959, she applied for it and was chosen to run. In October 1959 she was elected. It was not a happy period in her life, however. Her first two years in Parliament (1960–1961) involved more paperwork and other drudgery than she'd expected, and though Prime Minister Harold Macmillan appointed her secretary to the minister of pensions in 1961, she was dissatisfied. She didn't agree with Macmillan's economic policies.

The unhappy period worsened. In July 1963, Macmillan resigned and Alec Douglas-Home became prime minister. The next year, Douglas-Home called a general election. Thatcher was reelected, but with a small majority. The worst part was that the Conservative party lost the election. Thatcher and her party withdrew to the opposition until 1970. The bad situation continued. In the general election of 1970, the Conservatives returned to power, and Thatcher was elected again. But though the new prime minister, Ted Heath, appointed her secretary of state for education, serious problems began to emerge for her.

Thatcher demanded that "children not be allowed to drop out of school before the age of 16."[92] This decision angered large segments of the public. When she quipped before an audience of 5,000 women that "if you want something said, ask a man; if you want something done, ask a woman,"[93] she became unpopular even with the members of her party.

That wasn't all. Thatcher's bad season caused more mistakes. Her next step as minister of education, in 1970, antagonized so many people that it nearly ended her political career. She cut the free milk from schools for children aged seven to eleven. As her biographer Libby Hughes says, "The country went into an uproar, the press called her a milk snatcher, and cartoonists made endless fun of her in their drawings."[94] It was such a bad time for Thatcher that her husband asked her why she didn't "chuck it all in."[95]

In February 1974 came the final blow: The Conservatives called an election, but they lost; the Labor Party returned to power. Thatcher was reelected, but she was now in the opposition. She gave up her lavish facilities and went back to a small office.

## The New Good Season from 1974 On

In the spring of 1974, the situation changed for Thatcher. The Conservative Party was in a deep political crisis: The members disliked Prime Minister

Heath. Someone asked Thatcher whether she wanted to succeed him. She laughed and said: "I don't see it happening in my lifetime."[96] But a new good season had entered her life. When she later put her name as the leader of the Conservative Party, the miracle happened: After the final election in February 1975, Thatcher was elected the leader of the opposition.

Thus, a new era began for her. She started traveling abroad to solidify her knowledge of foreign affairs. She went to the United States to meet President Jimmy Carter, as well as to Hong Kong, China, and Japan. The Russian news agency TASS gave her a name that would stick to her: Iron Lady. "That's the greatest compliment they could ever have paid me,"[97] she said.

The decisive moment came on March 30, 1979. The British people had been angry with the Labor government all winter because of repeated workers' strikes (lorries were not delivering oil, petrol stations had no gas, "trains stopped running, unheated schools closed."[98]) Thatcher asked for a vote of no confidence against the Labor government, and after a seven-hour debate in the House of Commons, the great victory arrived: the government lost. Thatcher was excited: "A night like this," she said, "comes once in a lifetime."[99]

A new election was scheduled for May 3, 1979. During the campaign, Thatcher was tireless, and though the press predicted a Labor victory, in the end Thatcher and her party prevailed. Thatcher became the prime minister of Great Britain. As her biographer, Libby Hughes, said, Thatcher's "eyes filled with tears. . . . This would be a historic night to remember."[100] Outside her new residence at Ten Downing Street, "a cheering crowd and the news media were waiting for her."[101]

Thatcher's first priority was the restoration of the British economy. The following summer she made large cuts in the budget to decrease the trade deficit. Also, in 1980, she went to the United Nations and spoke at many international summits. During the Conservative Party's annual conference in 1981, "party members gave [her] . . . a six-minute standing ovation."[102]

In April 1982, the historical moment arrived. The "summer" of this good season entered Thatcher's life: She faced, with courage and grace, the great challenge of the Falklands War. On March 31, 1982, Argentinean ships had set out to attack the islands. They would get there in forty-eight hours. The British cabinet was in an uproar, and the majority of the members were against fighting. But Thatcher disagreed: "Gentlemen, we shall have to fight,"[103] she said. Her good season helped her to succeed: The war cabinet then agreed to send two aircraft carriers and other ships to defend the islands.

Meanwhile, the Argentinean ships landed on the main island and seized control of its population—mainly British citizens. When a British submarine sank an Argentinean cruiser, an enemy plane sank a British ship. But the British prevailed, and on June 14, 1982, Argentina surrendered. Thatcher's good season had again won. When she heard the news, she said, "It was the most marvelous release I have ever had."[104] The people also rejoiced.

For her conduct of the war, Thatcher won the respect of international leaders, and became the hero of her party. In January 1983, she went to the Falklands. The local people responded with an outpouring of affection. If becoming a prime minister was a great event for Thatcher, the Falklands victory raised her even higher to success. In May 1983, Thatcher called a general election the following month. She was triumphantly elected to a second term.

In March 1987, Thatcher was invited to visit Moscow to meet with the Soviet Union's new leader, Mikhail Gorbachev. The visit reinforced "the public's faith in Thatcher's abilities as a world leader."[105] And she had fulfilled almost all her campaign promises: More Britons now had their own homes, and Britain was "again becoming a prosperous and powerful nation."[106]

So she set a new election date, June 11, 1987, when she won an unprecedented third term. It seemed that she would "stay in power for years to come."[107] In 1989, she had in the budget a surplus of $20 billion, and she was planning to make "her philosophies a way of life for Britain."[108]

# The New Bad Season from 1990 On

But in November 1990 came the end of Thatcher's political life: The Conservative Party's members disagreed with her tax policy, and so she was forced to resign. It was the most bitter moment of her life. At first, she hoped she would return soon. But she didn't know she had entered a bad season that couldn't be reversed. From that point, the situation worsened. Thatcher lost the magic influence she exercised over the British people, and so she remained far removed from politics. Her grandchildren became her only joy. When they visited England, she'd take them "to the public gallery of the House of Commons . . . to show them where their grandmother once presided,"[109] Libby Hughes said.

Thatcher's bad season continued into the next years. She lost her beloved husband, her son was accused of serious criminal actions, and she was entirely removed from the political scene.

# Conclusion

Thatcher's alternations of seasons show that her life's good and bad seasons alternated every 16–17 years in 1941, 1957, 1974, and 1990. These dates are the same as those of the Dalai Lama and Gorbachev in the two previous chapters. This confirms that the alternations of seasons described in this book are valid not only for men but also for women.

But Thatcher's life also shows how you can benefit knowing that you are in a good season at a certain moment. Recall the case of the Falklands War. Though the majority of the British cabinet's members were against fighting, Thatcher disagreed. Still, her risky action ended in triumph: Argentina surrendered. Her good season had helped decidedly. That confirms what we've seen in chapter 2: Don't hesitate to risk bold actions when you know you are in a good season of your life—luck is with you.

In the next chapter we'll continue and extend our confirmation by seeing how the good and bad seasons alternated in the life of famous American actress Elizabeth Taylor.

Chapter 9
# ELIZABETH TAYLOR

Elizabeth Taylor was born in London to American parents who soon returned home. Since we do not have many details on her early years, we can't know whether she was happy or not at that age, and, therefore, whether she was in a good or bad season. She apparently had a normal childhood, attending school and playing with friends. But we do know that in 1941 a really good season, a spectacular one, started for her.

## The Good Season from 1941 On

Thanks to her mother's connections, little Taylor signed in 1941—at age nine—a contract with Universal Movies. This is when her career as an actress began. Though the next year she was dismissed—because she was talentless, according to a studio executive—her career soon continued. In 1943, Metro-Gold-wyn-Mayer, the most important movie studio at the time, signed Taylor up with a one-year contract for a role in the upcoming movie *Lassie Come Home*. The movie became a box office hit.

Taylor's successes would continue into the next years, too. In 1944, she played an impressive role in *Jane Eyre*, as well as a small part in *The White Cliffs of Dover*. In 1945, her passionate performance in *National Velvet* brought her a new contract and a salary of $1,200 per month. She had thus become her family's major breadwinner. Acknowledging her success, *Life* magazine featured her in a cover story in 1945 on her thirteenth birthday.

In 1946, Taylor starred in *The Courage of Lassie*, and in 1947, she starred in the Broadway hit *Life with Father*—as well as *Cynthia*, where she had her first on-screen kiss. In *Cynthia*, she performed a very touching role, and the film had enormous success. As a result, the studio now treated her "like a beautiful princess, kept behind protected walls."[110]

The successes continued. In 1948, she starred in the films *A Date with Judy* and *Julia Misbehaves*, while in 1949, there were *Little Women* and the *Conspirator*. In 1950, she appeared in two more films: *The Big Hangover* and *Father of the Bride*, which became an immediate box office hit. The same year, Taylor announced her engagement to hotel heir Conrad "Nicky" Hilton, "America's most eligible bachelor,"[111] and they got married on May 6 of that year. She was eighteen and he was twenty-three.

Though Taylor soon became disillusioned with her marriage—after only seven months, she asked for a divorce—she was completely undisturbed by that fact, and she continued to play starring roles. In 1951, she appeared in *A Place in the Sun* with Montgomery Clift, and the film met with much critical acclaim. After her divorce, she starred in *Love Is Better Than Ever* (1952), during which she had a love affair with Stanley Donen, the director of the film. Soon after—in London this time—Taylor starred in the extravagant film *Ivanhoe* (1952), where she fell in love with Michael Wilding, a star of British cinema. Wilding was married, but after his divorce—early in 1952—he and Taylor got married. A year later, she had her first child.

In 1954, Taylor appeared in other major productions, including *Beau Brummel* and *Elephant Walk*. But by 1955, when her second son was born, her marriage to Wilding began to deteriorate. He was out of work and his nonchalance about it disturbed Taylor. It was in this situation when she met the famous producer and showman Mike Todd, forty-nine years old, who soon proposed marriage. Dazzled, she separated from Wilding, and then married Todd, early in 1957. Soon after her marriage, she began living a much more lavish lifestyle. Todd wined and dined her with champagne and caviar, showered her with diamonds and furs, and made his Rolls-Royce and private plane available.

# The Bad Season from 1958 On

On a blustery night in March 1958, Mike Todd's plane was engulfed in fog over New Mexico and crashed to the ground, killing everyone aboard. The man who had enthralled Taylor was gone forever, after only a year of marriage. When she learned the terrible news, Elizabeth became hysterical: In her nightgown, she ran down the stairs heading to the front door, where she collapsed.

From then on, Taylor's private life would be in ruins. Immediately after Todd's funeral, his best friend, singer Eddie Fisher, was sent by his wife—actress Debbie Reynolds—to comfort Taylor. Soon, however, "their counseling sessions turned into something more,"[112] her biographer Larissa Branin says. By the next year, Fisher admitted publicly that he and Taylor had become lovers—and after the Fisher-Reynolds divorce, they "conducted their affair openly and defiantly."[113]

Those circumstances inevitably caused public animosity and even death threats. Everywhere "Taylor and Fisher went, they were heckled by crowds and various organizations upholding decency. Even the pope . . . [deemed] Taylor a lascivious, immoral adulterer,"[114] a fact that would nearly ruin her career, and though the couple got married in 1959, nevertheless the event had destroyed Taylor's chances of obtaining an Oscar for her role in *Cat on a Hot Tin Roof* or in *Suddenly Last Summer*.

Further, Taylor was not happy in this period of her life. While still a new-lywed, she confided that "her marriage to Fisher was clearly a mistake, and ... [though] she had tried to keep Mike's memory alive through Fisher,"[115] she only had his ghost. In the meantime, she had another reason for being dissat-isfied: Fisher's career began to deteriorate. He became more and more restless; he spent his time drinking heavily and losing lots of money when he played cards.

That was the state of affairs when Taylor—while filming *Cleopatra* in Rome in 1962—met famous Welsh actor Richard Burton, playing the role of Marc Antony in the film, and a love affair was kindled between them. Both, how-ever, were married. "Le Scandale" was soon known worldwide. Once again, Taylor "was condemned as a wanton woman, a shameless home wrecker."[116]

After divorcing their respective spouses, she and Burton married in 1964, but their union marked the beginning of a tumultuous period in Taylor's life. A year before her marriage to Burton, she had signed a million-dollar contract to perform in *Cleopatra*, also receiving ten percent of the film's gross sales. As a result, she earned about $7 million in 1965. So, when she and Burton got together, she was "living like a queen."[117] That lifestyle escalated after their marriage. Both actors commanded huge salaries, and had "a fleet of Rolls-Roy-ces, a yacht adorned with original . . . [works by famous artists], and later, their own jet."[118]

But the season was still a bad one for Taylor, and the "winter" of this season had already entered her life. The couple's lifestyle isolated them from the outside world and caused them boredom and heavy drinking. At the same time, Taylor had serious health problems—"chronic back pain, sciatica, a partial hysterectomy"[119]—that caused a severe dependence on pain-killing drugs and hard drinking. Soon, she became an addict, a situation that lasted until 1984. All this put big pressure on her marriage. Burton tried many times to turn things around, but in vain. The bad season couldn't be reversed.

Also, Taylor was not as happy in her career as before. Though she won the Academy Award for best actress in 1966 for her role in *Who's Afraid of Virginia Woolf*, critics said that the role "marked the peak of her career, for none of her future roles would match it."[120] When the film *X, Y and Zee* was released in 1972, critics said it was her worst performance.

Later in 1972, a tragedy destroyed Taylor and Burton's relationship: Burton's brother died, and he began drinking heavily. Severe quarrels with Taylor followed, and finally Burton was led to adultery. As a result, they separated in 1973. The next year (1974) they reunited, but Burton "was still succumbing to the charms of other women."[121] So, Taylor walked out—though she loved Burton very much—and their divorce followed soon after.

But this bad season of Taylor's life was at an end. A new season would begin now for Taylor, a good one again, during which she would live a dignified and quiet life, would be cured of her drug and alcohol addiction, and through a lucrative perfume business, would recoup the money she had lost since her multi-million dollar days.

# The New Good Season from 1975 On

In 1975, Taylor lived a happy year: She remarried Burton. But since nothing had changed in Burton's behavior, Taylor decided to free herself forever from the problems he caused her. The couple received the final divorce decree in 1976. From then on, Taylor would pursue happiness another way: through a quiet life. After her divorce from Burton, she met John Warner, a handsome and wealthy politician from Virginia, who was elected a US senator several years later. Soon he became her seventh husband. Taylor told reporters that "all she wanted to do was to live her life on [her husband's] farm"[122] in Virginia. So the next two years she did exactly that.

Later, Taylor decided to put some fun into her life. In 1979, she frequently appeared at the nightclub *Studio 54* in New York, where she "presided over the trendy scene . . . and spent many dizzying nights under the disco ball."[123] In 1980, she decided to return to her acting career. This time it was in the theater, in the Broadway production of *The Little Foxes*. The play was an immediate hit. But because her husband, a senator by then, had objections, Taylor decided at the end of 1981 to separate.

Three years later, in 1984, a new big event was added to Taylor's personal life—the "summer" of her good season had started. She entered a clinic in California and emerged from it completely cured of the drug and alcohol addiction—and "stronger, both physically and mentally,"[124] her biographer Larissa Branin notes. Taylor's good season had caused a miracle.

Then, in 1985, Taylor became involved with another sphere of activity that soon brought her great satisfaction: She joined the fight against AIDS. At first, she spearheaded a crusade to educate the public about the disease and to help raise money for research. For that purpose, she became one of the cofounders of the American Foundation for AIDS Research. At the same time, she was the first person to testify before Congress to solicit funding for the National Institute of Health. Taylor's efforts were enormously successful; her support and personal appearances reaped millions of dollars for AIDS research. She had now become a humanitarian and felt very happy.

In 1987, she would reach another milestone: She started a new career—in the perfume business by creating a perfume, "Passion," which soon became "a phenomenal success grossing an estimated $70 million a year."[125] She had recouped the money she had lost since her multi-million dollar days. Over the next three years (1988–1990), Taylor would continue her successful AIDS work, "helping to raise millions for the cause, while [at the same time] keeping up a rigorous schedule to promote her lucrative fragrance enterprise."[126]

But this good season would end in 1990.

## The New Bad Season from 1990 On

In 1991, Taylor entered another marriage: She married a construction worker, Larry Fortensky, her eighth husband. But the marriage caused her many troubles. First, many thought that her marriage to a construction worker was not in line with her status as a movie star. The couple also had a large age difference; she was fifty-nine, he was thirty-nine. Then, Taylor faced serious health problems, and, in 1995, had her hip joints replaced. The prolonged convalescence that followed damaged her relations with Fortensky, and, in 1996, the couple divorced. Taylor's, "lawyers battled with Fortensky over his exorbitant monetary requests."[127]

In the meantime, Taylor appeared in mediocre made-for-television movies that many said were not "worthy of an Academy Award-winning actress."[128] And, in 1997, her bad season continued: The health problems worsened. She suffered a seizure caused by a brain tumor. She faced a dangerous surgical procedure and was terrified she'd die. During the operation, a tumor the size of a golf ball was removed from her brain, leaving a scar from her ear to the top of her head.

The calamities did not stop here. After "several falls and many broken bones"[129] in 1998–1999, Taylor remained in bed for almost one year. At that age (Taylor was seventy-four in 2006), health was for her the main factor shaping her season. The indications weren't, however, favorable; her health problems were not over.

# Conclusion

From Taylor's alternations of seasons we see that her life's seasons alternated every 16–17 years in 1941, 1957, 1974, and 1990. These dates are the same as those of the Dalai Lama, Gorbachev, and Thatcher seen in the previous three chapters. We reconfirm further that the alternations of seasons described in this book are again valid not only for men but also for women.

Also, from Taylor's life we see that even the people we think of being hugely successful throughout all their lives also have had bad seasons. Recall that Taylor and Burton commanded huge salaries, had a fleet of Rolls-Royces, a yacht, and their own jet—and Taylor "was living like a queen." But the couple's lifestyle isolated them from the outside world and caused them boredom and to drink heavily. Taylor had serious health problems that caused a severe dependence on pain-killing drugs and hard drinking, so she soon became an addict.

In the next chapter we'll continue and extend our confirmation by seeing how the good and bad seasons alternated in the life of former US First Lady Jackie Kennedy Onassis.

# Chapter 10
# JACKIE KENNEDY ONASSIS

Jackie Kennedy Onassis was born as Jacqueline Bouvier, on Long Island, New York. The 1929 stock market crash had severely hurt the fortunes of her father, John Bouvier, giving her "a sense of insecurity and fear of poverty."[130]

When she was seven or eight, her family started to crumble. Her parents quarreled frequently over her father's pursuit of other women, and then they separated. The other kids needled Jackie, and she was "like a motherless kitten,"[131] her biographer Sarah Bradford says. In 1940, the humiliation went public: The news of the separation of her parents became known in the local press, with details of her father's womanizing. That fact caused Jackie deep insecurity and shyness toward the world.

## The Good Season from 1941 On

But from 1941 on, things would change: A good season was about to begin for her. In 1941, at the age of twelve, she had her first big success, winning a prize for horsemanship at a horse show. In 1942, things became even better: Her mother married a rich man, heir to an oil company with two luxurious houses. Jackie embraced her new family with love, experiencing a stability she had never known before.

In 1944, she enrolled in a school for wealthy girls, where she soon became an outstanding pupil. In 1946, she won first prize in a literature competition, and when she left school in 1947, she was "a bright, confident, imaginative seventeen-year-old"[132] girl, looking forward to unlimited possibilities. The same year, she entered a prestigious college for women, Vassar. In 1948, Jackie was dubbed as "Queen Debutante of the Year," a fact that immediately "put her almost on the level of a Hollywood star."[133]

The good season continued into the following years—the "summer" of this season had already entered Jackie's life. Between 1949 and 1951, she traveled to Europe, visiting England, Switzerland, Italy, and France, where she plunged into the cultural scene. In 1952, a lifelong dream came true for her when she was hired as a columnist at the *Washington Times,* where she soon established herself. The same year, her biggest moment arrived.

Jackie met the man who was to have the most profound influence on her life: Congressman John F. Kennedy, "America's most eligible bachelor"[134] and one of the richest members of Congress. Soon, Kennedy proposed to her, and in September 1953 they were married; he was thirty-six and she was twenty-four. It was the happiest day of Jackie's life.

The couple spent their honeymoon in Acapulco. Deeply in love with her husband, she wrote a poem for him while there. For the next three years (1954–1956), Jackie lived a life full of grandeur and satisfaction. The parties given by Kennedy's fabulously rich friends were endless. In 1957, she had one more joy: Her first child, Caroline, was born, something she had eagerly anticipated.

But 1957 was the last year in this good season of Jackie Kennedy's life.

# The Bad Season from 1957 On

The first clouds in Jackie's life began appearing immediately within 1957. Soon after her daughter's birth, Jackie started to decorate and redecorate her home. But her husband objected. He was furious. "What's the point of spending all this money?"[135] he demanded. It was her first clash with him. The turn in Jackie's own life had started. So, when he campaigned in 1958 for re-election to the Senate, she accompanied him with "a phony show of enthusiasm,"[136] Sarah Bradford, Jackie's biographer, notes.

The next year, Kennedy announced his candidacy for the presidency. But Jackie was unhappy. The previous year, her husband was so tired while he was campaigning that they barely spoke. What would happen if he was elected president? So, while Kennedy and his friends were celebrating their victory in the 1960 West Virginia primary, Jackie was so miserable that she disappeared from the scene and "went out to the car and sat by herself."[137]

The same situation persisted when Kennedy gave his speech accepting the Democratic nomination for president. While all the Kennedy family members were present, Jackie was not. She watched the speech on television at home, feeling that she "was all alone in the country,"[138] as she said later. When Kennedy was elected president in November 1960, Jackie again was not happy. When she heard the news, she "put on a raincoat and a headscarf and headed for the beach for a solitary walk as the other members of the family were dressing for a victory photograph."[139]

Jackie became First Lady after the inauguration in January 1961. But she soon found herself "buried behind a façade of suspicion, mistrust, and . . . [a sense of] imprisonment."[140] Most devastating was the fact that she became aware of her husband's many "other women"—among them Hollywood star Marilyn Monroe—a fact that started to terrify her. As if all that was not enough, she became increasingly aware that her husband's health was not good at that time. He had Addison's disease, and his back pain was so severe that he needed cortisone for relief and had to rely on crutches to be able to walk. As she said later, too, she and her husband were at that time "emotionally, twin icebergs."[141]

So, in the next year (1962), Jackie decided to go away. She traveled to India and Pakistan, then to Rome and London. The press was increasingly critical of Jackie's Italian vacation and of her night-clubbing activities: "Doesn't she have enough respect for her husband to be a good wife?"[142] they asked. (The news about Kennedy's "other women" was not known publicly at that time.)

The following year was even more devastating for Jackie, a year of tragedy. First, she was pregnant, but the baby arrived almost a month early and was stillborn. Withdrawal and depression followed. Then in that same year, the end came. On November 22, 1963, while campaigning in Dallas, Texas, together with Kennedy, her husband, he was assassinated. At thirty-four, Jackie was a widow. The "winter" of her bad season had started.

The first year of mourning (1964) was a year of emotional turmoil. The now former First Lady was disturbed and couldn't sleep at night; she felt her life was over. At the same time, she began to worry about money: The $50,000 annual appropriation she was receiving from the government was not enough, especially after the kind of life she had become accustomed to in the White House. She drank too much and sometimes wanted to commit suicide. She lived in an atmosphere of profound anxiety and grief, describing herself as a "living wound."[143]

Another cause of concern at that time was her desire to find another husband, a desire that really started to surface in 1965. This goal was not soon fulfilled. In the year after her husband's death, Jackie had worked with a successful architect, Jack Warnecke, on the design for Kennedy's grave. By 1966, they were contemplating marriage. But he was not rich and had no private plane, and no yacht. So Kennedy's brother, Robert, objected. Jackie "had to return to the stratosphere of the superrich,"[144] her biographer says.

Such a superrich person appeared in 1967, the Greek tycoon Aristotle Onassis. Jackie had first met Onassis in 1955 aboard his yacht *Christina*, where she and her husband had been invited for cocktails. The second time was in 1963, when Jackie was despondent over the loss of her baby: Onassis invited her for a cruise on the *Christina*. Jackie was impressed by his charm, so, on the day of her husband's funeral in 1963, Onassis—invited by Jackie—was a guest at the White House.

Ever since, Jackie and Onassis had kept in touch by phone. In the summer of 1967, Onassis invited her for a vacation on Skorpios, his private island in Greece. There, she agreed to marry him—and they married the next year. She was thirty-nine, and he was sixty-two. But her bad season couldn't be reversed. Jackie's marriage immediately caused her a new reason for worry: It was greeted by worldwide hostility—everyone felt that Jackie was betraying John Kennedy's memory. Also, the Vatican accused her of being "a sinner, who would be banned from taking the sacraments,"[145] because Onassis was a member of the Greek Orthodox Church while Jackie was a Catholic.

The marriage was not a happy one for Jackie. Soon after the wedding, Onassis went back to Maria Callas, at that time the most famous Greek opera singer with whom he had a lasting love affair, and they continued their relationship. (We'll see Callas' biography later.) Jackie learned about it and was furious. The next year, 1969, was boring and more disturbing for her: She remained alone and sad on the island of Skorpios when Onassis flew off on business, and she would burst into tears, saying she felt she would never again be really happy. (Jackie's daughter Caroline and son John, though they had no objection to their mother's marriage—they were then at the age of 11 and 8 respectively—never stayed in Skorpios, except on the day of the wedding ceremony.)

In 1970, the situation worsened: Onassis and Callas were photographed in Paris dining together at the famous restaurant *Maxim* and the nightclub *Régine*. It was no longer possible for Jackie to pretend she didn't know her husband met Callas every time Jackie wasn't present. Jackie's marriage started to disintegrate further. Though she did everything she could to please him, Onassis "was constantly complaining, . . . yelling and screaming at her,"[146] and humiliated her publicly by calling her "stupid" and so on, in front of their friends.

The situation continued into 1971. In 1972, Onassis presented Jackie with a legal document stating that she relinquish any rights to his estate. Jackie signed it. Two months later, Onassis started gathering evidence against Jackie to ask for a divorce. She soon found out about it and was unnerved. In 1973, the crucial moment came: Onassis's beloved son, Alexander, was killed in an airplane accident at the Athens airport—as we'll see in another chapter—and the next year (1974), Onassis's health began to deteriorate. He was diagnosed as suffering from the incurable disease *myasthenia gravis.*

But the approaching end of Onassis's life also meant the end of Jackie's bad season from 1957 to 1974.

# The New Good Season from 1974 On

In the first year of this season, 1974, Jackie ceased worrying any more what would happen to her marriage or to her husband, Onassis. When he died in Paris in March 1975, Jackie wasn't there at the moment of his death; she was in New York at a party her daughter was giving. At the funeral, "she appeared fierce, icy, remote, uncaring"[147]—and she didn't weep at all.

Also, Onassis's death gave her the means to become at last financially and personally independent. After his death, negotiations started between Jackie and Onassis's daughter, Christina, for a financial settlement regarding Onassis's estate. Though Jackie had signed the document stating that she relinquished any rights to Onassis's estate, the season was a good one for Jackie: Christina's lawyers informed her that the document wasn't valid according to Greek law. So, in May 1975, a settlement was reached under which Jackie received the sum of $20 million. Also, under a second settlement in 1977, it was agreed that Jackie would receive an additional lifetime income of $150,000 per year. Jackie's life had entirely changed.

With all that money in hand, Jackie moved back to New York. It was here that she would come into her own as an individual. During the two years after Onassis died (1976–1977), her life changed drastically. She revived her old dream of being a writer, taking a job in 1977 as a journalist. In 1978, she took "two major steps toward independence and self-fulfillment."[148] First, she bought a magnificent house in Hyannisport, Massachusetts. Then, she fulfilled her dream of having a literary career: she became an editor with one of the most prestigious publishing houses in New York.

There, Jackie "revealed a side of her that … [no one had] been aware existed."[149] Within four years of joining the company, she had become what a colleague described as an "incredibly positive life force."[150] With her status, she attracted many big-name authors to the publishing house. Meanwhile, a new, more satisfying element was added to her life: the presence of Maurice Tempelsman, a partner in one of the biggest diamond firms in the United

States. Almost the same age as Jackie, Tempelsman left his wife in 1982 and moved into Jackie's apartment. He loved her deeply and was very protective of her.

For the next five years, "Jackie felt free to lead an independent life, to travel, to see old friends and to make new ones"[151]—and to return to her beloved horsemanship. In 1988, she became a grandmother, at age fifty-nine, when her daughter, Caroline, gave birth to her first child. Jackie had now also become the head of the family; everyone turned to her for advice—a situation that lasted into 1989.

But in 1990, this good season would end for Jackie.

## The New Bad Season from 1990 On

After becoming a grandmother, Jackie began to change drastically: She altered her look from that of "sexy opulence . . . to . . . [a] more ladylike restraint"[152]—especially after Caroline gave birth to two more children. In 1993, she began to experience bouts of ill health, soon diagnosed as cancer. A painful swelling in her groin was diagnosed first, then it was found that her brain had been affected. She began experiencing mental confusion, so in March 1994, she drew up a will.

In April 1994, she collapsed and was taken to a hospital: The cancer had invaded her liver. The next month she died at the age of sixty-four. The woman, who was wife to two of the most famous men of the twentieth century, had left this world.

## Conclusion

Jackie Kennedy Onassis's alternations of seasons show that her life's good and bad seasons alternated every 16–17 years in 1941, 1957, 1974, and 1990. These dates are the same as those of the Dalai Lama, Gorbachev, Thatcher, and Taylor seen in the four previous chapters. This shows again that the alternations of seasons described are valid not only for men but also for women.

In the next chapter, we'll continue to extend our confirmation by seeing how the good and bad seasons alternated in the life of the great navigator Christopher Columbus.

Chapter 11
# CHRISTOPHER COLUMBUS

Christopher Columbus was born in Genoa, Italy, in 1451. We know almost nothing about his childhood and early youth years—until 1479. We cannot know, therefore, whether those years were good or bad for him. We only know that at the age of nine, in 1460, he went to sea. Later, in 1473, at the age of twenty-two, we find him as a sailor on a ship near Sardinia. In 1476, the ship on which Columbus was serving sank during a naval battle off Lagos, Nigeria. Wounded, he came close to drowning. He managed, however, to swim to the shore. After being rescued he was sent to Portugal, and from there he went to sea again. In 1477, his employer sent him to the then unknown north—perhaps to Iceland or Greenland.

## The Good Season from 1479 On

From 1479, however, we have lots of facts on Columbus's life. These facts show that a good season began for him—in fact, a triumphant season. He would discover the New World, win widespread admiration, and become a symbol of courage and virtue.

From the beginning of this season, Columbus—about twenty-eight to thirty years old—began to think of becoming a sea captain. A revolutionary goal—almost inconceivable in that period—occurred to him: to try to reach India not by the eastern route through which the explorers tried then to arrive, but by sailing westward across the Atlantic.

Columbus became obsessed with the idea, and the only thing that distracted him were the practical problems involved in its realization. To carry out the plan he needed official assistance. His first step was to apply to King Alfonso V of Portugal in 1481. But the royal council was skeptical and rejected Columbus's proposal. The visionary was persistent, however, and turned next to the Spanish court for help. Sometime between 1482 and 1484, he left Portugal for Spain. Initially, he stopped at a monastery near the borders, which had well-educated monks; one was applying himself to astronomy. When Columbus explained his plans for India, he found unexpected support.

The monks introduced Columbus to a duke in Seville who was also a ship-owner. The duke was impressed by Columbus's plans, and he solicited the help of others on Columbus's behalf. Seville had a large Italian population, including a banker and other wealthy individuals. With their help, the duke managed, in 1485, to assemble three to four caravels for Columbus, enough for the long trip.

State assistance was also needed for such an enterprise. The duke sought the help of Spain's Queen Isabella, who expressed interest and asked that Columbus come to Cordoba to meet her. Filled with enthusiasm, he arrived in Cordoba in 1486 and was received by both Queen Isabella and King Ferdinand. To the king, Columbus's idea did not appear attractive, but the queen was fascinated.

However, the queen was then embroiled in the Granada War, which had started three years earlier, so she could not give immediate attention to Columbus's case. But the great visionary wasn't disappointed—he realized he had to wait. The same situation also happened in 1487, when the king informed Columbus that he was willing to help. Filled again with enthusiasm, he rushed to the royal court at Cordoba. But there they continued to talk only about the Granada War.

In 1491, however, the "summer" of this good season entered Columbus's life: Queen Isabella again invited Columbus, toward the end of the year, to the royal court. An advisory committee she had formed had given a favorable assessment of the great enterprise. And so the dream began. Only the terms and conditions remained to be finalized. Columbus asked for "one-tenth of the profits to be produced by the exploitation of the land he would discover—as well as one-tenth of the gold, precious stones, and other goods he would bring back."[153] He also demanded the title "Admiral of the Ocean,"[154] as well as the position of "governor and viceroy of all the countries he would discover."[155]

The royal court at first reacted negatively to those demands. But Columbus was unyielding, and threatened to abandon everything. The season, however, was a good one for him: When he walked out, a messenger was quickly sent to ask him to return. Finally, all his terms were accepted, and the agreement was signed on April 17, 1492. Everything was in place for the great adventure.

On August 3, 1492, the adventure started. Columbus set out from the Spanish port of Palos, with a fleet of three caravels and an eighty-seven-man crew. After a stop in the Canary Islands, he sailed toward an unknown world. While many of the sailors were terrified of what lay ahead, Columbus was jubilant. "Thanks God," he wrote in the ship's log, "the air here is sweet and fragrant, and it is a great *pleasure* breathing it."[156]

On October 11, 1492, after about two months at sea, Columbus arrived at the first island he would discover in the New World. It was San Salvador—as he named it—in the Bahamas. When he found a suitable place for the ships to anchor, a crowd of curious and frightened natives ran to the shore to see the ships, the "sea monsters with the big white wings,"[157] which had suddenly appeared out of nowhere. When the sailors set foot on land, they "knelt down, kissed the earth, and thanked God."[158]

During the next three months, Columbus explored almost all the other islands in that area—including Cuba and Haiti—and at the end of December, he headed back to Europe. He stopped first at the Azores—on February 15, 1493—then returned to the port of Palos, Spain, from which he had sailed. He had realized his dream.

News of Columbus's return, after a seven-month absence in uncharted waters, immediately spread throughout Spain. The delighted king and queen welcomed him with a triumphal reception in Barcelona. Huge crowds—nobility and commoners alike—greeted him. He was feted like royalty and crowned with a special crown. Six natives Columbus had brought back with him—"live trophies"[159] of his success—were baptized Christians before the crowd.

In September 1493, Columbus—now forty-two—set sail on his second voyage to the New World. This time it was a much bigger undertaking: seventeen ships, 1,200 men, and provisions for six months. After forty days, he reached the islands again. He stayed there for more than two years, until March 1496. He explored other islands, too—Puerto Rico, Jamaica, Santa Cruz—and, in June 1496, he returned to Spain.

# The Bad Season from 1496 On

At the second half of 1496, Columbus's psychological state suddenly changed dramatically. Immediately after his return to Spain that year, he discarded his admiral's uniform and "adopted a Franciscan monk's frock, which he never took off again."[160] And shortly after he returned to Spain, he was charged in a

Spanish court with serious offenses that he had committed, according to his accusers, during his second voyage to the New World: He was charged with trying to challenge the king's authority in the new lands.

Columbus was eventually acquitted, but his reputation had been tarnished. The trouble he'd been in, and his failure to bring back the gold he'd promised to Isabella and Ferdinand, could have meant the end of his voyages. But the queen and king agreed to support him on a third expedition. He sailed, in January 1498, with eight ships. After two months, he arrived at Trinidad. But he suffered from arthritis and eye problems. When he reached the island of Hispaniola (today Haiti and Dominican Republic) in August of the same year, he found that the Spanish colonists he'd left behind during his previous visit had revolted.

Columbus did his best to quell the revolt, but Isabella and Ferdinand sent an independent governor to investigate the situation. Based on the depositions of some of the rebels, the governor accused Columbus of being culpable—and sent him back to Spain, bound in chains. Columbus's humiliation had been completed. When he reached Spain, in October 1500, he never got over the humiliation of appearing before the people, in his Franciscan monk's frock and in shackles. He expressed a desire to be buried in his chains. His reputation had sunk to such depths, he felt, that "no one—no matter how worthless—hesitated to deprecate"[161] him.

After his arrival in Spain, Columbus was transferred to a monastery in Seville, still in chains, to await his fate. Six weeks later the chains were removed and he was brought to the royal palace of Alhambra in Granada. The king and the queen received him in a friendly manner, and they promised "justice would be done."[162] But that promise was not fulfilled.

The worst blow for Columbus came next year (1501). After his meeting with the king and queen, he again withdrew to a monastery and started examining the results of his explorations. He suddenly realized the terrible mistake he had made: The islands he had explored were *not India* as he had thought, but some other part of the world. The disappointment was unbearable.

To find out what happened, he decided to make another voyage to try to find a passage to India. He again applied to the king and the queen who immediately agreed to his request—either because they believed in him, or, as his biographers suggest, "Because they wanted to get rid of him forever."[163] On May 9, 1502, Columbus set sail again—this time with four small ships—on his fourth expedition to the New World.

But he wasn't in a position to reverse his bad season: the fourth trip was ill fated. When he reached Hispaniola on June 29, 1502, a terrible hurricane struck, but the governor of the island did not permit him to land. For the next three months Columbus explored the islands and the coast of Central America in the midst of terrible storms—always looking for a passage to India. But his ships were badly damaged; "The sails were tattered and anchors, masts, rigging, boats, and provisions had mostly been lost."[164]

When Columbus arrived in Panama, late 1502, his bad season prevented him from seeing that the passage he was seeking was there—what separated him from the Pacific Ocean was a strip of land "only 40 miles wide."[165] Disappointed, the great navigator returned to Jamaica in June 1503. But his ships couldn't hold out any longer; only two of the original were left, and he was forced to abandon them. He was now essentially shipwrecked.

Ill and exhausted, Columbus waited for help. His men mutinied, and the natives also attacked them repeatedly. Finally, Columbus made his way to Hispaniola; from there he sailed, in September 1504, for Spain. He "would never see the lands he discovered again."[166]

Columbus arrived in Spain in November of 1504. It was a sad return; nobody was there to greet him. A few days later, he lost his main support when Queen Isabella died. Alone and seriously ill—he could not even go to the queen's funeral—Columbus again retreated to a monastery. He felt old, tired, and above all, embittered. On May 20, 1506, the greatest navigator of all seasons died in obscurity at the age of fifty-five.

# Conclusion

From Columbus's alternations of seasons we can see that his life's seasons alternated every 16–17 years in 1479 and 1496. Columbus lived more than 500 years ago. If we extend Columbus' dates every 16–17 years, we arrive at the year 1990—this way: 1496, 1512, 1529, 1545, 1562, 1578, 1595, 1611, 1628, 1644, 1661, 1677, 1694, 1710, 1727, 1744, 1760, 1776, 1792, 1809, 1825, 1842, 1859, 1875, 1892, 1908, 1925, 1941, 1957, 1974, 1990. That is a period of more than 500 years. We then have confirmation that the alternations of seasons started more than 500 years ago, as indicated in Chapter 1.

But Columbus's life also shows how you can take advantage of knowing which season of your life you are in at a certain moment—good or bad. Recall how the good season of Columbus's life helped him to succeed in discovering the New World, despite of the fact that almost everybody—the Spanish royal council included—were skeptical and had rejected his idea. Columbus's example again confirms, therefore, that as noted earlier, you too can dare when you know you are in a good season of your life—fate is with you.

On the contrary, when you know you are in a bad season, you have to act very carefully. Remember how Columbus's bad season destroyed him during his fourth trip to the New World. His bad season prevented him from seeing the passage to India in front of him in Panama. When he returned thus to Spain—disappointed and shipwrecked, ill and exhausted—his glory had been lost forever. You have to be very careful when you know you are in a bad season of your life.

In the next chapter we'll see how the good and bad seasons alternated in the life of Queen Elizabeth I of England.

Chapter 12
# QUEEN ELIZABETH I OF ENGLAND

Queen Elizabeth I was born in 1533 at Greenwich Palace, London. Her father was King Henry VIII; her mother was Anne Boleyn, Henry's second wife. Soon after her birth, Elizabeth was sent far from London, to Hatfield, and her parents rarely visited her. When Elizabeth was three, her mother was accused of adultery by Henry VIII and was executed, while her marriage to the king was annulled (as we'll see later in detail in King Henry's biography). As a result, Elizabeth then legally became a bastard. She was deprived of her title of princess, and Henry VIII no longer paid any attention to her upbringing. She didn't even have enough clothes to wear and suffered from headaches and other maladies. That situation lasted until 1544, when Elizabeth was eleven. But the next year, a good season began for her.

## The Good Season from 1545 to 1562

Elizabeth had a half sister—Mary—whose mother was Henry's VIII first wife, Katherine of Aragon; she also had a half brother—Edward—from the King's third marriage to Jane Seymour. In 1544, Henry VIII was preparing to invade France, but his official successor was his son, Edward, then only seven years old. Afraid of leaving the country in the hands of one child, the King "decided to restore his two daughters to the line of succession."[167] Elizabeth thus became a princess again, by parliamentary statute, and was now third in line to succeed the king—after Edward and Mary.

This change hadn't at first any immediate effect on Elizabeth's life. The favorable impacts began appearing by the next year (1545). In 1545 and 1546, she was living in the countryside but made frequent and extensive visits to court. When her father died early in 1547, that fact didn't cause her any worry: She knew her father had executed her mother. After her father's death, she inherited an annual income of $6,000, while at the same time she was invited to live with her stepmother, Queen Katherine Parr—Henry's VIII widow and sixth wife—at her residence in Chelsea.

It was there that Elizabeth had her first love interest. After Edward ascended the throne—at the age ten—the widow Katherine Parr secretly married Lord Thomas Seymour. But Seymour immediately started showing an interest in the young princess, who "blushed hearing Seymour's name and smiled if he were praised in her presence."[168] However, it was too soon for her to have serious feelings of love.

Though in May 1548 Queen Katherine noticed what was happening and sent Elizabeth to Cheshunt, in October 1549, Elizabeth returned to court— Queen Katherine had died in August 1548. By 1550, Elizabeth had her own house in London, though she was invited many times to lodge at the palace. She also became a great landowner after her father's will was settled. Her household consisted of 120 persons and "when she rode into London, in March 1552, to visit her brother, she was accompanied by a retinue of some 200 horsemen."[169]

In the spring of 1553, she moved ahead in the line of succession—the "summer" of this good season has started in her life. King Edward became seriously ill and died four months later, at the age of sixteen. Elizabeth's half sister, Mary, became Queen of England, according to the terms of Henry's VIII will, and Elizabeth became first in line to succeed her.

Early in 1554, a rebellion burst out. English courtiers conspired to overthrow Mary and place Elizabeth on the throne—which of course would have advanced Elizabeth's interests, though she was unaware of the plot. The conspirators failed, however, and were captured. Believing that Elizabeth knew of the plot, Mary ordered her arrest and imprisonment. But the season was a good one for Elizabeth: Not having any evidence against her, Mary soon released Elizabeth; she only put her under house arrest far from London. This situation had the unintended effect of making Elizabeth very popular. "Throughout her journey [to her new residence], men and women flocked to see her . . . [offering] cake and wafers . . . while church bells were rung to celebrate her freedom."[170]

Elizabeth stayed far from London for only about a year. In April 1555, Mary was forced to bring her back, because she feared that in case she died, Mary

Stuart (Mary, Queen of Scots), would claim the throne, since she was the granddaughter of Henry's VIII sister, Margaret. Elizabeth, therefore, should be ready to ascend the throne if necessary.

In London, Elizabeth returned to the life of the court. She had her own household, was free to travel, and resumed her studies. Extremely well educated, she was taught by a series of tutors, and though, in 1556, her household became "the center of another plot against Mary"[171], the plot failed, andElizabeth was not arrested. Mary was in poor health and again wanted Elizabeth at liberty to block Mary Stuart's claim to the throne.

Two years later, Elizabeth reached the height of her good fortune, though at her half-sister's expense. Mary's health worsened, and late in 1558 she died. Elizabeth became the new Queen of England at the age of twenty-five; her coronation took place on January 15, 1559. The child that had been proclaimed a bastard twenty-two years earlier and had been deprived of the title of princess was now at the top of her country's hierarchy.

The following three years (1559–1561) were very satisfying for Elizabeth. In 1559, she negotiated a peace treaty with France regarding the occupation of Calais—a treaty that, under the circumstances, was the best possible solution. The following year she negotiated another treaty with France by which it was agreed that the claimant to the English throne, Mary Stuart of Scotland (who was married to King Francis II of France), "would neither bear the title nor quarter the arms of England."[172]

In 1562, however, this good season for Elizabeth would end.

# The Bad Season from 1562 to 1578

In October 1562, Elizabeth fell seriously ill with smallpox. She feared she would die, and lacking a successor, appointed John Dudley, duke of Northumberland, as "Protector of England"—though nobody knew what this title meant. (During the previous two years, Elizabeth contemplated marrying John Dudley, but in the summer of 1561 she changed her mind). Luckily, however, Elizabeth recovered, but that illness would soon bring her lots of worries. In the same month (October 1562), Elizabeth also learned a bitter lesson. She ordered that a campaign be mounted against France, but the project wasn't well conceived, and the result was a failure. In July 1563, "the remnants of the English army surrendered and returned home. . . . Calais was irretrievably lost"[173] for England.

The same year (1563), the situation worsened. Because of Elizabeth's recent illness, Parliament "petitioned the queen to marry or, if not . . . to lay down the succession in a parliamentary statute."[174] But Elizabeth only wanted to marry a man she could trust; the fact that her father had ordered the execution of her mother may have made her leary toward any potential husband. Also, she didn't want to name a successor, fearing that she might be assassinated by that person. So, she rejected Parliament's petition.

The rejection caused great difficulty in her relations with Parliament, a situation that continued for several years. In 1566, Parliament submitted the petition again, but Elizabeth rejected all marriage proposals—including one from the Archduke Charles of Austria, the son of the Holy Roman Emperor.

As if the pressure to marry wasn't enough cause of worry, a new threatening element was added. Queen Mary Stuart of Scotland was forced by the Scottish lords to abdicate, and, in 1567, she fled to northern England. Elizabeth originally offered refuge, but since Mary was "the strongest contender"[175] for the English throne, Elizabeth decided to hold her prisoner. Their rivalry was not only political; as a Catholic, Mary posed a major religious threat to Protestant England under Elizabeth.

In 1569, that threat was realized: A rebellion against Elizabeth burst out—the "Northern Rebellion"[176]—led by the Catholic earls of Northumberland and Westmorland, who wanted to put Mary on the throne. The rebellion was suppressed, but in January 1570, a new rising occurred. Though this, too, failed, Elizabeth was badly shaken. It was the first time in her reign that she seriously feared for her throne—the "winter" of this bad season had already entered Elizabeth's life.

In 1571, another plot was uncovered—the plan was for "Elizabeth to be assassinated and for a small Spanish army to invade England."[177] As a result of this plan, the relations between England and Spain deteriorated. In the next few years (1572–1576), England was in a state of siege by a combined Franco-Spanish offensive. It is not surprising, therefore, that, in 1577, Elizabeth was troubled with a leg ulcer and was suffering from terrible toothaches.

But this bad season ended in the middle of 1578.

# The New Good Season from 1578 to 1595

In the summer of 1578, Elizabeth finally decided to get married. She was forty-five. Her choice was Francis, Duke of Anjou—brother of France's King Henry III. Francis was more than twenty years her junior, and Elizabeth believed she could trust him. In August 1579, Anjou arrived in London to court the Queen. Though Elizabeth's council of ministers was divided over the marriage because Anjou was French—seven members of the council were opposed, while five were in favor—Elizabeth announced, in 1581, that she would marry Anjou.

But an objection immediately broke out, and she retreated—after all, she wasn't enthusiastic about getting married, viewing marriage only as a duty. After renouncing her intended marriage, however, Elizabeth became extremely popular among her subjects. For the next few years (1582–1585), she walked carelessly in public, traveled in open carriages and barges, and when underway ate and drank without fear of being poisoned. In 1586, an opportunity arose for Elizabeth to get rid of the threat posed by Mary Stuart forever. From Mary's secret correspondence, a plot to assassinate Elizabeth was uncovered. Elizabeth was outraged. She ordered a trial, and the court sentenced Mary to death. On February 8, 1587, Mary was executed.

The next year, the greatest moment in Elizabeth's reign arrived—the new "summer" of her life had started. Spain's King Philip II decided to invade England. In July 1588, a Spanish "Armada of 125 vessels"[178] was in the Channel, off Calais, where it anchored. But there, "English fire ships loaded with explosives were released and drifted"[179] by the currents towards the Spanish fleet. Panic ensued. The Spanish Armada dispersed, and "driven by strong winds northwards . . . [was] forced to return to Spain by circumnavigating the British Isles."[180] On the journey home, about forty vessels shipwrecked, and about 15,000 Spanish seamen were drowned.

The defeat of the Spanish Armada brilliantly enhanced Elizabeth's reputation. As her biographer, Susan Doran, says, "sermons, ballads, pamphlets, and commemorative medals celebrated the victory,"[181] all demonstrating Elizabeth's courage and success as a leader in war. That triumph dominated her life for the next five or six years (1589–1594/5). Her happiness was palpable and could be seen in the stylish clothes and fabulous jewelry that she began to favor.

# The New Bad Season After 1595

In 1595, a rebellion erupted in Ireland against England. But Elizabeth's coffers did not contain enough money to handle the new situation. England was in a bad economic recession. On the other hand, Elizabeth's "generals and naval commanders frequently disobeyed her or deliberately misconstrued her instructions."[182] As a result, she was under stress, made more difficult by the fact that she was no longer young (she was sixty-two). She increasingly withdrew to her chamber, and "accusations of [her] indecisiveness"[183] began to be heard.

Among her accusers was the second earl of Essex, who showed great disrespect for her. "In the midst of an argument in council [in July 1598] . . . [Essex quarreled with Elizabeth and] turned his back on her. . . . She . . . gave him a cuff on the ear . . . Essex laid his hand upon his sword and had to be restrained by another councilor."[184]

Finally, Elizabeth agreed, in 1598, to quell the rebellion in Ireland, and she sent an army of 17,000 men under the command of Essex. But her decision would soon cost her a lot. Essex didn't achieve anything; on the contrary, he negotiated a truce and returned to London in September 1599, despite Elizabeth's instructions to the contrary. Outraged, she put Essex on trial in 1600; he was found guilty and was "suspended from all his offices."[185] In a state of despair, he decided to plan a coup, and, in February 1601, "he marched with about 200 armed men through the streets of London."[186]

Though Essex failed—and Elizabeth ordered his execution—she sunk into a state of melancholy after his death. She knew that the rebels who had followed Essex were, as her biographer, Susan Doran, notes, "representative of a wider group of soldiers, gentlemen, and aristocrats who were disaffected and disillusioned with Elizabeth's rule."[187]

The final blow on Elizabeth came in March 1603. At first she suffered from insomnia; then she had problems with her throat. Soon, she had a stroke and couldn't speak. On March 24, England's warrior queen died at the age of seventy.

# Conclusion

Queen Elizabeth I's alternations of seasons show that her life's good and bad seasons alternated every 16–17 years in 1545, 1562, 1578, and 1595. Elizabeth lived more than 450 years ago. If we extend Elizabeth's timeline, these dates every 16–17 years, we arrive at the year 1990 this way: 1545, 1562, 1578, 1595, 1611, 1628, 1644, 1661, 1677, 1694, 1710, 1727, 1744, 1760, 1776, 1792, 1809, 1825, 1842, 1859, 1875, 1892, 1908, 1925, 1941, 1957, 1974, 1990. That is a period of more than 450 years. We, therefore, have confirmation that the alternations of seasons, started more than 500 years ago, are not only for men but also for women, as indicated in Chapter 1.

But Elizabeth I's life also shows how she was radically affected by the alternations of her good and bad seasons. When she was in a good season, she became queen, as you remember—though *she hadn't made any effort* to achieve that outcome—only because her half-brother, King Edward, died at the young age of sixteen, and soon her half-sister, Queen Mary—who had succeeded Edward—died five years after him, though she was only forty-two. We confirm that you have to be patient in your bad seasons: Luck will decide how far you will go in a good season of your life—and how low you will go in a bad season.

In the next chapter we'll see how the good and bad seasons alternated in the life of Napoleon I.

Chapter 13
# NAPOLEON I

Napoleon I (also known as Napoleon the Great) was almost an exact contemporary of Beethoven. Napoleon was born in 1769 while Beethoven was born in 1770; and Napoleon died in 1821 while Beethoven died in 1827.

## The Bad Season from 1776 to 1792

The available biographical facts for Napoleon's childhood are less detailed than we would like. But the limited information we have suggests that the period from 1776 to 1792 was a bad season for him. Between the ages of ten and sixteen, Napoleon was enrolled in a military academy. After graduating, he was appointed as a young officer in an artillery regiment in the provinces of France. But he hated life there and asked for repeated leaves so he could get away.

In 1789, he abandoned the army out of disillusionment and returned to his home, the island of Corsica, where he got involved in politics. But he got into a dispute with local party leaders there, who accused him of disloyalty. So he abandoned politics and returned to the army, where he hadn't any significant success until 1792.

## The Good Season from 1792 to 1809

In 1793, Napoleon participated enthusiastically in France's military invasion of Sardinia's island of Mandalena. Though the undertaking failed, Napoleon's brilliant season had started. He left Corsica with his entire family—mother, brothers, and sisters—and returned to France. There he was promoted to captain and participated in an expedition to expel the English from Toulon. On this expedition, his exceptional abilities were acknowledged, and he was promoted to major general. Later the same year (1793), the French Parliament promoted him to the rank of brigadier-general—at the age of only twenty-four.

The promotions continued the following year. Napoleon went over to the political party of Robespierre and was appointed commandant of the artillery and sent to the Italian front, where he soon distinguished himself and won the esteem of his superiors. But a vernal storm descended: Robespierre was expelled from power and suspicion fell on Napoleon, so he was arrested and put in prison. His superiors needed him, however, and ordered his release. Napoleon returned triumphantly to his position in the army.

Further advancement lay ahead. In 1795, Napoleon was brought back from Italy to Paris, where he was commissioned to defend the French Parliament against the rebellious mob. He carried out that task so successfully that the French government officials appointed him major-general and supreme commander of the army of Paris at age twenty-six.

The next year, Napoleon took another important step: He married Josephine, the widow of a French general, thus cementing relations with the military regime. (We'll see Josephine's biography later.) Napoleon's military acumen and his connections soon led him to his appointment as supreme commander of the army of Italy—turning a fantastic dream into reality.

He lost no time defeating the Austrians at Genoa, and triumphant, he entered Milan. There he created a royal court for himself: He took up residence in a tower, and surrounded himself with nobles and servants, living like royalty. Though he had learned that his wife, Josephine, who had remained in Paris, was "unfaithful to him,"[188] that fact didn't distress him: He immediately brought Josephine to Milan and thus everything settled.

In 1797, his success continued. After a victorious campaign, Napoleon forced all of Italy to surrender. When he returned triumphantly to Paris, "crowds rushed into the streets to welcome him."[189] Napoleon had become a hero. Soon afterward, in 1798, he persuaded the government to entrust him with "the conquest of Egypt,"[190] too. He crushed the Egyptian army at the Battle of the Pyramids, and he took over as a monarch and a "modernist" in that country, surrounded by a team of lawyers, civil employees, artists, and others he had brought from France. (While in Egypt, Napoleon learned again that Josephine continued being unfaithful. He decided to divorce her, but when he returned to France, Josephine stayed all night before the locked door of his room, weeping and begging him, so he finally forgave her.)

In 1799, Napoleon had a new success: He "abandoned his army in Egypt with the command of one of his generals,"[191] and returned to Paris—without the government's permission. He made the trip from Egypt to Paris despite not having the government's permission and despite the risk of being captured by the English ships that dominated the Mediterranean. His good season held out, however, and he managed to cross the Mediterranean unscathed. When he arrived in France, Napoleon received a hero's welcome, and though he had abandoned his post in Egypt without the authorization of the government, the regime did not dare bring charges.

On the contrary, in November 1799—in a period of political turbulence, when the Directory was overthrown in France and replaced by the Consulate, consisting of three consuls—Napoleon was appointed by the Senate as the third consul. He and the other two consuls would conduct the destiny of France from now on. Napoleon's political career had begun. Jubilant crowds rushed into the streets to celebrate.

Napoleon's first act was to abolish the Parliament—with the intervention of Paris's military forces, which were under his command. This brought "the French Revolution of 1789 to an end."[192] Now, a period began in Napoleon's life, which would bring him unmatched success and worldwide fame—the "summer" of this good season had started in his life.

In the first year of this period—1800—Napoleon was appointed, at the age of thirty-one, first consul of the French government—that is, head of state. His selection was confirmed by a referendum in which he received 99 percent of the votes. He settled in the royal palace with Josephine and his mother and became "the absolute monarch of France."[193] From that position he created real miracles in the public life of the country: He "codified all the laws and reorganized the administrative machinery, educational system, and judiciary into a new system"[194]—which acquired his name and was destined to last almost to the present day.

In the same year (1800), Napoleon also became commander-in-chief of the army, and he set in motion the great expedition against Austria. Leaving Paris, he crossed the Alps, as Hannibal had done—an undertaking that "captivated the imagination of the French people"[195]—and arrived on the outskirts of Milan. There, in two great battles, he routed the Austrians. When news of the victory reached Paris, "jubilation broke out throughout the city."[196] In 1801, the Austrians were forced to sign a humiliating peace treaty.

The same year (1801), Napoleon signed another treaty, this one with the Pope, thus bringing much-needed religious harmony to France. The summer continued: In 1802, Napoleon signed another peace treaty, this time with England. The French were so appreciative, Napoleon was appointed by the

Senate a consul for *life*, supplanting his previous ten-year term. The following year (1803) reflected the same climate of achievement and satisfaction.

The biggest event came in 1804: The Senate proclaimed Napoleon Emperor of France. The decision was confirmed by a referendum in which he received a crushing majority. At his coronation in the church of Notre Dame in Paris by the Pope—who "had come to Paris just for that purpose"[197]—Napoleon took the crown from the Pope's hands, and he put it on his own head and then on Josephine's. That was an indication of his sense of superiority.

As emperor, Napoleon began to live an exalted life. He created an imperial court with a large staff of servants for him as well as for Josephine, while at the same time surrounding himself with a new aristocracy of princes and princesses (among them his sisters), and other dignitaries. Women—who had often slighted him in the past—swooned at his feet.

Napoleon's ascent in Europe continued. In 1805, Great Britain, Austria, Russia, and Sweden formed an alliance, and they prepared to attack France. But Napoleon preempted them by attacking first. He resoundingly defeated the Austrians at Ulm. Marching on, he delivered a crushing defeat to the Austrian and Russian forces at Austerlitz. This was Napoleon's most brilliant victory and the primary basis for his military glory. Three weeks later, the Austrians were forced to sign a demeaning peace treaty.

Napoleon was on the move. In 1806, he attacked the Prussians, destroying their army at Jena and nearly captured their king and queen. He entered Berlin where he took possession of the royal palace. From Prussia, Napoleon invaded Poland, attacking the Russians who occupied that country. There he became acquainted with a Polish countess, Maria Walewska, who later gave him his first child. Chasing the Russians from Poland, Napoleon clashed with them at two decisive battles in 1807 and then forced Czar Alexander I to enter into a peace agreement.

The two emperors met to work out the details of the peace treaty at Tilsit, Prussia. The czar was enchanted by Napoleon, and Napoleon confessed later that this was the happiest moment of his life. At the top of his form, he returned triumphantly to Paris, where his arrival was celebrated with unprecedented processions and parades.

And the summer continued. In 1808, Napoleon captured the king of Spain in battle; he "replaced the deposed king with his own brother, Joseph."[198] When the Spaniards rebelled, Napoleon invaded Spain, crushed the revolt, and entered Madrid triumphantly. He then revolutionized the whole social and political system of the country: He abolished by decree the notorious Inquisition, as well as the feudal system that had prevailed for centuries.

# The New Bad Season from 1809 On

From the first days of 1809, the situation began to turn against Napoleon. While he was in Madrid, some of his generals back in Paris plotted to overthrow him. Napoleon hastened back from Spain and neutralized the conspirators, but he could not punish them because Austria had declared war on France and he needed all his generals for the battles that lay ahead.

Napoleon attacked the Austrians and made headway, but he did not succeed in destroying their forces. He himself "was shot in the foot."[199] He tried again to overcome them near the Danube, but failed. Though a month later Napoleon managed to defeat the Austrians, his casualties were huge: He lost his best warriors, and his army was in disarray.

Meanwhile, the conditions in France had become tragic: A severe economic crisis was underway, and the public was showing alarming signs of unrest. Unemployment was skyrocketing, while French products were accumulating unsold in warehouses. For a time, there were no more battles for Napoleon to fight—and thus no victories, either.

This situation continued in 1811. In 1812, the clouds began to thicken: In April 1812, the Russian czar sent an ultimatum to Napoleon demanding the withdrawal of the French army from Prussia. Instead of replying, Napoleon decided to attack Russia. But his bad season didn't help: The Russian army pulled back in order to draw the French further in. When "Napoleon entered Moscow—without any resistance from the Russians—he found the city deserted and in flames."[200]

An embarrassed Napoleon sent a letter to the czar proposing peace—but he did not receive an answer. The severe Russian winter arrived and the French army could no longer hold out in Moscow—Napoleon's bad season was against him. He decided to retreat, but as his soldiers trudged through the ice and snow—without any provisions—"the Russians decimated them."[201] When his army crossed the frozen Berezina River, the Russian artillery smashed the ice in the river, and what followed was total destruction. Most of Napoleon's forces—the famous "Grande Armée"[202] included—were exterminated.

Napoleon abandoned the remnants of his troops in disgrace and, disguised as a Russian peasant wrapped in fur on a sledge, he headed back toward Paris, escorted by a handful of men loyal to him. After having traveled through all of Europe under such miserable conditions, he arrived at last in Paris, totally humiliated.

The failures mounted. In 1813, the Prussians decided to shake off Napoleon's yoke and declared war. In the battles that followed, Napoleon initially won in Saxony, but then he was defeated in Leipzig, where he faced the united Prussian and Austrian forces. A united Europe now marched against Napoleon: "The Russians, Austrians, and British invaded France from every side."[203] The French army—composed "mainly of young boys"[204] after the loss of the experienced troops in Russia, the famous "grenadiers" included—was unable to pass muster. Napoleon won some battles, but the end was near.

The definitive defeat came next year (1814). The "allies"—the British and Germans—invaded France. Napoleon was defeated in the battles that followed and within two months the allies entered Paris—which "Napoleon's army had already abandoned."[205] Empress Marie-Louise—whom Napoleon had married in 1810 after divorcing Josephine—and their son had already gone, too. Napoleon's generals pressed him to quit; he asked them to continue the war, they refused, and then he attempted suicide—but the poison he took didn't do the job. Napoleon was forced to resign unconditionally.

Immediately after that, the allies arrested him and exiled him to the island of Elba. When he was en route, infuriated Frenchmen tried many times to lynch him, but he was saved by his guards. On Elba, Napoleon was forgotten by all. He was visited only "by his mother and by the Polish countess Maria Walewska and their son."[206] Empress Marie-Louise was dancing and being entertained at receptions all over Europe. Josephine had died soon after Napoleon was exiled to Elba.

After a stay of ten months on Elba, Napoleon decided upon a desperate deed that led him to his end. He escaped in February 1815, and made his way to Paris. He again settled at the royal palace, resumed leadership of the army, and mobilized against the English and Germans. But because of his bad season, he was completely unable to reverse things. In the historic battle of Waterloo, Napoleon was defeated and suffered total destruction—the "winter" had entered his life for good.

Disgraced, he returned to Paris, where the infuriated citizenry demanded his resignation. He abdicated—for a second time—and tried to escape, but finally he was forced to surrender. He "hoped for asylum in England."[207] But the British government, having learned a lesson from his escape from Elba, banished him to the remote Atlantic island of Saint Helena, where he arrived in October 1815.

In Saint Helena, Napoleon lived a miserable life. He slept in a wooden shed built to serve as a stable, while at the same time he suffered from stomach ailments and could eat almost nothing. His skin was yellow and swollen, he was in severe pain, and he couldn't sleep on the narrow bed provided for him. He woke at night and recalled, as he confessed to his guards, how far he'd fallen. He was nostalgic for his childhood in Corsica, and he suffered unbearably at the thought that he couldn't leave Saint Helena. He said he would rather have died in the Russian campaign or at Waterloo.

Finally, on May 5, 1821, the greatest military leader of modern times died, as a terrible storm was battering the island of Saint Helena. He was only fifty-two years old.

# Conclusion

Napoleon's I alternations of seasons show that his life's good and bad seasons alternated every 16–17 years in 1776, 1792, and 1809. In these same dates Beethoven's good and bad seasons alternated in his life, as we've seen in Chapter 3. But the seasons of these two men are opposite: In the dates when, for Beethoven, a good season begins, for Napoleon a bad one starts—and vice versa: when a bad season starts for Beethoven, a good one begins for Napoleon.

That is a first indication and confirmation that there are two opposite courses of seasons in our lives, as we've seen in Chapter 1. Since Beethoven belongs to the first course of seasons, we confirm that Napoleon belongs to the opposite course—the second, as indicated in Chapter 1.

Also, Napoleon's life confirms that, as indicated in Chapter 2, there is a great advantage to knowing that you are in a bad season of your life. If Napoleon knew that, in 1812, he was in a bad season of his life, he may not have attacked Russia that year, an action that led to his humiliating defeat there, which marked the beginning of his end. Also, he may not have attacked the English and Germans in 1815 at Waterloo where he suffered total destruction that led him to death. Things may have taken another course for Napoleon: Maybe he wouldn't have died at that early age, and so a new good season, perhaps a glorious one again, may have started for him.

In the next chapter we continue and extend our confirmation by seeing how the good and bad seasons alternated in the life of the great French author, poet, and playwright Victor Hugo—who was born thirty-three years after Napoleon.

# Chapter 14
# VICTOR HUGO

From the few known facts, Victor Hugo's early years seem to have been rather bad years. His father—an army officer—had to move incessantly during the campaigns of Napoleon I, and at the same time had taken up with another woman, whom he later married. For the young Hugo, his father was thus a shadowy, somewhat unreliable figure. The situation worsened when, in 1814—Hugo was twelve years old then—his father asked his wife for a divorce, which was granted four years later. Hugo, together with his mother and brother and sister, then went to a poorhouse, where years of misery followed.

In that setting, the seventeen-year-old Hugo fell in love, in 1819, with a girl younger than him, Adela Fouché—but his mother disapproved and broke off the relationship. After two years, in 1821, his mother—who was everything to him—died suddenly of the flu. In despair, Hugo ran to Adela for consolation, and a year later they were married. The young couple had no means of support, so they lived with her parents. In one respect, their marriage was shrouded in sadness: Hugo's brother, Eugene, was also in love with Adela, and his jealousy ended in madness, which led to his confinement to a mental asylum, where he died after a few years.

## The Good Season from 1825 to 1842

But from 1825 on, things improved—Hugo's first good season of his life began. At first, he was awarded a royal grant of 3,000 francs per year, allotted to him for his novel, *Hans of Iceland*, published two years earlier. With this money, the couple could face the future with more security, so they moved to a bigger house. Around the same time, the novel attracted the attention of a famous literary critic, who opened his house to Hugo. Thus Hugo suddenly found himself mingling with many other novelists, poets, and artists.

The same year, the young writer—who had just published another work, the *New Odes*, a poem—was named by the king of France as "Knight of the Legion of Honor,"[208] at the age of twenty-three. He was also invited to be present as a distinguished guest at the coronation of King Charles X, which took place with great splendor at the Cathedral of Rheims. After the ceremony, Hugo described his impressions in his *Ode on the Coronation*, which was published by the royal printing house. His reward: a porcelain serving set from Sévres.

In 1827, Hugo published his first drama—titled *Cromwell*—but it was too long to be performed. In 1829, however, his second drama, *Marion Delorme*, was performed and aroused great interest, though "the government soon banned it for political reasons."[209] In 1830, Hugo's drama, *Hernani*, was performed, and its premiere created "a turning point in the history of the French theater."[210] It aroused mixed reactions: Some people were in favor, while others were critical. But the play was a milestone for Hugo. It ran for "a hundred performances and brought him huge earnings: He collected more than 6,000 francs."[211]

In the meantime, Hugo's family had increased in size: He and Adela now had four children—two sons and two daughters. His earnings from *Hernani* allowed him, however, to purchase a mansion big enough both for his family and to entertain large numbers of writers, artists, and other creative people. Things improved even more. In 1831, Hugo published his works *Ruy Blas* and *Notre Dame de Paris*, as well as his collection of poems titled *Autumn Leaves*. *Notre Dame de Paris*, a novel of about 700 pages, with unforgettable characters like Esmeralda and Quasimodo, sold out almost immediately.

Hugo's good season continued into the next years—and as a "summer" now. In 1833, his work *Lucretia Borgia* was performed with great success in Paris. Hugo formed a close relationship with actress Juliette Droué that would last more than fifty years. She remained devoted to him for the rest of her life. At the age of only thirty, Hugo was recognized as the greatest living author. His literary output was prodigious. In 1833, he published *Maria Tudor*, simultaneously with *Lucretia Borgia*. In 1834, he published his books *A Study for Mirabeau, Literature and Philosophy*, and *Claude Gué*. In 1835, his *Angelo, the Tyrant of Padua* was performed with great success, and at the same time, he brought out his poems *Songs of Twilight*. In 1837, his collection of poems titled *Inner Voices* was circulating.

In 1838, Hugo's drama *Ruy Blas* was performed, and in 1840, he published his collection of poems *Rays and Shadows*. The following year, Hugo reached the apex of his career: At the age of thirty-nine, he was elected as a member of the French Academy. At the ceremony that followed, all of France's high society "gathered under the dome of the Academy."[212] And when, in 1842, Hugo published his book *Le Rhin*—containing his impressions from a trip on the Rhine two years earlier—the book achieved great success: Honoré de Balzac, the novelist, found it a masterpiece.

# The Bad Season from 1842 to 1859

At the beginning of this season, Hugo published his play *Les Burgraves* (1843), inspired by the ancient German castles on the banks of the Rhine. But this work did not have the success that *Le Rhin* had. The critics pronounced *Les Burgraves* "the beginning of Hugo's decline."[213] Cruelly, they suggested that "at the age of 41, Hugo had said all he had to say."[214] From "a literary perspective, he was considered dead."[215]

The same year, Hugo suffered a second blow. Theater critic Charles Sainte Beuve published a book in which he revealed that he had been the lover of Hugo's wife, Adela, for about ten years. They had apparently met secretly at her home as well as in other places all those years. The humiliating news became widely known and, of course, wounded Hugo's ego and prestige.

But the worst blow was to follow. His beloved oldest daughter, Leopoldine, got married in 1843—at the age of nineteen—to the son of a wealthy shipowner. Seven months later, she and her husband drowned at sea. Hugo learned the news "as he was returning home from a trip he and Juliette had taken to Spain, from a newspaper that lay on the table of a provincial café."[216] As Juliette said, "she saw a man thunderstruck, with eyes that were looking but not seeing."[217] The pain his soul suffered remained for many years and was imprinted on several of his works.

To forget, Hugo tried to find consolation in his work. In 1845, he began his great social and historical novel *Les Misérables*. But he soon put it aside, and he didn't take it up again for ten years. The same year he became embroiled in a scandal; he was "caught in the act"[218] with the wife of a painter named Biarre. She was escorted to jail, while Hugo avoided persecution. His title as a Peer of France, which King Louis Philippe had just granted him, helped decidedly, but he was forced to leave Paris for several weeks.

Soon the situation worsened. Hugo stopped writing and got involved in politics, trying to bring about reforms. In 1848, he was elected a deputy of the right wing of the French Parliament, and with a newspaper he published, he supported the bid of Louis-Napoleon (nephew of Napoleon I) to become president of the French Republic. But when Louis-Napoleon finally became president, he disappointed Hugo deeply by dissolving the French Parliament. He also eliminated democracy and restored the monarchy, proclaiming himself Emperor of France and taking the name Napoleon III.

Hugo's enraged reaction was to be expected: He assailed Napoleon III openly in 1851, calling him "Napoleon the Small."[219] As an immediate consequence, both of Hugo's sons were confined to prison. At the end of 1851, the situation for Hugo became even more unpleasant. He joined the mobs demonstrating against Napoleon III in Paris and spoke out openly against him. But the season was bad for Hugo: He couldn't reverse things. Soon the rebellion turned bloody, and then he secretly escaped from Paris in 1852, with the aid of a forged passport, and went into exile. He wouldn't return for nineteen years—the "winter" of this bad season of his life had already started.

Hugo's first stop was Brussels, Belgium. Only Juliette was with him. He began writing about the events he had just lived through in Paris, but soon gave up, though he continued attacking Napoleon III with a libel titled *Napoleon the Small*. He and Juliette then left Brussels for the British island of Jersey, in the English Channel. His whole family joined them—his wife, Adela, had come to accept Juliette's presence, and they all lived there together.

On Jersey, Hugo became acquainted with other exiled French citizens, and they published a newspaper with a revolutionary slant. But because of this newspaper, Hugo was expelled from Jersey in 1855 and was forced to go to the island of Guernsey, also in the English Channel. There he completed his collection of poems titled *The Contemplations*, published in 1856. With the money he made, he bought a house on Guernsey. This attempt to put down roots was a sign of his disillusionment with conditions in France. He felt the monarchy would last forever and that he would never return.

He furnished that house in a heavy, even oppressive style, with heavy armchairs, huge tables, and inscriptions on the walls like "Exile is Life."[220] In that environment of complete disappointment, Hugo worked on various writing projects from 1856 to 1859, including the novel *Les Misérables* —which he had started more than ten years earlier—but he couldn't finish it.

# The New Good Season from 1859 to 1875

In 1859, Hugo's bad season finally ended. In August 1859, Napoleon III gave general amnesty to all French exiles. Hugo could now return to France. But he couldn't tolerate the regime that still prevailed there. Thus, he replied to Napoleon III that "he would go back to France only when democracy returned, too."[221] Besides, he had come now to love Guernsey. He would go for walks on the beach, swim, and work in a room he had built at the top of the house, with large windows that provided a beautiful ocean view. He was thus reluctant to leave the island.

In 1861, he wrote that "though people assumed he was depressed, he was in fact very happy."[222] In the island's pleasant environment, Hugo returned to *Les Misérables*, finishing most of the book in 1861. Only the description of the Battle of Waterloo remained. To write this piece, he left Guernsey and set foot—for the first time in nearly ten years—in continental Europe. He went to the Waterloo battleground in Belgium to relive the details of the battle. Returning to the island, he threw himself into his work. He wrote at night; in the morning Juliette organized the manuscript pages and copied them neatly. The work was completed in about a month.

*Les Misérables* was published in 1862, initially in Brussels and then in Paris. Triumph followed: The bookstore in Paris was mobbed by crowds, and Hugo's profits amounted to sums huge for that era. The characters in the novel—Jean Valjean, Javert, Mario, and Cosette—immediately became familiar to everyone, and they remain unforgettable. A new Hugo emerged—at the age of sixty and beyond.

In the island's tranquility, he continued the new phase of his literary work with undiminished intensity, and he published his *William Shakespeare* (1864), *Songs of the Forest* (1865), *The Workers of the Sea* (1866), and *The Man Who Laughs* (1869). In 1870, his dream was realized: Napoleon III's monarchy in France collapsed, the country was again proclaimed a democratic one, and Hugo returned to Paris. The new "summer" of this good season of his life had started. Hugo's arrival in Paris attracted crowds of doting admirers, who welcomed him at the railway station. Deeply moved, he greeted them from a balcony.

Soon, Hugo became as prosperous as he'd ever been. In September 1871, a brilliant era began for him. His drama *Ruy Blas* was performed again, and after that, "all the theaters of Paris asked to perform his works."[223] Because of the rehearsals Hugo was obliged to attend, he had no time to write anything new. To find some peace, he left Paris in August 1872 and went to his beloved Guernsey, where he wrote his new work *Ninety-Three*.

He returned to Paris a year later, in July 1873. An astonishingly productive period followed. In 1874, his works *Ninety-Three* and *My Sons* (dedicated to them) were published. He also wrote a three-volume work on his experiences in exile. His other publications in this period included the second volume of *The Legend of the Centuries* and *The Art of Being a Grandfather*, as well as the first and second volumes of *The Story of a Crime*. The poet Paul Valéry said that during the last period of his life, Hugo also wrote verses incomparable in conception and imagination.

But what most vividly characterized this good season of Hugo's life was his social life. His home in Paris was frequented by the best representatives of the arts and politics in Paris. The seventy-year-old Hugo also had many women admirers; among them was the novelist and playwright Judith Gautier, as well as a young—later famous—actress, Sarah Bernhardt. (We'll see Bernhardt's biography later.)

# The New Bad Season After 1875

In 1876, Hugo decided to reenter politics, for the first time since 1848. But though he was elected a senator, he faced tremendous disappointment. He tried again, through intervention in the Senate and by means of public speeches, to bring about political reform, but in vain. In 1878—at the age of seventy-six—Hugo experienced a major blow. After eating and drinking too much and engaging in heated debate, he suffered a stroke. The doctors prescribed rest, and Juliette took him to Guernsey.

Hugo would not write any more. Nor would he feel joy again. In 1881, a huge birthday celebration was organized under the windows of his home in Paris. Despite the cold weather, a huge crowd gathered to wish him well. But "the bouquets of flowers the people brought remained on the street, frozen: Hugo was sitting in front of his fireplace, and for the first time in his life, he remained silent."[224]

Two years later, he lost the most precious asset he had in life: Juliette, after spending fifty years with him, died of cancer. After Juliette's death, Hugo wrote in his will: "I wish to be carried to the graveyard on the cart used for paupers' funerals. I do not wish any prayers in church; I ask for private prayer by everyone. I do believe in God."[225] Two years later, in 1885, France's most prolific writer was dead—at the age of eighty-three.

# Conclusion

Hugo's alternations of seasons show that his life's good and bad seasons alternated every 16–17 years in 1825, 1842, 1859, and 1875. Connecting Napoleon's dates we've seen in the previous chapter to those of Hugo, we find this continuous row of dates: 1776, 1792, 1809, 1825, 1842, 1859, and 1875. We see confirmation that the seasons of these two men alternated in the continuous row of dates indicated in Chapter 1. But though Hugo's dates are the same as Verdi's, as you can recall, their seasons are opposite: When a good season begins for Hugo, a bad one starts for Verdi—and vice versa: When a bad season starts for Hugo, a good one begins for Verdi. That confirms that since Verdi belongs to the first course of seasons, Hugo belongs to the second course, as indicated in Chapter 1.

In the next chapter, we continue and extend our confirmation by seeing how the good and bad seasons alternated in the life of August Rodin, the great French sculptor.

Chapter 15
# AUGUST RODIN

The few details we possess about August Rodin's early years suggest that these years were bad. Rodin's parents were poor, and he was brought up in a poor section of Paris. His mother worked as a seamstress and sometimes as a maid to supplement the income of his father, a policeman.

When Rodin was ten years old, he went to school for the first time, but he left after three years. He said "he felt like a prisoner" there and never went again. Later, in 1857, when he was seventeen, he took the exams to enter the School of Fine Arts to study sculpture, but he was rejected. It was a humiliating experience that he never forgot. To support himself, he worked for an ornament maker.

## The Good Season from 1859 On

In 1859, a good season began for Rodin. While working with the ornaments and jewelry, he created some small masterpieces that people liked very much and he started earning enough money. This situation continued for the next two to three years, and, in 1863, it became even better. Rodin was now earning so much money that he rented a studio for himself. At the same time, he became acquainted with many famous artists, writers, and other notables.

In 1864 when he was twenty-four, Rodin had a girlfriend: Rose Beuret, who would remain with him for the rest of his life as both his wife and his model. The same year he was hired, at a very satisfying salary, as a designer in a famous art gallery. Two years later, he began enjoying life—the "summer" of this good season had entered his life: He and Rose moved into a new apartment, he was receiving a better salary, his working conditions improved—he decorated, among other things, the mansion of a marquis—and Rose gave birth to their first child.

In 1870, he left Paris and settled in Brussels—together with his employer and many of his colleagues—under very good working conditions. Rose followed, and the couple "lived an idyllic life."[226] In 1875, at the age of thirty-five, he was financially successful enough to be able to realize his big dream: to travel to Italy to see the great sculptures of the Renaissance. He visited Genoa, Florence, Naples, and Venice. As he wrote to Rose, "he was thrilled to see Italy's great art,"[227] and he was enjoying everything.

# The Bad Season from 1875 On

During the first two years of this season, Rodin lived in Brussels. There he constructed his first sculpture—*The Age of Bronze*—a piece that would soon cause him huge problems. When, in 1877, Rodin returned from Brussels to Paris and exhibited there *The Age of Bronze*, the work faced unbelievable reactions. Rumors said that "he had used his model's body as the mold of the sculpture."[228] The great painter's worry was unbearable. At the same year, new worries were added: Rodin's beloved mother died, his father became blind and helpless, and his eleven-year-old son turned out to be mentally handicapped. Also, Rodin's relationship with Rose took a turn for the worse, and he took up with various other women.

Rodin's misfortunes continued in 1878. That year, a piece he had done for another sculptor was exhibited at the Paris Salon; the other sculptor—named Laouste—took credit for it. Ironically, that work won a gold medal, while another work by Rodin, *The Man with the Broken Nose* (later considered a masterpiece)—and exhibited at the Paris Salon under Rodin's name—failed to win an award. Rodin was inconsolable.

His bad season would continue fiercely: More disappointments were in store for him. In 1879, he entered his sculpture *Call to Arms* in a competition sponsored by the City of Paris. But the jury found no merit in that work and eliminated it even before it reached the finals of the competition. (Years later, that work was installed by the French government on the battlefield of Verdun as a reminder of what happened there during World War I.) The same year, Rodin began a sculpture commissioned by the French government—the *Gates of Hell*—to which he would devote the next ten years. But the remuneration was almost nothing, leaving Rodin nearly destitute.

In 1880, he exhibited his work *St. John the Baptist* at the Paris Salon and won a minor award, but he had to relive the experience of being accused of using the body of his model as a mold. Many of his other works also lost favor. Disillusioned, Rodin abandoned Paris and returned to his old employer, the Sévres factory, where he decorated vases and table ornaments. (Those works by Rodin later made the Sévres factory known all over the world.) He was living a withdrawn and lonely life. One of his biographers says that "he was so shy that he blushed when someone addressed him,"[229] though he was a man of forty.

In 1881, Rodin went to England in an effort to find there what he had not found in France. But he didn't have any luck and returned to Paris a year later. He now lived in a poorhouse, together with Rose. His affairs with other women—models, students, servants, and others—understandably drove a wedge between them. In that atmosphere, Rodin tried to work on the *Gates of Hell*, but without any success. That work—two huge gates, each twenty feet high and twelve feet wide, with 180 distinctive figures, which were to form the entrance to a decorative arts museum in Paris—would never be finished.

In 1884, Rodin began work on *The Burghers of Calais,* later deemed a masterpiece. Initially, it created huge problems for him. When the citizen's committee of Calais saw a cast of the work in 1885, they were so enraged that they immediately asked Rodin to redo it. His life had been turned upside down—the "winter" of this bad season had already started for him. Around this time, he became acquainted with a woman twenty years younger—he was forty-six and she was twenty-six—named Camille Claudel, also a sculptor. Their tumultuous relationship would last for eleven years, and would cause a real storm to Rodin's life.

In 1889, the problems with *The Burghers of Calais* intensified. He had modified the statue, but the citizen's committee that had ordered it rejected the work because it had not been placed on a pedestal. Soon, his "winter" became more severe. The next year, Rodin finished the statue of Victor Hugo that the French government had commissioned. But the result was disastrous. The statue—representing Hugo "naked among naked women"[230]—was rejected and caused general disdain.

Rodin lost favor to such an extent that it seemed as if he had already died. That disfavor was reinforced when he completed his statue of Claude Lorrain, the painter, a short time later. The statue was considered so ugly that everyone turned against him. In 1891, Rodin began work on the statue of Honoré de Balzac, the great French novelist. But he was at a loss as to how to proceed and missed the 1892 deadline.

# The New Good Season from 1892 On

From the beginning of this season, the people's reactions against Rodin had ceased. He set back to work with enthusiasm: During the next years, he continued Balzac's statue, and he exhibited it at the Paris Salon of 1898. The statue was found to be a masterpiece by the critics and other famous people— including "Clemenceau, Lautrec, Debussy, Anatole France, and others"[231]— though it still displeased the public. As a result of this difference of opinion, a great dispute broke out in Paris that worked to Rodin's advantage. Newspapers all over Europe reported the tumult in Paris, and thus Rodin gained an international reputation.

From now on, Rodin's good season continued undiminished. In 1898, Camille Claudel left him, bringing their tempestuous relationship to an end. Rodin returned to the always faithful Rose, with whom he again found peace. The next year brought him greater recognition and financial success. His works now attracted huge crowds, and his earnings were correspondingly high. He even exhibited his works in Brussels and Rotterdam, where the sales mounted steadily. His "wounded ego was finally beginning to be restored,"[232] his biographers say.

In 1900, the successes were even more impressive —the new "summer" of this Rodin's good season had entered his life. At the International Exposition that opened in Paris that year, Rodin erected a pavilion of his own—at his own expense—and so became independent of the judgment of the Exposition's various committees. He displayed all his great works in the pavilion: *The Man with the Broken Nose, The Burghers of Calais,* Balzac's statue, even a frame of *The Gates of Hell.* The results surpassed every expectation: The sales of his works generated huge sums, and the world's most influential museums acquired his works at tremendous prices.

That situation continued for several years. Rodin was recognized as a brilliant sculptor and was honored at receptions and other events throughout Europe. As an example, at a celebration in London in 1902—at which a representative of the British government was present—art students were so in awe of him that they "unhitched the horses of his carriage and pulled it themselves."[233]

Also in 1902, the city of Prague bought Rodin's *The Age of Bronze* and held a magnificent reception to honor him. The next year, Rodin was elected—in London again—president of the International Society of Painters, Sculptors, and Engravers. A year later, the French government promoted him to the high rank of Commander of the Legion of Honor.

The greatest form of recognition came immediately after that. In 1905, the French government installed his superb work *The Thinker* in a place of honor in front of the Panthéon in Paris—the statue had been considered equally "great" as all the great men of France who are "sleeping" in this mausoleum.

The prices Rodin now asked for his works were fabulous, and influential men from all over the world came to his Paris studio to have him make busts of them.

Among them was George Bernard Shaw, the great Irish playwright, who went to Paris in 1906 for that purpose and stayed at Rodin's studio for a month. Delighted by the results—a bust in marble—he wrote Rodin that he felt extraordinarily humble in his presence. Even more illustrious clients sought him out. In 1908, King Edward VII of England visited Rodin's Paris studio and commissioned a bust of a female favorite. Rodin's revenues at that time were staggering: While his total assets in 1900 amounted to about 20,000 francs, in 1908 he was earning around 300,000 francs *per year*.

# The New Bad Season After 1908

In 1908, Rodin—now sixty-eight—became acquainted with an alcoholic duchess who began to destroy his life. She isolated him from his friends, slandered them, and in some cases personally drove them from his house. Rodin started drinking heavily, was often depressed, and neglected his work. He was far less productive than he'd been in the past.

In this atmosphere, in 1911, Rodin made a bust of France's Prime Minister Georges Clemenceau—the man who had praised Balzac's statue thirteen years earlier while others had scoffed at it. But Clemenceau rejected the bust, claiming it looked "like a Mongolian general,"[234] and asked Rodin to title it "Bust of an Unknown."[235] In 1912, a new humiliation awaited the great sculptor. He produced a statue of Vaslav Nijinsky, the then-famous dancer, but everyone turned against him because of rumors that Rodin had had homosexual relations with the dancer. A friend of Rodin's had found the two men "drunk and asleep on the floor, with Nijinsky on Rodin's feet."[236]

The calamities continued. The same year, the government ordered Rodin to vacate the house he was living in because the government intended to use it as a public mansion. The news came as a shock; Rodin had planned to renovate the house at his own expense as a museum for his works, which he would bequeath to the state. The seventy-two-year-old Rodin could not withstand that blow; he suffered a stroke that left his left hand paralyzed.

Two years later, in 1914, World War I broke out. Frightened, Rodin left Paris for England, then sought refuge in Rome. He returned to Paris in 1915. But now he was unable to manage his affairs, and began to crumble mentally and physically. In 1916, he suffered a second stroke. The deterioration continued into the next year: Rodin found himself alone in life. His only companion, Rose—whom he had married two weeks earlier after fifty-three years of life with her—died. He had broken off with the alcoholic duchess several years earlier.

He now lived alone in a house the French government had permitted him to stay in until his death. In exchange, he had donated his fortune and all his works to the state—and the government had already taken everything, the furniture included. The house was now quite empty, and in the whirlpool of the war, the public authorities neglected to supply the house with coal for heat, and so "wrapped in blankets, its aged resident"[237] had to cope as best he could.

Late in 1917, the greatest sculptor of modern times died at the age of seventy-seven, neglected and forgotten by all.

# Conclusion

Rodin's alternations of seasons show that his life's good and bad seasons alternated every 16–17 years in 1859, 1875, 1892, and 1908. Adding these dates for Rodin to Napoleon and Hugo's row of dates we've seen in the previous chapters, we find this continuous row of dates: 1776, 1792, 1809, 1825, 1842, 1859, 1875, 1892, and 1908. We can confirm that the seasons of these three men alternated every 16–17 years in the continuous row of dates indicated in Chapter 1.

But though Rodin's dates are the same as Verdi's, their seasons are opposite, as you can see when you compare them. That confirms that since Verdi belongs to the first course of seasons, Rodin belongs to the second course, as indicated in Chapter 1.

Also, Rodin's life confirms what we've seen in Chapter 2: If you are a talented artist—a sculptor like Rodin, for example—but your works are rejected in your bad season, don't despair: You will be recognized at some time later. Rodin had seen his works being rejected again and again during his bad seasons, but later they were considered masterpieces, as we've seen in this chapter.

In the next chapter, we continue and extend our confirmation by seeing how the good and bad seasons alternated in the stormy life of Winston Churchill, the great British politician.

# Chapter 16
# WINSTON CHURCHILL

As Churchill himself has written in his memoirs, the years of his childhood and youth—until the age of eighteen—were the worst of his life. They form, he wrote, "a somber grey path upon the chart of my journey . . . [and they were] an unending spell of worries . . . a time of discomfort, restriction and purposeless monotony."[238]

Young Churchill went to school at the age of seven, in 1881, as a boarder. The school atmosphere was one of extreme cruelty, as was typical of elite English schools at that time. His first traumatic experience was with a Latin teacher. When he asked him why it was necessary to say "Oh, table!" in Latin, since we never address tables, the teacher retorted that "if you are impertinent, you will be punished . . . severely."[239]

That threat was realized many times over, and with great cruelty: Churchill was often beaten. The situation was so unbearable that he began to stammer and developed health problems. His parents then sent him to another school, but the damage had already been done. The new school was equally unbearable. Churchill was not disposed to study, and he failed his exams again and again. His biographers say he was essentially "on strike"[240] at school—for twelve years! He also formed few friendships. When he finished school in 1892 at the age of eighteen, he was "profoundly ignorant," as he himself said later.

Something else made those years among the worst of Churchill's life: His relations with his father, Lord Randolph Churchill, were poor to nonexistent. The senior Churchill had high expectations for his son and condemned him for his poor performance as a student, considering him incompetent and a failure. Whenever he dared approach him, the son said in his memoirs, he made young Winston feel frozen "into stone."[241] That contempt poisoned young Winston's soul.

Churchill's relationship with his mother was not much better. In that era in England, children became completely acquainted with their parents only after reaching adulthood. Not long after birth, upper-class children were given to nannies, who would raise them. Churchill's nanny meant everything to him. When she died, he was twenty years old, and people said they saw him crying at her funeral. Her photograph hung on the wall of his office even when he was prime minister during World War II.

After the end of his studies, in 1892, Churchill took the entrance exams for Sandhurst, the Royal Military Academy. His father had decided he was fit only for the army. But there was more disappointment: He failed the exams.

## The Good Season from 1892 to 1908

The next year, Churchill retook the Sandhurst exams and passed. But at first, this year was something of a cool springtime for him. Since he had entered Sandhurst with a poor academic record, he was placed in the cavalry, not in the infantry where the best students were assigned. The cavalry cadets had to buy their own horses; the horses were expensive, and Churchill's father didn't have enough money to buy one. His father was furious about this expense and lashed out: "If you continue on that path," he wrote him, "you will end up a zero."

But the situation soon changed. The same year, Churchill's father, already in his last days, became reconciled with his son, asking forgiveness and expressing his unqualified love. In his life, he said, many "things . . . [didn't] always go right with me."[242] That is why he asked young Winston to show understanding toward him. That unprecedented show of emotion remained in Churchill's memory for the rest of his life.

In the following five years, the situation would improve even more. These years, Churchill would later write, "were the happiest time of . . . [my] life."[243] In 1895, at the age of twenty-one, he graduated from Sandhurst and was named an officer. From now on, there were no obstacles in his path. From the age of twenty-one, his biographers say Churchill was "like a coiled spring that was suddenly released." He himself wrote later that from 1895 on, "I was . . . the master of my fortunes."[244]

In 1896, while peace prevailed throughout Europe, Churchill found a way of doing what he most wanted to do—go to war—and for that purpose, he went to India. There, he was overcome by a desire to learn and began studying furiously: Plato, Darwin, Schopenhauer, and many others. He also began to write. In 1897, Churchill returned to England, then left in 1898 to participate in an expedition to the Sudan. In the same period, his mother—who had previously shown little interest in him—finally entered his life. She gave him money and introduced him to London's high society, where she had various connections. As a result, Churchill was now present wherever anything important was happening—and more crucially, he managed with his mother's connections to be sent everywhere that a war was taking place.

In the same period (1895–1899), Churchill discovered he had another talent besides fighting: literature. His literary prowess would soon make him famous and would net high earnings; later it would bring him the Nobel Prize for Literature. Churchill started as a reporter and went to Cuba as a war correspondent in 1895 (at this time, army officers were not yet prohibited from writing for newspapers). The articles he sent from Cuba were especially successful, and his income was rising steadily.

In 1897, he began to write books. His first book, on military history, received favorable reviews because of the graceful descriptions of battles it contained. His next book—also on military themes—was equally successful. The primary benefit Churchill reaped from these publications was that they brought him to the attention of England's most powerful statesmen. Ministers and deputy ministers, eventually including the prime minister himself, sought him out.

Churchill then discovered he had a third talent: politics, a talent that would give him a brilliant future. In 1899, he left the army and became a Conservative candidate for Parliament, representing a small workers' electoral district (constituency). But his time hadn't come yet, and he lost the election. Success, however, was waiting for him the same year in another sphere: war. At the end of 1899, Churchill became a national hero. The opportunity came with the Boer War that broke out that year in South Africa. Though he had resigned from the army, Churchill sped to the war and was one of the first to arrive on the scene—as a war correspondent.

Things, however, were not going well for the English: one defeat after another occurred, and an oppressive psychological climate had begun to prevail. But then news spread of an incident in which Churchill was the protagonist and reversed everything. In a battle that was going badly for the English, the young former army officer resumed leadership of the fighting force in the midst of general confusion, saving them from certain capture: He loaded the wounded onto the locomotive of a train and removed them to safety. He also tried to free the other prisoners on the train but was taken prisoner himself. He soon managed to escape from a prison camp in the enemy's capital, however. After wandering for several days in unfamiliar territory and without understanding a word of the language, he finally arrived, hidden in a train loaded with coal, in neutral Mozambique. His good season had caused a miracle.

That heroic achievement convulsed England. Churchill became a national hero, and the government restored him with honors to the ranks of the army. As an officer now, Churchill returned to South Africa, where he continued his military feats. In 1900, he led an invasion of the capital, Pretoria, and with the help of his good season again, he freed all English prisoners from the prison camp. All of England was now talking about Churchill—and the "summer" of Churchill's good season had already started.

At the end of the same year, it became clear that the war would end victoriously for the English, and the government, wishing to take advantage of the jubilant atmosphere, proclaimed general elections. Taking advantage, too, of the glory he had attained, Churchill again resigned from the army, declaring his candidacy for Parliament in the same electoral district he'd tried to represent previously. This time he was elected a Member of Parliament by an overwhelming margin. He was only twenty-six. Later, when Churchill traveled to the United States to give some lectures, Mark Twain addressed him as the "future Prime Minister of England."[245] Indeed, from that point on, Churchill's political career took off—a career that would culminate in his taking the country's highest political office.

From 1901 to 1904, Churchill served in Parliament. But he aspired to a cabinet-level position. The Conservative Party to which he belonged, however, had been losing ground—after eighteen years in power—and Churchill anticipated that the party would lose the next election. Chances were slim that, as a Conservative, he could get a ministerial position. Thus, he did something that shocked the political world: In May 1904, he switched to the rival Liberal Party. His good season again helped him. As a famous young man who had left the Conservatives, Churchill was treated well and assured he would get the kind of position he sought.

And indeed: When in the next election, in 1906, the Liberal Party came to power, Churchill was appointed undersecretary of the colonies at the age of thirty-two. Two years later, he became president of the Board of Trade (minister of state economics). In only a short time, he'd had a meteoric career. In 1908, he took another important step, this one of a personal nature. He married a woman of excellent character, beautiful, clever, and polite—not rich—with whom he would live "a lifelong and exemplary union."[246]

# The Bad Season from 1908 to 1924

Soon after the happy event of his marriage in 1908, however, Churchill faced his first failure in politics: He lost his seat in Parliament in the elections of that year. The newspapers of the rival Conservative Party exulted: "Churchill is out [of Parliament,] Out, OUT!"[247] But the season was still "fall": Another electoral district was soon found that reelected him. The descent, however, had begun. Churchill now started to slide toward the extreme left of the Liberal Party, almost to a radical position. That tendency would eventually cause him very serious problems.

The cause of that turn was David Lloyd George, the famous politician from Wales, also a member of the Liberal Party and a radical. He was a "political genius, demagogue, incomparable . . . [speaker]."[248] Seeing Lloyd George as the future prime minister of the country—as he, in fact, later became—Churchill decided to become his principal ally and supporter. That alliance, however, not only horrified the Conservatives but also the Liberal Party leader, Prime Minister Herbert Asquith, who decided to break up the alliance.

For that purpose, Asquith appointed Churchill first lord of the admiralty in 1911, at a time when war was imminent; World War I got underway three years later, in 1914. In that position, Churchill was forced to ask for more and more money for military purposes, in spite of other pressing financial needs in society. That fact caused a rift with Lloyd George, and the two men parted company.

Though Churchill's position was unpopular, he realized that England was not prepared for war; more preparations and more resources were necessary. Neither Prime Minister Asquith nor Minister of War Horatius Kitchener—with whom Churchill had particularly tense relations—saw his point of view. Even his own assistants were disdainful. The public was against him as well: He was considered an extremist and a warmonger, as well as an opportunist for having changed political parties. When he submitted a memorandum to Parliament predicting the bad consequences of the war for the English, no one paid any attention.

Churchill spent the next two years (1912 and 1913) in that unpleasant atmosphere. In 1914, he experienced his first humiliating defeat. World War I had begun, and the Battle of the Marne was underway. Churchill—as first lord of the admiralty—saw that the only salvation for England was to land at Antwerp, Belgium. But no one agreed with him.

Then he did something unbelievable. He went alone to Antwerp, assumed leadership of a small body of sailors, and ordered two divisions "of recruits still in training"[249] to be transferred from England to Antwerp. But the season was bad for Churchill: What followed was a catastrophe. The operation was a complete failure, and the sailors were all captured by the Germans. The anger that swept through England because of that senseless sacrifice was explosive. Churchill's prestige was irreparably wounded.

He was involved with an even greater calamity in 1915. Churchill believed that a second front behind the German troops—in the Balkans—should be opened so that the war could be won. Minister of War Kitchener, however, again disagreed. Then Churchill, first lord of the admiralty, decided to do what he had done the previous year: to open that front himself—with the navy alone, without the support of the army.

For this purpose, he ordered British naval forces to land at Gallipoli, in Balkan Turkey. But due again to his bad season, what followed was another disaster. Although Kitchener later sent troops there, the Turkish resistance could not be overcome. The campaign was lost. Prime Minister Asquith dismissed Churchill from his admiralty post on May 17, 1915. To punish him further, he appointed Churchill a member of a "Committee for Gallipoli" whereas Churchill was the accused. "I am done," he said over and over: "I am finished."[250] He didn't know that a new good season was to start later for him.

Then, the situation worsened. In the same year, idle and distraught, Churchill asked to return to the army. His petition was accepted, and as a lieutenant colonel, he left for the front in France. But he wasn't able to reverse his bad season—on the contrary, the "winter" of this season would soon follow. His hopes for a meaningful role in the army were dashed; all he was allowed to do was to take part in procedures to rid the soldiers of lice. As a result, the other officers in the regiment treated him contemptuously. As if that was not enough, "members of Parliament and diplomats touring the front . . . came to inspect the miraculous beast,"[251] a former minister in such a bad state. He was obliged to stand at attention before them.

Naturally, Churchill could not endure that situation for long. In 1916, he left the army again and returned to England. His resignation was accepted with the humiliating stipulation that he never again would be permitted to resume an officer's duties during the war. In England, Churchill returned to his Parliament seat. But there, too, the situation was no better. The prime minister was now Lloyd George, who—knowing Churchill's value but also weaknesses—decided in 1917 to bring him to the government. But he placed him under close supervision to prevent him from making false steps. He did not permit Churchill to take any serious initiative and always insisted on having the final say. For the next five years (1918–1922), Churchill was only "Lloyd George's shadow,"[252] as he himself said.

As a result, Churchill was deeply displeased with the Liberal Party. He was trying to find an opportunity to return to the Conservatives, where "by tradition" he belonged. But he did not dare do that. Besides, Lloyd George had warned him during an intense discussion: "A rat could desert a sinking ship," he told him, "but it couldn't climb back if the ship didn't sink after all."[253] And when, in 1922, Lloyd George fell, Churchill also fell with him: For the next two years, he was not even elected a member of Parliament.

# The New Good Season from 1924 to 1941

In the first year of this season, 1924, Churchill accomplished the daring deed he had hesitated to do for so long: He went over again to the Conservative Party. While that action would have had destructive consequences for any other person, Churchill escaped unscathed. Stanley Baldwin, the new leader of the Conservative Party, not only opened the party's doors to him—and thus Churchill was reelected a member of Parliament—but he also gave him a ministerial position immediately after the election.

The season was still "springtime," however: The ministry to which Churchill was appointed was Chancellor of the Exchequer, a financial position not to his liking. For that reason, in the five years he stayed at that ministry (1925–1929), Churchill was occupied more with his other great love—literature—and less with politics. During those years, he wrote his renowned five-volume work *World Crisis*, a history of World War I, which was recognized immediately as a wonderful achievement and brought him enormous profits.

In 1930, Churchill left his government post and retained only his parliamentary position, which he kept for the next nine years. A new life, free of worry, filled with social pleasures, and envied by all, now began for him. The "summer" of this season had started. First, with the money he had earned from his book, he bought a luxurious mansion in London, where he was preoccupied with the garden, the goldfish, the exotic butterflies, and with painting. The mansion echoed every evening with the sound of visitors—politicians, writers, and others—who listened to him with respect until late in the night.

Churchill now began smoking expensive cigars from Havana—which later became his trademark—and drinking exquisite liquors and wines. He was also preoccupied with his children—three daughters and a son—as a strict but magnanimous father. "In the last few days," he once said to his son in this season, "we have spoken together more [things] . . . than [I discussed with my father] in his entire lifetime."[254]

In this period, Churchill continued his involvement with his great love, literature. At first he wrote newspaper articles about international politics—articles that were published in other countries, too—and was well paid for them. He also produced a colossal work, the four-volume biography of his ancestor, *Marlborough*. As soon as he finished that study, he began writing the multivolume *History of the English-Speaking Peoples*.

Churchill was also a politician, of course, and he could not forget it. In Parliament during that season he gave some of his most famous speeches, and everybody listened with politeness and admiration. His speeches were mainly cautionary. He saw World War II (as he named it later) approaching, and believed that England was not prepared to face it. He was warning his fellow citizens to arm themselves. Initially, they could not see the threat he perceived from Nazi Germany, so when war finally broke out in 1939, England was caught off guard. Churchill—the prophet, the great man, the only one who could save them—was "back"[255] in favor. On September 3, 1939, Prime Minister Neville Chamberlain invited Churchill to enter the government. Churchill resumed his old post as first lord of the admiralty.

But the situation became increasingly precarious. Chamberlain was forced to resign, then died. Then, the crucial moment arrived: On May 10, 1940, Parliament appointed Churchill, then sixty-six, prime minister. He had become the most powerful person in England. He ruled everything, he later wrote in his memoirs, and "had the authority to give directions over the whole scene."[256]

Churchill's first objective as prime minister was the removal of all pacifists from the government. Second, he created a new Ministry of Defense, making himself a Field Marshal. After that, he mobilized the country's industry and thus converted England in six months into a fully armed war machine. His third concern was the forging of a firm alliance with the United States—an alliance that he established through a secret personal correspondence with President Franklin Roosevelt, without going through diplomatic channels.

By 1941, Churchill was at the zenith of his power: Hitler and Stalin were embroiled in a war in the depths of Russia, Rommel had been defeated in the Mediterranean and Africa, and the British airplanes were hammering Germany. When America entered the war that year, Churchill celebrated. The only thing that remained now was the great leap to victory—a leap he was planning to start from the Mediterranean.

# The New Bad Season After 1941

Though some people may think that the years from the middle of 1941 to 1944 were something of a triumph for Churchill, this is not so. The truth is that while in 1941 Churchill was preparing the great leap forward—the landing of the Allied forces in a Mediterranean country—in 1942, everything began to go wrong. Japan—which, in the meantime, had entered the war—occupied Burma in Southeast Asia and was threatening India, still a member of the British Commonwealth, while Rommel defeated the English in Egypt. Further, Singapore—a British colony—surrendered to the Japanese with 100,000 British soldiers, while Tobruk in Africa also fell into German hands. The British Navy was decimated: in the Pacific, the Indian Ocean, the Mediterranean, even in the Arctic.

This situation naturally had unfavorable consequences for Churchill. In July 1942, a loss-of-confidence motion against him was submitted to Parliament. Though with much effort he managed to overcome it, in September a government crisis loomed again and Churchill's position as prime minister was threatened. Another member of Parliament, Stanford Cripps, prepared to challenge him for the position. However, the season was still fall with its "Indian summer." Churchill finally succeeded in convincing Cripps to postpone his decision to run. But the Churchill of 1942 was no longer the Churchill of 1940 to early 1941.

In 1943, the situation worsened. Churchill believed that the best way to achieve victory was a landing in the Mediterranean—and he thought he had convinced Roosevelt of that, too. But at the summit conference that took place in Tehran that year, Roosevelt and Stalin opposed Churchill. The landing would be realized in France—from England, across the Channel. This decision was a real slap in Churchill's face. One implication was that Russia would not be excluded from Europe, as Churchill hoped, but that it would join the Allies in the heart of Europe, in Germany. Also, the fact that Roosevelt and Stalin kept exchanging glances during the conference—as if they were laughing at him—had not escaped Churchill's attention.

Then Churchill's condition began to decline. He became aged and spoke with a hoarse voice that could barely be heard. At the conference he warned of a future war—with Russia—for which these three leaders in Tehran would be responsible. "There might be a more bloody war," he said, "[but] I shall not be there."[257]

Returning from Tehran to England, Churchill became seriously ill from pneumonia during the trip and nearly died. When he arrived back in London at the end of 1943, he was psychologically in a shambles. That same situation, and worse, continued into 1944. Churchill began to have trouble concentrating, and his speech was sometimes inchoate. Yet he suddenly decided to do something unacceptable: At the age of seventy, he wanted to personally participate in the Allied invasion of France. Not surprisingly, his decision caused an outcry, and the king "threatened [to accompany him to the front] if Churchill insisted on going."[258]

Churchill's policy, in 1944, consisted of a series of measures that didn't seem to lead anywhere. He visited the front in Italy, seeking a way to promote the landing from there, but of course this move was in vain. Then he visited Stalin in Russia, trying to detach some countries from Communist domination, but again he was unsuccessful. In 1945, the final blow came. The war ended, and on May 8, 1945, Churchill announced England's victory. But that was the bitterest moment of his life. The end of this war meant, according to his opinion, the start of a frightful World War III with Russia.

In the general elections that followed two months later, his compatriots punished him in the worst manner: The Conservatives lost control of the government, and Churchill was relegated to the opposition party—to inaction. To console himself during the next few years, he wrote his memoirs and the history of World War II, for which he later won the Nobel Prize. But in the summer of 1949, he suffered his first heart attack.

In the general elections of 1951, the Conservatives returned to power, and Churchill again became prime minister. But his bad season couldn't be reversed: Though his return to power could be considered as an upturn, in fact it wasn't. The "winter" of his bad season had already entered his life. Churchill was now a shadow of his former self. At seventy-seven he had trouble hearing, and his memory often abandoned him: He sometimes even forgot his ministers' names. Instead of attending to the problems of the country, he would read novels for hours. By the following year, disenchantment with his performance was spreading.

In June 1953, he suffered a stroke. He became paralyzed on one side and was unable to speak. He was initially confined to a wheelchair, and many times he was crying. Later, he managed to walk with the aid of a cane but couldn't stay on his feet for long.

In that disturbing condition, Churchill did something in 1954 that caused a stir in the government. Without informing anyone, he began corresponding with the leaders of the United States and Russia in order to set up a conference that would address the problem of the "Cold War" (a term he had coined). His cabinet members were appalled and requested his resignation. At first he refused, but it was evident by now that he could not perform his duties properly. He was losing his mental faculties and also suffered from depression. When his closest associates again asked him to resign, he finally gave in: On April 5, 1955, he submitted his resignation.

Churchill's resignation was not only a farewell to politics, but also to life itself. Soon after his resignation, he became mentally dead. He lived for another ten years, but it was as if he was non-existing. He lost most of his hearing, he was not speaking, and he would sit for hours absentminded in front of the fireplace, looking but not seeing. In fact, his life had really ended a little after 1955.

# Conclusion

Churchill's alternations of seasons show that his life's good and bad seasons alternated every 16–17 years in 1875, 1892, 1908, 1924, and 1941. Adding these Churchill dates to Napoleon, Hugo and Rodin's dates as we've seen in the previous chapter, we find this continuous row of dates: 1776, 1792, 1809, 1825, 1842, 1859, 1875, 1892, 1908, 1925, and 1941. We can confirm that the seasons of these four men alternated every 16–17 years in the continuous row of dates indicated in Chapter 1.

But although Churchill's dates are the same as Picasso's, their seasons are opposite, as you can see when you compare them. That confirms that since Picasso belongs to the first course of seasons, Churchill belongs to the second course, as indicated in Chapter 1.

Also, Churchill's life confirms another advantage mentioned in Chapter 2: If you have problems in your career in your bad seasons, wait and you will see it solved. As we've seen in this chapter, Churchill said during a moment of one of his bad seasons, after the disaster he caused at Gallipoli, as first lord of the admiralty: "I am done, I am finished." But later, he became the prime minister of his country. Also, if you have difficulties with your studies in school or university in your bad season, don't worry: This will not have any influence in your future. Churchill failed his exams in school again and again, as we've seen—the same as with Verdi's application to enter the Milan Conservatory had been rejected.

In the next chapter we continue and extend our confirmation by seeing how the good and bad seasons alternated in the life of Greek tycoon shipowner Aristotle Onassis.

Chapter 17
# ARISTOTLE ONASSIS

The few facts available suggest Aristotle Onassis's childhood was difficult. Born in 1906 in the Greek town of Smyrna (later occupied by Turkey), he lost his mother when he was still a baby, and his father remarried a year and a half later. His relationship with his stepmother was extremely bad: They were in a state of continuous warfare: "He regarded . . . [her] as a usurper,"[259] and refused to obey her. At one point, the situation with his stepmother became so bad that the young boy was sent to a friendly neighbor's house to stay for a while. His relationship with his father was not much better. A wealthy wholesale merchant in Smyrna, he was a strict father who was feared by his son.

As a result of these problems, Onassis was mostly brought up by his grandmother. He also did poorly in school, which he entered at the age of seven in 1913. He did not like studying and constantly skipped class. He was extremely disruptive and annoyed his classmates. As a result, he was expelled from all the schools he attended. His desperate father then wrote one of Aristotle's teachers that he was contemplating "suicide because of . . . [that boy]."[260] Under those circumstances, it was not surprising that Onassis never finished his studies. When he took the final exams required for a high school diploma in 1922, he failed—and he never tried again.

The same year, the situation became even more difficult for him: The Turks invaded Onassis's town of Smyrna after defeating the Greek Army. Young Onassis—then sixteen—was caught up, as he would often recall later, in the disaster that followed. The Turkish Army swept the town from one side to the other for many days, killing, looting, and burning. Men and women were taken forcibly out of their homes and "killed in the streets."[261] Churches filled with refugees were covered with oil and set on fire, while people trying to come out "were bayoneted on the church steps."[262] When the mayhem ended five days later, about 120,000 Greeks had been lost. Smyrna was entirely destroyed.

Onassis's father gathered his family inside their home when the Turks entered the town and closed the doors and windows. Terrified, they watched the destruction through cracks in the walls. Their only source of income, the shop in the town, had been destroyed. On the fifth day, the Turks entered the house and arrested the father, leaving young Onassis as the only male there. The next day, Onassis took on the responsibility of rescuing his family. He went out into the chaotic streets of Smyrna, and there by chance he met the American vice-consul. With his intervention, the Onassis family was transferred immediately on a small boat to the nearby Greek island of Lesbos. But Onassis stayed behind to rescue his imprisoned father.

He soon managed to visit his father in prison, where he found him ill and distraught. When Onassis was leaving the prison, the Turks arrested him. But he managed to escape; terrified, he ran to the vice-consul's office. The next day he was on his way to Lesbos disguised as a sailor on an American warship. Three weeks later, the Onassis family arrived at the Greek port of Piraeus in a miserable condition as war refugees.

Onassis's father was later released and joined them. But the family's uprooting was, for young Onassis, an oppressive experience. Throughout the next year (1923) he had "a feeling of futility,"[263] as he said later, and spent his days in Athens lonely and withdrawn. He didn't have any contact with his former classmates who'd also come to Greece, and he was not willing to get involved in any way in the business that his father had started under difficult circumstances—tobacco trading.

In desperation, he got the idea to immigrate to the United States. But he could not obtain a visa, so as a second choice, he decided on Argentina. Unfortunately, his father was vehemently opposed, so much so that he refused to even give him the money for the tickets. Onassis was forced to ask some of his friends for a loan. He obtained a small amount, and with it embarked on a risky venture. In August 1923, he departed from the Greek port of Piraeus arriving a month later in Buenos Aires. He was only seventeen, clutched a torn suitcase, and was penniless.

His first priority was of course to find a job. He soon realized that wouldn't be easy. To keep himself alive, he had to wash dishes in restaurants and haul bricks on construction sites. Finally, in March 1924, he found a job at the Telephone Company of Buenos Aires as an electrician. Since he wasn't making enough money, he had to request the night shift, so that he could do another job during the day. This was not the Argentina Onassis had dreamed of.

# The Good Season from 1925 to 1941

In 1925, Onassis's fate changed. As soon as he found a decent job, his next step was to work out a deal with his father so that he could start selling Greek tobacco in Argentina. Early in 1925, he began corresponding with his father and soon they'd repaired their relationship. Before long, he convinced his father to send him samples of high-quality Greek tobacco. With the samples in hand, Onassis started visiting the cigarette manufacturers of Argentina to try to sell them tobacco. He quickly received his first order, for $10,000. Since the quality of the tobacco was excellent, a second order followed soon, for $50,000. The orders came faster and faster. Onassis couldn't even find time to sleep. By May 1925, he had managed to put $25,000 in the bank—not bad for someone who had recently been penniless.

The same month, he quit his telephone company job and started a business of his own: He began manufacturing his own cigarettes in the small room he was living in. That business was very successful, and soon Onassis started living the high life. He frequented music halls and clubs, and formed friendships with wealthy young men. Early in 1926, he moved out of the small room he had been living in and took a hotel suite in the most distinguished part of Buenos Aires. He also bought a car and took French and English lessons.

Although the season was still "springtime", there were some rain showers, too. In the summer of 1929, the Greek government increased the import duties from countries with which it did not have commercial agreements by 1,000 percent. Argentina was among those countries, and Onassis feared that Argentina would retaliate by increasing the import duties for the Greek products, making the trade of Greek tobacco impossible. He decided to return to Greece the same year (1929) to persuade the authorities to exempt Argentina from the increased duties. After a stormy discussion with the Greek prime minister, Onassis—then only twenty-three—finally won the battle. The spring shower had passed.

Onassis's visit to Greece had another benefit: Not only was he reunited with his family, but the reunion had a touch of triumph. He was the successful son who had come back, the son who was sending money to the widows in the family for the educational expenses of their children. The reconciliation with his father was now complete. Returning to Argentina later in 1929, Onassis made his first foray into a field of activity that would eventually bring him staggering wealth: shipping. He bought a dilapidated 7,000-ton ship that was twenty-five years old.

A great deal of money came from the tobacco trade. Between 1930 and 1931, he expanded the business to Cuba and Brazil. A year later, a new source of profits was added: The Greek government acknowledged his commercial potentials and appointed him the country's consul in Buenos Aires—at the age of twenty-six. In that position, Onassis could now obtain foreign currency at official rates and resell it in the free market at huge profits. That position also gave him two more advantages: He was able to acquire Argentinean citizenship, and he made many important contacts in the international shipping world.

In the fall of 1932, Onassis assembled all of his savings—around $600,000—and sailed to London, the maritime world's capital, to buy ships. Because of the economic crash of 1929–1932, ship prices had declined precipitously. A "ten year-old freighter which had cost $1 million to build in 1920"[264] could now be obtained for $20,000. Onassis didn't take long to find what he was looking for: A whole fleet of ten such ships was for sale in Saint Lawrence in Canada. In the winter of the same year, he went to Saint Lawrence. After brief negotiations, he bought six of those ships in 1933—for $20,000 each. Onassis's career as a shipowner had begun. Simultaneously, the "summer" of this good season entered his life.

The next year, a new and important element was added to his life: During a trip from Buenos Aires to Genoa, he met Ingse Dedichen, the daughter of one of Norway's biggest shipowners, and a love affair developed between them that would last for more than ten years. After they met, Onassis abandoned Argentina and settled in Norway, to be with Ingse. Over the next two years, the doors of that country's shipowners and upper classes opened to him.

In 1937, Onassis entered a new field of business activity: that of tankers. He ordered his first 15,000-ton tanker from the Swedish shipyards, about 3,000 tons bigger than any other tanker at that time, valued at $800,000. He was prudent enough to lease the ship in advance for one year to the oil company of US tycoon J. Paul Getty. In 1938, the Swedish flag flew over the tanker.

The following year, World War II broke out. Onassis was not anxious at all—he didn't know that a bad season would begin for him. On the contrary, he predicted the hostilities would end soon. To avoid any trouble, he left Europe in June 1940 and settled in New York in a luxurious apartment on Park Avenue. Within a few days, Ingse followed.

# The New Bad Season from 1941 to 1957

Soon after the declaration of war, Onassis realized that things were not as simple as he'd thought. Most of his fleet—particularly the tankers—were immobilized in hostile countries. Only the aged small ships he had bought in 1932 in Canada were available. His revenues were beginning to decline dramatically. To resolve the situation, he resumed the tobacco trade, based in New York this time. He added olive oil, too. But the profits were limited.

For the first time, Onassis started living a tedious and unsatisfying life. He rented an old house in New York, while his relationship with Dedichen began to sour. As she said later, Onassis told her at the time that "the years were passing him by,"[265] and he had not lived his life. He had given all his attention to business, he lamented, and had neglected everything else. As a result, he now lived a dissolute life, carrying on with various women, mainly Hollywood's marginal young actresses—with whom he became acquainted during his trips to California, where two of his ships were chartered. He also pursued a wealthy heiress in San Francisco, but in what was a humiliating experience for him, she rejected his marriage proposal.

Whenever he came back from California, he would see Dedichen, but their relationship was in serious trouble—especially after he beat and kicked her. Dedichen says Onassis had begun drinking heavily in those years. That situation lasted for three more years (1942–1944). Finally, after repeated quarrels and abuse, Ingse decided to leave him.

With the end of the war, in 1945–1946, things got even worse for Onassis. During the war, all Greek shipowners had put their ships at the disposal of the military in the fight against Hitler's Germany—for transporting equipment and materials—*and they had lost all of them.* The only exception was Onassis, who had not made any ships available. That advantage, however, ultimately proved to be a great disadvantage for him.

In 1946, the US government had the biggest commercial fleet in the world. They were the Liberty ships, which had been built by the thousands to meet the needs of the war, and now were immobilized in various ports around the country. To get rid of them, the US government decided to give them to the Allied countries' shipowners who had lost their own ships during the war. This transfer was made under very favorable terms. While each ship had cost about $1,500,000 to build, the price was fixed at $550,000 per piece, with a down payment of $125,000 and the remainder to be paid in seven years. The sole condition was a guarantee by each country's government for the payment of the installments. A hundred such ships were given to Greece, and they went to those shipowners who had lost their own ships in the war. Having lost none of his ships, Onassis got none of the Liberty ships—though he had asked for thirteen.

The other Greek shipowners now had the most competitive fleet in the world—the Liberty ships were in excellent condition and, for the most part, were modern ships. Onassis, on the contrary, had been left with an antiquated fleet. The game, it was evident, would be unequal: Onassis would not be able to overcome the competition. So, he made desperate attempts to obtain Liberty ships from the Greek government. But he didn't know he was in a bad season of his life: His attempts failed.

Then, in 1946, Onassis made another attempt to acquire ships, but this one would soon land him in an American prison. The US government was offering many tankers of 16,500 tons each, again under favorable terms, but only American citizens could buy them. Onassis submitted a petition to buy twenty of these ships, but of course he was rejected. Then he created phony companies ostensibly run by American citizens and was able to acquire the tankers he was previously prohibited from buying. But that illegal act would later prove costly. In 1946, Onassis married Tina Livanos, the daughter of the then greatest Greek shipowner Stavros Livanos—she was seventeen and he was forty. If he thought he would profit financially from the connection with his wealthy father-in-law, that did not happen. However, later Onassis would become a self-made tycoon.

Onassis's business problems persisted in 1947. The US government again offered to Greek shipowners seven tankers of 16,500 tons each—like those offered to American citizens the previous year—under equally favorable terms. Onassis immediately asked to buy all seven tankers. But for the same reason as before, the Greek government would not acquiesce.

Then he did something unprecedented for that time—his bad season continued. He borrowed money from American banks and bought tankers, and he also borrowed the dizzying amount of $40 million from the Metropolitan Life Insurance Company of New York to build new ships. These acts astonished the shipping world, since buying or building ships with borrowed money was then considered too risky for a dangerous business such as maritime transportation. Indeed, the above loans later drove Onassis to the threshold of bankruptcy.

In 1948 with the $40 million loan in hand, Onassis went to Germany to negotiate the terms under which his ships would be built. But he became indecisive and was unable to complete the deal. On the contrary, the next year he decided to take up a line of work quite different from shipping: hunting and killing whales—a pursuit that would soon make him notorious. For that purpose, he assembled a fleet of seventeen ships and hired a number of Norwegian and German whale gunners. That act provoked protests from the Norwegian Whaling Association.

In 1950, Onassis finally decided to proceed with the construction of his ships in Germany—on borrowed money. This was a huge, complicated order that caused him many sleepless nights. It involved sixteen ships of 20,000 tons each, and two ships of 45,000 tons each—a total of more than 400,000 tons. At the same time, Onassis's business troubles worsened. The American government started investigating the illegalities involved in his 1946 purchase of the tankers only US citizens were permitted to buy.

Onassis anxiously tried to avoid the consequences. But the "winter" of his bad season had already entered his life. In August of 1950, with the Korean War underway, he sent a cable to the US Department of the Navy, setting "five [of his] newly built supertankers"[266] at the department's disposal in case of need. Of course, his offer was rejected with a polite pro-forma letter. The investigation continued. More troubled now, in October 1950, he sent another cable offering not only his ships but also his own services as a sailor. This offer, too, was rejected.

In 1951, Onassis added to his notoriety. Not satisfied with the results of his whaling enterprises, he decided to continue hunting the whales well after the season was over, flouting international regulations. The season had ended on March 9, and he continued for two more months, until May 10. The news spread, and a general outcry arose damaging his reputation.

The same situation prevailed in 1952. In 1953, the US government decided to institute legal proceedings against him for the problem with the tankers. Onassis sent another cable offering his ships—but without any results. On the contrary, the government now took severe measures against him: Each time an Onassis ship arrived in a US port, a customs official "would inform its master by letter that the ship [as well as its profits] was under seizure."[267]

The same year, Onassis bought the majority of shares in the Casino of Monte Carlo, which belonged to the principality of Monaco—a purchase he made without previously informing the principality's Prince Rainier. While Onassis expected huge profits from that investment, the profits were disappointing. In 1954, Onassis suffered a major blow: The US government ordered his arrest.

As soon as he learned the news, he sent a cable to the Department of Justice and placed himself at the disposal of the attorney general. The next day, gloomy and "accompanied by his legal entourage"[268] and several newsmen, he presented himself at the attorney general's office. He assumed he would arrange some kind of settlement there. But he didn't know he wasn't able to reverse his bad season: Just the opposite of what he had hoped for happened. After having been fingerprinted and photographed from all angles, he was put in jail—in the company of a group of Puerto Rican terrorists. Later, he was released on bail, but Onassis was not a free man any more. Most important, he had been profoundly humiliated. (After negotiations lasting another two years, the case was closed: Onassis would pay a fine of $7 million.).

Also in 1954, a second humiliating experience awaited him. He wasn't satisfied with the results of his whale hunting in Norway, so he decided to hunt off the coast of Peru. The Peruvian government sent two warships to prevent him from doing it. But he persisted, and five of his ships with 400 German sailors were arrested and escorted to the nearest port. The remaining ships, chased by Peruvian planes, took refuge in Panama. Soon after, a Peruvian court fined Onassis about $3 million. The fine was paid by the insurance companies, but Onassis's name and fame had been badly wounded.

The same year, Onassis did something else that drove him to the brink of destruction. After a series of negotiations that lasted many months, and after having bribed some of the highest officials, he concluded an agreement with the king of Saudi Arabia that would give him the exclusive rights to use his tankers to transport that country's huge oil output. As soon as the agreement became known, however, a storm of protest broke out against him—not only from the big US oil companies, which had the exclusive right to produce the Saudi Arabian oil, but also from the government of the United States itself.

The oil companies protested officially to Saudi Arabia, and simultaneously made clear to Onassis that each time his ships would arrive in that country's ports to load crude oil, they would not let him have it. US Secretary of State John Foster Dulles warned the Saudi Arabians that if they insisted on upholding the agreement with Onassis, the American oil companies would stop oil production in that country. In the face of that reaction, the king of Saudi Arabia was forced to cancel the agreement. For Onassis, that was still another mortal blow—and soon it would have even worse consequences.

In 1955, the Norwegian Whaling Association issued a report indicating that, for years, Onassis had systematically violated the whaling regulations by hunting off season and killing very young whales, pregnant females, or whales belonging to a protected category. The damage he had caused, the report said, was incalculable. Because of the general disapproval the report created, Onassis was forced to abandon whaling in 1955 for good.

The most devastating blow came that year as a result of his questionable agreement with Saudi Arabia. The US oil companies decided, out of revenge, to discontinue any cooperation with him. Each time a charter contract for any of his ships expired, they would not renew it, giving it instead to other shipowners. At the end of 1955, half of Onassis's tanker fleet was idle. His main source of income was drying up at tremendous speed.

That situation continued into 1956 as well. More and more of his ships were becoming idle, and those ships were mortgaged with the huge loans he had borrowed to build them. But Onassis no longer had sufficient income to repay the loans. In despair, he went around to the American banks to which he was indebted, asking them to take over management of his ships. That was "the worst time of my life,"[269] he said. The international shipping community expected him to announce bankruptcy at any moment.

# The Second Good Season from 1957 to 1974

The bankruptcy never happened, however. In October 1956, the Suez Canal closed to shipping because of the crisis between Egypt and Israel. As a result, ships had to circumnavigate Africa, adding considerable time to each trip. Too few ships were available to meet the demand, and freight costs skyrocketed to unprecedented heights in 1957. The only shipowner who had ships available was Onassis. Because of the boycott the American oil companies had imposed on him, he had a huge number of ships standing idle in various ports. The results were predictable: His ships were chartered by desperate merchants, the boycott ended, and the acrimonious relationships with the oil companies were forgotten.

Instead of destruction, triumph had arrived. Onassis's new good season had started. He began to realize dizzying profits: In 1957 alone, he earned $70 million—while ten years earlier, he had been head over heels in debt with the $40 million loan he had taken out. The profits were huge. Onassis didn't know what to do with all this money. His first act was to repay all the loans he owed. His second act was to commission the building of new ships—among them a 100,000-ton tanker, the biggest in the world at that time. His third act was to give a resplendent reception in Monte Carlo to celebrate his improved fortunes. That same year, Onassis also became the first private individual in the world to own a *national* airline company: He transferred his business activities also to Greece, where he established Olympic Airways.

From 1958 on, Onassis began to become an international celebrity. He invited many international personalities to cruise the seas on his yacht *Christina*, the most luxurious yacht in the world. Originally a 2,200-ton frigate in the Canadian Navy, Onassis had transformed it into a floating palace. Celebrities seen relaxing on the yacht included Hollywood's famous actors and actresses, like Marlene Dietrich, Greta Garbo, Ava Gardner, and others. Even aged ex-Prime Minister Winston Churchill—in a wheelchair—was hospitably received. Every time the *Christina* arrived in port with Churchill aboard, ambassadors, other distinguished visitors, even prime ministers and kings, paid their respects.

In 1959, Onassis got to know Maria Callas, at that time the most famous Greek opera singer, as we'll see in her biography later. The bond created between them piqued intense global interest for many years, with scores of reporters and photographers following the couple closely "from one end of Europe to the other."[270] Because of that bond, Callas separated from her husband, Giovanni Meneghini (an Italian), later that year; Onassis divorced his wife, Tina Livanos, the following year.

That situation in Onassis's social—as well as business—life continued through 1962, causing a great deal of interest all over the world. In 1963, he impressed international society even more by buying a whole Greek island—Skorpios—which he converted into a fabulous summer resort. In the summer of that year, gossip-mongers had a field day: The wife of the president of the United States, Jacqueline Kennedy, cruised the Greek islands aboard the yacht *Christina*—as Onassis's guest. (In November of that year, President Kennedy was assassinated).

In 1964, Onassis began to increase his fleet at a tremendous pace. He arranged for ships of 50,000–60,000 tons each to be built, while the next year he acquired a newly built 100,000-ton tanker. In 1966, he commissioned the building of huge tankers of 175,000–200,000 tons each. The size of his fleet now amounted to 4 million tons—while in 1950, when he had taken out huge loans, he had only 400,000 tons.

In 1967, Onassis realized staggering new profits: the Suez Canal closed again to shipping because of a renewed conflict between Egypt and Israel, and freight charges rose to unprecedented heights. Onassis ordered the building of six super tankers in 1968, so that the tonnage of his tankers alone amounted to 2,500,000 tons. The same year, Onassis's rise to social prominence culminated in his marriage to Jackie Kennedy in a fabulous wedding ceremony on his privately owned island. That was the social event of the year; Onassis was now known all over the world. That triumph, success, and world admiration would continue for the next four years. By 1973, however, Onassis's brilliant season would end abruptly. What followed was a tragic season, the last of Onassis's life.

# The New Bad Season from 1973 On

In January 1973, Onassis's son, Alexander, was killed in a plane crash at the Athens airport at the age of nineteen. At first Onassis seemed that he had overcome that tragedy. Immediately after his son's funeral and burial on the island of Skorpios, he started expanding his fleet. While the fleet then consisted of more than 100 ships—among them fifteen supertankers of 200,000 tons each—Onassis commissioned six more tankers to be built, two of them of 400,000 tons each, the biggest tankers in the world.

But from 1974, things began to get worse. That year Onassis's marriage to Jackie began to deteriorate. In a visit to Acapulco—where Jackie had spent her honeymoon with John Kennedy—she asked him to buy her a house there. He understood that the reason was sentimental and refused. During the quarrel that followed, Jackie said she now expected nothing from him.

However, the worst blow was to Onassis's health. Maybe because of his son's death, he began in 1974 to suffer from *myasthenia gravis*, an incurable disease affecting the eyes and other parts of the body. He couldn't hold his eyelids open, and had to keep them up with tape. He had also a hard time swallowing food and slurred his words when speaking. Not surprisingly, he was full of complaints: about his life, about himself, about his marriage, about everything.

Next year, 1975, was the last in Onassis's life. Olympic Airways, his Greek airlines company, suddenly found itself in a precarious financial situation. Onassis asked the Greek government to lend him money to resolve the situation, but the government refused. On the contrary, he was informed that the government intended to nationalize the airline. "Against his doctors' orders,"[271] he then escaped from the hospital in New York where he was undergoing treatment, and returned to Athens in an effort to reverse the nationalization— but in vain. On January 15, 1975, he was forced to accept his company's takeover.

A few days later, Onassis became seriously ill from pneumonia. In an awful condition, he entered a hospital in Paris, where he was operated on to no avail. On March 15, 1975, the wealthiest man in the world died—at the age of sixty-nine. Only his daughter, Christina, was at his bedside.

# Conclusion

Onassis's alternations of seasons show that his life's good and bad seasons alternated every 16–17 years in 1925, 1941, 1957, and 1974. Adding Onassis's dates to Napoleon, Hugo, Rodin, and Churchill's dates we've seen in the previous chapters, we find this continuous row of dates: 1776, 1792, 1809, 1825, 1842, 1859, 1875, 1892, 1908, 1924, 1941, 1957, and 1974. This confirms that the seasons of these five men alternated every 16–17 years in the continuous row of dates indicated in Chapter 1.

But though Onassis's dates are the same as Picasso's, their seasons are opposite, as you can see when you compare them. That confirms that since Picasso belongs to the first course of seasons, and Onassis belongs to the second course, as indicated in Chapter 1.

Also, Onassis's life confirms once more that you mustn't be seized by despair in your bad seasons, as the good season—maybe a fantastic one—will come later. For example, when Onassis was at one of his bad seasons, almost all his ships were idle in various ports around the globe because of the boycott the US oil companies had imposed on him. The international shipping community expected him to announce bankruptcy at any moment. That bankruptcy never happened, however. Soon, the Suez Canal closed to shipping and freight costs skyrocketed to unprecedented heights. The only shipowner who had ships available was Onassis. He began to realize dizzying profits—and in the next few years he became the wealthiest person on earth. Instead of destruction, triumph had arrived.

In the next chapter, we continue to extend our confirmation by seeing how the good and bad seasons alternated in the life of South Africa's national hero Nelson Mandela.

# Chapter 18
# NELSON MANDELA

Nelson Mandela was born in 1918 in a village near Umtata in the black South African territory of Transkei. As a boy—from 1924 on, after the age of a six—he lived a fulfilling life. He was loved deeply by his mother and thrived within his extended family of cousins, stepmothers, and half brothers and sisters. His father, a hereditary chief, had four wives. "I had four mothers who were very supportive and regarded me as their son,"[272] he recalled. He also vividly recalled the richness of his life as a child in the country, where there were hills and streams to explore and pools to swim in.

His father was a political leader, and the young Mandela commanded respect in the community. His family was privileged, and in 1927 at the age of nine, he was exposed to even greater privilege. That year his father died, and his mother took him to the Regent of Tembu, who had been his father's friend. It was here that Mandela lived his most constructive years—fourteen years in total, from 1927 to 1941—and acquired a kind of kingship that influenced all his life. There, "he saw himself as a member of the royal family,"[273] and experienced a much grander lifestyle than before.

At the age of sixteen, in 1934, the Regent sent Mandela to Clarkebury, the largest educational center of Tembuland, to board at the great Methodist Institution there, where distinguished British missionaries were teaching. There, Mandela's eyes were opened to the value of scientific knowledge, and he entered a much wider world. In 1936, he transferred to a bigger Methodist Institution at Healdtown, and in 1939 he went on to the University of Fort Hare, where he was seen by his teachers and other students as a prince ready to become the leader of his people.

Mandela bloomed at that university. He not only took advantage of its academic offerings, but he also learned to dance, among other things, and made many new friends. During his second year (1940–1941), he was elected to the student council.

# The Bad Season from 1941 to 1957

The majority of the students had not voted in the elections for the council, because they wanted improvements in their food. Thus, Mandela resigned from the council. The president of the university warned him that he would be expelled, but he insisted—and was expelled. He then went home to the Regent, but the Regent became angry and demanded that Mandela go back to the university. He refused, and so the Regent brought things to a head: He tried to arrange a marriage for Mandela, but he wasn't interested and decided to run away secretly to find his fortune in Johannesburg. This meant the end of Mandela's good season.

Suddenly, his expectations were dashed. "All my beautiful dreams crumbled, and the prize that was so near my grasp vanished like snow in the summer sun,"[274] he said later. It was April 1941, and he was twenty-three years old. To make matters worse, Johannesburg was not what Mandela expected. An increasing African migration into the city in the last five years had produced disorderly hut-towns near the city and had caused the Afrikaners to seek a kind of segregation, the *apartheid*.

Mandela first looked for work in the gold mines. But as soon as it became known that he had left his home, he was fired. He then tried to get a job at a black-owned real estate agency and a law firm. "It was the most difficult time in my life,"[275] he wrote later. For the next five years, he wore a decayed suit, which one of the lawyers had given him. He lived in a slum with no electricity or indoor plumbing. He was very poor, and had to walk miles per day to go to the office.

But Mandela always wanted to become a lawyer. Thus early in 1943, he enrolled at the University of Witwatersrand for a law degree. He spent six years there, but it was often a painful experience. He encountered a great deal of racism—for example, white students would move away when he sat down near them. In the same year, 1943, Mandela met a young black woman, Evelyn Mase, and, in 1944, they married—he was twenty-six, she was twenty-two. In 1945, Evelyn gave birth to a son and, in 1946, to a daughter. But this was a difficult period: Mandela was forced to help his wife by bathing the babies and preparing the meals, while at the same time he was attending the university and working at the law office.

At the same time, he became a member of the African National Congress (ANC), the black political union, and, in 1952, he and four other members of the ANC wrote a letter to the government asking for the annulment of some laws they considered unjust. But the season was a bad one for Mandela: That letter did not have a positive result, but on the contrary, it marked the entrance of the "winter" of this bad season in his life. Soon he experienced his first imprisonment—he stayed in jail for two nights. In July 1952, he experienced a worst treatment: He was sentenced to nine months imprisonment (which was suspended for two years), while at the end of 1952, the situation worsened: He was prohibited "for six months from attending any meeting or from talking to more than one person at a time, and was forbidden to leave Johannesburg without permission."[276]

In 1953, he received another ban, again restricting him to Johannesburg for two years, and after that ban expired in 1955, he received a new one for another five years. "I found myself treated like a criminal,"[277] he said later. At home Mandela also faced severe problems. His wife, Evelyn, disapproved of his political activity and did not want to hear anything about politics. Finally, in 1956, their marriage fell apart. Evelyn left, even taking the curtains with her.

But the final blow came at the end of 1956: In December of that year, Mandela and another 155 leaders were charged with high treason. The preliminary hearings got underway in January 1957.

# The New Good Season from 1957 to 1974

In 1957, a year after Evelyn's departure, Mandela met a beautiful young woman from Transkei. Her name was Winnie Madikizela and she was awed by his political acumen. A new good season started for Mandela. They got married a year later—he was forty, she was twenty-four—and his image now "acquired a new dimension: not just the lawyer and the revolutionary, but the lover with the adoring partner,"[278] his biographer, Anthony Sampson, says. They were deep in love, and while Mandela was on trial for treason, their affair seemed like "a wartime romance."[279]

The trial started in February 1959, and in August 1960, Mandela testified with a speech that revealed a thoughtful politician: It was the most powerful speech he had made until then. In March 1961, the court announced the victory: a verdict of not guilty. Mandela and the other accused celebrated the verdict with a spontaneous outburst of joy.

Soon after his release, Mandela went underground—as the chief ANC leader—and from then on became more famous than he had ever been. Seeking help in liberating black South Africans, he traveled in 1961 and 1962 throughout South Africa and visited Tanzania, the nations of West Africa, Egypt, Tunis, Morocco, Ethiopia, Britain, and other countries. When he returned home in August 1962, he did what he had already planned: He let himself be arrested for leaving the country without a passport. As his biographer, Anthony Sampson, says, "he seemed . . . to be *courting* [his] arrest."[280]

In the trial that followed, he played an almost theatrical role; the court was his theater. "The leader of a new type emerged in South Africa," a local newspaper wrote: "the leader who would neither surrender . . . nor flee the country."[281] During the trial he did not dispute the facts, and he was sentenced to five years imprisonment. From prison, Mandela "established him [self] as the lost leader who had defied the system, [and though] hunted and underground . . . [he was] yet in the midst of his people,"[282] Anthony Sampson says.

But though he waited to be free in five years, scores of documents incriminating him were found by the police in 1963, and a new trial opened. Mandela and the other accused now faced the death penalty. However, he was jubilant and confident, his morale was high, and he had decided to accept responsibility, despite his lawyers' warnings. He was prepared to face even death if that was necessary. When, in 1964, the court sentenced him and the other accused to life in prison instead of giving them the death penalty, as had been expected, Mandela actually smiled: He had achieved what he had pursued.

Mandela "went to jail with all the glory of a lost leader, in an aura of martyrdom."[283] And many of his friends were with him. A kind of "summer" now started in his life. Soon, with Mandela as their leader, the prisoners began to exert pressure on their guards, until they gained control over them. Conditions in the prison gradually improved, and by 1967, there was even hot water for them to use. The prisoners' recreation included outdoor games, such as rugby and cricket, and Mandela's favorite form of relaxation was tending the small garden he had planted in the courtyard.

His wife, Winnie, visited him whenever she could, and he was particularly satisfied that she was, as he said, "a woman who is loyal to me, who supports, and who comes to visit me, who writes to me."[284] Mandela was thoroughly optimistic, insisting he was never depressed because he knew his cause would triumph. Although for most people, life in prison is not a good season, for Mandela it was: He believed his goals to free his people would be realized only if he remained imprisoned—and for that reason he was happy, though he wasn't free.

All the prisoners believed they would serve ten years at the most, from 1964 to 1974. But 1974 came and no hope of release loomed ahead. Mandela's optimism faltered, and this good season for him ended here.

# The New Bad Season from 1974 to 1990

By 1975, the majority of the prisoners started challenging Mandela's leadership. Some of the new prisoners regarded him as a "sellout" because he had reached agreements with the guards. "The year 1975 started off badly and was disastrous from beginning to end,"[285] Mandela told his wife. In 1977, Winnie was banished to a small, bare house in a desolate Afrikaner town, where she would stay for the next seven years. She was forbidden to meet with more than one person at a time, and she had lost almost everything else. Mandela felt guilty, and in that period he was tortured by the thought of what would happen to his wife and children.

By 1980, Mandela—now sixty-two—looked frail, sometimes spoke haltingly, and often seemed lost in thought. The conditions in the prison remained grim, and the monastic lifestyle caused much psychological strain: Mandela worried that his children would never forgive him for his absence. In 1982, the situation worsened—the "winter" of this bad season would now follow: Mandela was moved to a new prison, a colossal building for thousands of criminals. The government wanted to separate him from the other political prisoners, so he was transferred to that castle. There were six prisoners in each cell; the cell was dreary and the amenities were worse than before.

In 1985, Mandela had prostate surgery. After the operation, he was taken to an isolated section of the prison, in a damp, uncomfortable cell on the ground floor, where the prisoners who were ordinary criminals shouted racist insults at him. For the first time in his years in jail, Mandela felt alone and had lost every hope to be released. In 1986, he wrote to Winnie: "There is not a living soul in South Africa today . . . who knows when we will be released."[286]

The following year, Mandela was invited by the minister of justice to help negotiate the future of South Africa's black population. This turned out to be an ordeal for Mandela. He was alone in encountering the government; he had been cut off from his colleagues. "One false move could destroy his leadership,"[287] Anthony Sampson said. Between 1987 and 1990, there were twelve more such torturous meetings between the government and Mandela, with Mandela still in jail.

At the same time, Mandela's health was not good: He coughed, was sweating and vomiting, and had trouble standing up. In 1988, the doctors said he was suffering from tuberculosis. By 1987, he also faced severe problems with his wife; she had involved herself in outbreaks of violence and murder. In July 1988, Winnie's opponents set fire to her house. Mandela learned of it in jail and was mortified. In December 1988, Winnie's supporters stabbed and killed a fourteen-year-old boy, accusing him of being an informer. Winnie witnessed the assault. Mandela learned about it early in 1989 and was enormously worried.

In 1989 and early 1990, Mandela was faced with a diplomacy of intrigue: The government insisted on the abandonment of majority rule, which meant that the black population of the country could not govern. Mandela could not of course accept that provision—and thus he would remain in jail. By November 1989, Mandela was the only black leader still in prison. "His eyes looked so dead,"[288] a friend said.

# The New Good Season from 1990 On

But in February 1990, the big moment arrived. The government announced that the political prisoners—Mandela included—would be freed. Mandela was released on February 11, 1990. At last, he had won. As he walked through the prison gates, he received a hero's welcome from the thousands of well-wishers crowding around the prison. Soon, Mandela started negotiations with the government to peacefully transfer the power to the blacks, and a conference for that purpose was held in September 1991.

The next year, Mandela "began a new happy life."[289] He announced he would divorce Winnie because he could not ignore her infidelity and other misdeeds. Early in 1994, he started campaigning for the general election. Projecting a superb politician's charm and skill, he won the election easily. On May 10, 1994, he was inaugurated president of South Africa.

Mandela "occupied the presidency as if he had been born to it;"[290] he "seemed more like a [philosopher] king than a politician."[291] And, in 1995, he acquired a new love: He was enchanted by Graça Machel, the widow of the former president of Mozambique. By 1997, she became his consort. In 1998, they were married; he was eighty and she was fifty-three. "Late in my life I am blooming like a flower,"[292] he said. This feeling continued for many years. The "summer" of this good season had started for Mandela in 1998.

# Conclusion

Mandela's alternations of seasons show that his life's good and bad seasons alternated every 16–17 years in 1941, 1957, 1974, and 1990. Adding Mandela's dates to the dates for Napoleon, Hugo, Rodin, Churchill, and Onassis that we've seen in previous chapters, we find this continuous row of dates: 1776,

1792, 1809, 1825, 1842, 1859, 1875, 1892, 1908, 1925, 1941, 1957, 1974, and 1990.

That is a period of more than 220 years. You remember that a same period of 220 years also happens in the dates of Beethoven, Verdi, Picasso, and Gorbachev (see the end of Chapter 6). But the seasons in these periods are opposite. When a good season starts in one period, a bad season starts in the other—and vice versa: When a bad season starts in one period, a good one starts in the other.

For example, Napoleon's alternations of seasons happened at the same time as those of Beethoven (1776, 1792, and 1809). But while, in 1776, a good season started for Beethoven, on the contrary a bad season started for Napoleon. Similarly, when in 1792 a bad season started for Beethoven, on the contrary a good season started for Napoleon the same year. Also, in 1809 a good season started for Beethoven while a bad season started for Napoleon the same year.

The same phenomenon happens, as you have seen, with the dates of Verdi, Picasso, and Gorbachev compared with the dates of Hugo, Rodin, Churchill, Onassis, and Mandela. This confirms that there are two opposite courses of seasons in our lives—the first course and the second course.

Furthermore, with Mandela's biography we have confirmed that the phenomenon of the alternations of seasons is universal and happens in all kinds of human races, as indicated in Chapter 1. Specifically, Napoleon, Beethoven, Columbus, Verdi, and others were born and brought up in Europe, while John Glenn, Jimmy Carter, and Jackie Kennedy were born and brought up in the United States, and Gorbachev was born and brought up in Russia. Mandela was born and brought up in South Africa—that is, in the southern hemisphere of the earth—while the Dalai Lama was born and raised in Asia. Also, the Dalai Lama belongs to the Asian human race, while Mandela to the black one, and all the others belong to the white human race. That confirms that the alternations of seasons happen all over the world and in all kinds of human races.

Mandela's life confirms once more that you mustn't despair during your bad seasons; the good season will come with certainty in the future. Recall that when Mandela was in a bad season in 1985, he lost every hope to be released from jail—he wrote to his wife that "there is not a living soul in South Africa today who knows when we will be released." But after five years, he triumphantly walked out the prison gates, and, in 1994, he was inaugurated the president of South Africa.

## Understanding the Patterns of Your Life

In the next chapter we continue and extend our confirmation by seeing how the good and bad seasons alternated in the life of famous Greek opera singer Maria Callas.

# Chapter 19
# MARIA CALLAS

Maria Callas was born in 1923 in New York City to Greek immigrant parents (her father's name was George Kalogeropoulos, later changed to Callas). From the few facts available regarding her early years, it appears that the first years of her life were good. In her early childhood, one of her joys was to listen to the phonograph records her parents played. She had a very good voice and a phenomenal ear for a young child. She sang selections from the records, like "La Paloma" and others.

At the age of ten, in 1933, she sang Gounod's "Ave Maria" and Bizet's the "Habanera" from *Carmen* at a school performance. At her middle school graduation two years later she sang Ambroise Thomas's "Je Suis Titania" from *Mignon*. In the same year she sang in one of America's very popular talent-contest radio programs; she came in second and won a watch and $50, a large sum in that time.

At the end of the school term, early in 1937, Callas' mother—believing that her daughter needed education in music, which she could have only in Greece—took her, together with her sister, despite her father's objections, back to Greece. On the ship, Callas sang the "Habanera" again, and the captain gave her a doll as a gift, which she kept for years, decorating the headboard on her bed.

Later that same year, in Greece, Callas sang "La Paloma" at a tavern and the customers gave her an ovation asking for more. When she finished, a young tenor congratulated her; he was with the Athens Opera and proved to be of great assistance. He introduced her to Madame Trivella, a teacher at the National Conservatory of Greece. When Madame Trivella heard Callas sing the "Habanera," she was astonished. She immediately accepted Callas as her pupil with pleasure, and soon Callas won a scholarship at the Greek National Conservatory.

Thrilled, she sat down to work, not even taking time for a meal. The next year, she was invited to see Verdi's *La Traviata* at the Lyric Theater of Athens. She "was transfixed. She now knew ... [at the age of fifteen] that opera was to be her world,"[293] her biographer, Anne Edwards, says. The same year, Callas sang at a concert in Athens. When she finished, the applause was overwhelming, and when she sang her first role in opera—in Mascagni's *Cavalleria Rusticana* in 1939—the audience rose from their seats and cheered her. The following year, Callas became a member of the chorus of the Greek Opera at a salary of $15 a month—at age seventeen.

# The Bad Season from 1941 On

Early in 1941, however, Callas developed a slight tremor in her voice. Her alarmed teacher kept her off the stage for a year. She was extremely unhappy. In the meantime, the worst had happened: Hitler's army had invaded Greece in April 1941. Food was scarce; the Germans destroyed everything. The winter was severe and there was no wood for the fireplace. Callas was distraught: "The occupation of Athens was the most painful period in my life,"[294] she said later.

In 1942, Callas' life worsened: When the Germans again permitted public performances, Callas sang *Tosca* at the Athens Opera. But she returned home miserable, convinced that her performance had been ruinous. When, in 1943, Callas made the faulty step of giving a concert for the occupation army, the board of the Athens Conservatory decided that the concert was unpatriotic and discontinued her scholarship. She could not attend classes any more. She cried bitterly but in vain.

At the same time, Callas became enormously overweight. Despite the food shortage, she was eating huge quantities of nuts and dried figs. The next year, the situation worsened. The Germans left Athens after their defeat. But then the Communist Party's guerrillas seized the city of Athens in an effort to install their own government. Callas and her mother and sister were imprisoned in their apartment, and they hadn't any food or water.

When that situation ended in 1945, Callas decided to realize her long awaited dream to return to America, to be reunited with her father and to sing at the Metropolitan Opera House. Over her mother's strong objections, she sailed back to New York, in September 1945, alone. But she couldn't reverse her bad season: Things were not as anticipated. She first called a Greek tenor with the Metropolitan Opera who she knew from Athens before the war. But he refused to see her. She also tried to see opera agents and managers in New York but to no avail.

After six months of rejections, she managed to be heard by a famous tenor, but he told her coolly that she had to get further training. When at last, Callas was asked, in 1946, to sing at the Met, she made a terrible mistake: She didn't like the role offered to her—Leonore in Beethoven's *Fidelio*—and to the manager's great surprise, she refused it. She ruined any chance she had of making a name for herself in the United States anytime soon. Not long after that, she was asked to audition at the San Francisco Opera, but it didn't go well. The manager "treated her like a schoolgirl,"[295] saying that she should lose weight because she was too heavy, and that she had to get her career started in Italy first.

The opportunity to build her career in Italy came unexpectedly the following year. She was asked to sing at the Arena di Verona during the 1947 summer festival there. Though successful, however, her role did not produce enough excitement to make the opera companies want to ask for her services. To her great disappointment, "no agent or opera company in Italy displayed even the slightest interest in her,"[296] Callas' biographer, Anne Edwards, says. Only an Italian businessman named Battista Meneghini, who was a supporter of the opera and knew many important artists and conductors in Italy, offered—recognizing Callas' talent—to become her agent. She gratefully accepted. But his first effort to take her to an audition at Milan's La Scala failed: There was no audition.

Later, Meneghini succeeded in arranging for Callas to sing at La Fenice, the old opera house in Venice, in late December 1947 and early January 1948. She sang *Tristan and Isolde*, but the acclaim she had hoped for didn't come. Only some minor opera houses in Trieste, Udine, Genoa, and Rome sent her offers. On Meneghini's advice, she accepted them, but reluctantly. When she came back to Verona in the summer of 1948, she was dispirited. The problem with her weight had worsened (she stole food and hid it under her bed), and nights filled with anxiety began to torture her.

Another cause for concern was Callas' belief that Meneghini was indispensable to her life and that she had to marry him. But he had not proposed. Though she sang *I Puritani* in Venice with great success early in 1949—and "there was now a growing demand for her services, [while] articles about her . . . appeared in newspapers all over Europe and the States"[297]—nevertheless, she was again deeply depressed, gaining even more weight.

Finally, Callas became Meneghini's wife in April 1949; she was twenty-six and he was fifty-six. But the bad season continued, and the "winter" of this season entered into her life: The happiness she was expecting did not come. First, there were Meneghini's brothers, who were hostile toward her because she was not of an aristocratic origin. When she was to leave on a tour of South America the day after her wedding, Meneghini said he wouldn't accompany her. She became hysterical and warned the tour would be cancelled, but finally she went alone—a "bride of twenty-four hours,"[298] her biographer notes. In Buenos Aires, she sang *Turandot*, but the critics emphasized the unpleasant intonation of her voice. Not surprisingly, her earnings from the South American tour were modest.

In 1950, Callas was at last invited to sing at La Scala—three performances of *Aïda*. However, she wasn't satisfied: The La Scala production of *Aïda* wasn't suitable for her. Finally, her performance in it was a failure. Callas was depressed; her "disastrous engagement at La Scala . . . had seriously injured her self-esteem"[299] and reputation. That same year, Callas had a very successful tour in Mexico, where she sang *Norma*, *Aïda*, *Tosca*, and *Il Trovatore*. But when she returned to Verona, a big disappointment awaited her: She found that the money with which Meneghini had bought a new car was not taken from his earnings, but from hers. That fact raised serious doubts in Callas' mind about Meneghini's faithfulness for years to come.

In 1951, she realized that Meneghini was not as good at handling her contracts as she'd assumed—despite her success in many Italian cities, including Rome, Venice, Naples, Palermo, and others. She also hated having to stay in various hotels around the country while she was performing. For these reasons, her weight increased more, there was restlessness in her voice, and she had a bit of a sharp tongue.

When Meneghini arranged a series of performances in Mexico City during the hot summer months of 1951, she said that this was a a bad idea: the heat when she sang *Aïda* "was so intense that . . . she was suffering from heat exhaustion, . . . her legs and ankles had swollen painfully, [and] she spent two days in bed."[300] Later, in Rio de Janeiro, she had to cancel her performance in *Aïda* because she was still too ill. Her other performances in Brazil, furthermore, were frustrating: Though in *Norma* she had great success, in *Tosca* many members of the audience shouted against her. When she finished, the concert manager nearly refused to pay her, saying that her performances were awful.

The unpleasant situation continued into the next two years. Though in late 1951 and early 1952 she sang *I Vespri Siciliani* and *Norma* at La Scala with great success—and at the end of 1952 she sang *Norma* again, at London's Covent Garden, also with great success—she was not happy. When she was home in Verona trying to relax, the animosity with her husband's brothers was extreme. They were entirely disrespectful. Callas began to hate her own home and became hostile toward her husband.

In 1953, she went on a strict diet, and lost sixty-eight pounds (thirty kilos). But because of this diet, a new eating problem arose, the opposite of her previous weight problem. She couldn't eat sufficiently and her weight was only 117 pounds (fifty-three kilos). However, she sang seventeen operas in 1953 in many Italian cities. But when she was back home in Verona, she "still suffered the worst insults and indignation"[301] from her husband's brothers. She then swore to leave Verona and never to come back—and she never did.

In 1954, the situation worsened. Callas sang *Norma, La Traviata*, and *Lucia di Lammermoor* with great success at Chicago's Opera House. But she wasn't happy: She felt terribly alone. Her situation became worse when she fell in love the same year with the famous Italian film and stage director Luchino Visconti. Though Visconti was a homosexual, Callas's bad season prevented her from seeing that fact. When she sang *La Traviata* at La Scala under the direction of Visconti in 1955—and the audience became delirious—Callas had eyes only for Visconti. But unfortunately, he wasn't available.

In 1955, Callas had a second tour at Chicago's Opera House. Though she was again a big hit, she was still unhappy: She "was becoming less and less patient with . . . [Meneghini, since] her sexual appetite [was] unsatisfying."[302] At the same time, another worry was added: Her mother—who wanted to exert extensive influence on her daughter, a fact that Maria refused to accept, and thus their relationship was never good and had worsened during the last years—gave interviews to various newspapers blaming her daughter and describing her as a monster.

The next year, Callas sang at last at the Met in New York, *Norma, Tosca*, and *Lucia*. Though she received applause and many encores, her appearance was less successful than she had anticipated. At the same time, *Time* magazine published a cover story quoting Callas's mother as saying that when she asked her daughter for money, she replied: "Jump in the river and drown yourself."[303] The story was also broadcast on radio and television, causing Callas enormous worries and difficulties.

Early in 1957, Callas was feeling more alone than ever. Her mother had betrayed her, she didn't trust her husband any more, and she was extremely bitter with Visconti. But this bad season in Callas' life ended in the middle of 1957.

# The New Good Season from 1957 On

In April and May 1957, Callas sang Donizetti's *Anna Bolena (Anne Boleyn)* at La Scala under the direction of Visconti. But now, her feelings for him had suddenly changed drastically; she became less tolerant of his homosexuality, and she was no longer bewitched by his genius. Her love for him had evaporated. At last, she was free. Her role in *Anna Bolena,* furthermore, was an unprecedented triumph. The audience went mad, "the applause . . . rose in a tremendous crescendo . . . [and] continued for twenty-four minutes, a La Scala record."[304] The crowd outside the theater was so big that the police came to contain it.

On September 3, 1957, the crucial moment arrived: Elsa Maxwell, the famous American gossip columnist and socialite, arranged a party in Venice in Callas's honor. Among the guests were Greek tycoon Aristotle Onassis and his wife. When they met, he took Callas's hand and kissed it. Later, they had a short dance. "His touch seemed somehow magnetized and it set up an alarm in me,"[305] Callas said later. That was the start of a new life for her, a life she had always wanted but never achieved, a life full of love.

Simultaneously, her career continued on its meteoric ascent. In 1958, Callas sang brilliantly at the Metropolitan Opera, at La Scala, and at London's Covent Garden where Queen Elizabeth was present. Onassis, who was in London at that time, sent her a magnificent bouquet of roses. When at the end of the same year she sang—also with great success—at L' Opéra de Paris in front of the president of France, Onassis attended the gala, though he disliked opera. At the dinner reception that followed, he again took Callas's hand and kissed it. The touch was "so pleasing,"[306] she said later.

In June 1959, Onassis and his wife, Tina, invited the Meneghinis to a party they would give in Maria's honor in London. In the meantime, Onassis had sent Callas a superb chinchilla coat as a gift. She wore it immediately, despite the warm weather. When they had a tango at the party, and she said she loved that kind of dance, Onassis ordered the orchestra to continue with tangos. A month later, the Meneghinis were invited to a cruise on Onassis's yacht, the *Christina.* By the end of the first week, Callas spent little time with Meneghini, and she "was seen going in and out of Onassis's apartments . . . late at night and leaving the next morning."[307] After the cruise was over, Onassis arranged a suite for her at the Hôtel de Paris in Monte Carlo.

She was now extremely happy. "For the first time I understand what it means to be a woman. My singing, my career . . . come after Ari,"[308] Callas told her maid and confidante. Toward the end of 1959, Callas put an end to her unhappy marriage: A court decreed her separation from Meneghini—since divorce is not permitted in Italy. (At the same time, Tina Onassis filed for divorce in New York.)

That idyllic situation continued into 1960 and 1961. Callas had greatly curtailed her singing engagements so that she could stay with Onassis. When, in 1960, Onassis organized one more tour on the *Christina* with Callas, she was, as she admitted, "madly happy."[309] That summer, she sang *Norma* in Greece, at the ancient theater of Epidaurus. When she finished, the audience was weeping, and a few days later, she was honored with the Medal of Merit by the Greek government. When, in 1961, she sang *Medea*—in Epidaurus again—it was an amazing performance. The crowd shouted: "Greece's Queen of Opera!"[310]

In 1962, she and Onassis spent most of their time together in Monte Carlo and Paris, where he had bought a flat for her. Her passion for Onassis was undiminished. He was equally devoted to her, his gifts to her were extravagant, and the bills for the furnishings she ordered for her apartment weren't questioned. So, when Onassis told Callas, in 1963, that he was going to arrange a cruise on the *Christina* with President Kennedy's wife, Jackie, as a guest—a cruise on which Callas could not be present—she had no objections. She knew that the president's friendship was crucial to Onassis and that her presence as his mistress on the same cruise as the first lady of the United States would be problematic.

In late 1963, Callas found that she was pregnant—at the age of forty. But the only thing that interested her was her love with Onassis—the child had no meaning for her. So, early in 1964, she had an abortion. On her return from the hospital, a magnificent necklace was delivered to her apartment from Onassis. The summer of 1964 was "the most intimate time [Onassis and Callas had shared] . . . since the early days of their relationship"[311] on Skorpios, Onassis's private Greek island.

The next year, Callas's successes continued undiminished: She sang *Tosca* at the Opéra de Paris and soon after at the Metropolitan Opera. There, it was an unprecedented success: The cheers lasted for almost six whole minutes. The critics said that was the most superb *Tosca* New York had ever seen. After that, she sang at London's Covent Garden—*Tosca* again—before the Queen, with equally great success. This situation continued through 1967.

Then in 1968, Onassis told Callas that he was going to marry President Kennedy's widow, Jackie. Not because he loved Jackie, he said—he loved only

Maria—but because he *needed* her for his business in America. He always would love Callas, he added. Callas knew very well how much Onassis loved her. So, she did believe him, and Onassis was true to his word. Soon after his marriage to Jackie, in March 1969, he went back to Maria. Again, they were lovers, as we've seen in Jackie's biography.

Their lasting love continued for several years, until late 1973. When Onassis's son, Alexander, was killed in a plane crash at the Athens airport in January 1973, he went to Callas for consolation. In the meantime, Callas successfully continued to sing in various places around the world. When, at the end of 1973, Onassis stopped seeing or calling her, she wasn't disturbed: She soon found another love, Italian tenor Giuseppe di Stefano, who made her very happy. He planned to abandon his wife and to propose to Callas, he had told her.

# The New Bad Season After 1974

But in the fall of 1974, di Stefano's wife appeared suddenly and forced her husband to break off his relationship with Callas. Callas was distraught. She took lots of sleeping pills, and the next morning a friend found her in a coma. A doctor came, and Callas recovered over the next few days.

A worse blow came at the end of 1974. Onassis was admitted to a hospital in Paris; he suffered from incurable *myasthenia gravis*. Early in 1975, he was operated on. Callas was distressed. She wanted to go see him, but his wife, Jackie, had given orders to the hospital staff not to permit it. Callas stayed in her apartment waiting to hear news about Onassis.

When Jackie left for New York, a few days later, Onassis's daughter, Christina, and his sister, Artemis, called Callas and told her she could come to see him. When she arrived, they left her alone with Onassis. He "appeared to be unconscious, . . . [but] there was a moment when he opened one eye and seemed to recognize her."[312] "It's me," she said, "Maria—your canary."[313] Five days later, Onassis died. Callas said, quite inconsolable, that she felt she now was a widow. She shut herself up in her apartment, became moody and depressed, and kept the TV set on day and night because of her loneliness and fear of the dark. Onassis's photo rested on her piano.

This situation lasted throughout 1976 and for the first nine months of 1977. In September 1977, Callas called her sister in Athens and told her: "[since] Aristo died, I want to die, too."[314] A few days later, Callas' maid found her faint in the bathroom. The doctor who was called said she was dead—from a heart attack. She was only fifty-four. Onassis's "canary" had followed him as quick-ly as she could.

# Conclusion

Callas's alternations of seasons show that her life's good and bad seasons al-ternated every 16–17 years in 1941, 1957, and 1974. These dates are exactly the same as those of Onassis we've seen previously. Since Onassis belongs to the second course of seasons as we've also seen, that means that Callas belongs to the second course. This confirms that the alternations of seasons in a second, opposite course are valid not only for men but also for women.

Also, Callas's life confirms what is indicated in Chapter 2: To take more advantages from our findings, new studies by other persons (scientists or scholars) are necessary to complete our discovery. For example, should we marry a person belonging to the same course of seasons as us or to the oppo-site? Onassis and Callas belonged to the same course, and their relation was extremely satisfactory. But Onassis and Jackie Kennedy belonged to opposite courses, and their marriage was a failure, as we've seen in Jackie's biography. The question needs further research.

In the next chapter we'll continue and extend our confirmation by seeing how the good and bad seasons alternated in the life of famous French actress Sarah Bernhardt.

Chapter 20
# SARAH BERNHARDT

Sarah Bernhardt was born on October 23, 1844, in Paris, when her mother Judith was only sixteen. Her mother was a courtesan, while her father's name is unknown; he may have been Eduard Bernhardt, a "young French lawyer, whose name . . . [Judith] adopted."[315] In part because of these complexities, Sarah's childhood was the worst period of her life.

Soon after her birth, her mother sent her to live with a nurse, far from Paris. For the next few years, the nurse's family was the only family Sarah knew. They didn't have much money, and Bernhardt later recalled the house as dark and ugly. In 1852, when she was eight, Sarah was still unable to read or write. Her mother sent her to a boarding school, but she felt like a prisoner there, as she says in her memoirs. The other girls "made fun of her appearance,"[316] and she developed severe bouts of illness. During her almost two years at that school, her mother visited her only twice.

In the fall of 1853, Sarah was sent to a convent school. But she also hated life there and rarely saw her mother. Six years later, she was withdrawn from the convent school and went to live with her mother. Sarah was so ill at that time that the doctors said she would die young. She had a persevering cough and was spitting up blood. She was so depressed that she wanted to have her coffin ready. After repeated demands, her mother was forced to buy her a coffin.

But this bad season for Sarah ended abruptly in 1859.

## The Good Season from 1859 On
One afternoon in 1859, Sarah's mother took her to the Comédie Française to see a play. As her biographer, Elizabeth Silverthorne, says, "when the curtain slowly rose . . . [Sarah] thought . . . [she] was going to faint."[317] In fact, "it was . . .the curtain of my life which was rising,"[318] Sarah said later in her memoirs.

Shortly after that, she decided to enter the Conservatoire (Paris Conservatory of Music and Drama, considered the finest drama school in the world) to become an actress. A brilliant season started thus for Sarah Bernhardt that would lead her to repeated triumphs and glory.

During the audition at the Conservatory, Bernhardt's voice charmed. She threw herself into her work and was ready to graduate two years later. At the graduation ceremony, there was a competition among the students in which Bernhardt won second prize for comedy. A few days later, the Comédie Française sent her a letter asking for an interview. Bernhardt's career as an actress had begun.

She now lived with her mother and enjoyed spending time at the house of her aunt, Rosine. When her aunt gave a dinner party for her, a son of Napoleon I was a guest, as well as the famous Italian composer Gioacchino Rossini, "who accompanied Bernhardt on the piano as she recited a poem."[319]

The crucial moment arrived in August 1862. Bernhardt looked forward to her debut in the Comédie Française with the leading role in *Iphigénie* by Racine, the greatest French writer of tragedies. But because of stage fright, she became "paralyzed with fear,"[320] and her performance was disappointing. When after the performance, she slapped another actress, the Comédie Française terminated her contract. But this didn't influence Bernhardt. Over the next four years, she started to live another kind of satisfying life: She began to acquire and discard several lovers.

Early in 1864, she had an affair in Belgium with the Prince of Ligne Henri—and she became pregnant. Enjoying her independence, she returned to Paris and moved into a flat where her son, Maurice, was born on December 22, 1864. She was twenty and adored Maurice.

In 1866, Bernhardt signed a contract with the Odéon Theater, one of the most famous theaters in Paris. She achieved great success in Shakespeare's *King Lear,* in Alexandre Dumas's play *Kean* (this was Alexandre Dumas the father, not the son), and in two plays by novelist George Sand. Delighted, Dumas kissed her hand after the performance, while Sand said she performed "like an angel."[321] And when, in 1868, Bernhardt performed François Coppée's *Le Passant,* she had tremendous success: While the play was to run for only a few performances, it lasted for 150. The critics lavished praise on her interpretation, and the French emperor, Napoleon III, sent her "a magnificent brooch with the imperial initials in diamonds."[322]

In 1870, Napoleon III announced war on Prussia. While her family—mother, sisters, and son—went safely to Le Havre, Bernhardt stayed in Paris, transforming the Odéon Theater into a hospital, where she took care of the soldiers. (Later, the French government awarded her a gold medal for her efforts at the hospital.) After the war ended, in 1871, the Odéon reopened, and Bernhardt's appearance in several plays was well received. She was especially successful in Victor Hugo's *Ruy Blas*. The critics were effusive, the audience—which included England's Prince of Wales—went wild, and the crowds outside the theater "replaced the horses of her carriage and ran with it [as they transported her] through the streets to her apartment."[323] She had become a superstar. The "summer" of this season had already entered her life.

After Bernhardt's success in *Ruy Blas,* the director of the Comédie Française invited her to rejoin that premier theater—from which she had been fired ten years earlier—at a high salary. Bernhardt had arrived. She was now living stylishly in an opulent home she built, with eight servants and two carriages, and was enjoying a lavish social life. In 1874, she reached the pinnacle of success. She gave an amazing performance in Racine's *Phédre* at the Comédie Française. Other triumphs followed, including Alexandre Dumas's (son) *La Dame aux Camelias (The Lady of the Camelias),* and other plays.

# The Bad Season from 1875 On

From the beginning of this season, clouds in Bernhardt's relationship with the Comédie Française began to appear on the horizon and continued into the next years—despite her success in Hugo's *Hernani* in 1877. When, in 1878, Bernhardt left Paris for a few days without getting permission from the Comédie Française as she was required to do, the theater director asked her to pay a fine. She refused, and the director threatened to fire her. He kept her only because the Comédie Française was about to appear at London's Gaiety Theater, and the contract would be canceled if she wasn't in the company of actors.

The Comédie Française gave its first performance in London in June 1879, with *Phédre*. But the season was already bad for Bernhardt: She experienced "the worst stage fright"[324] of her life and was barely able to perform. The situation worsened shortly after that when noise and behavior problems associated with the menagerie of animals she'd accumulated in her temporary London home—including a cheetah, a monkey, and a parrot—led to public complaints. The manager of the Comédie Française cautioned her "to stop acting like a madwoman,"[325] while the French press criticized her behavior.

Not surprisingly, Bernhardt's relations with the Comédie Française worsened. Because of her scandalous behavior, the theater gave her, in 1880, a role she didn't like. The result was a poor performance, and she received the first bad reviews of her career. Bernhardt submitted her resignation, and the Comédie Française retaliated with a lawsuit, which remained in the courts for years. The French press also became increasingly hostile.

Bernhardt's only choice was to leave France. Earlier she'd refused offers of a North American tour, but late in 1880 she felt she had to accept. Her performances in New York and Boston were very successful, but the press treated her badly, criticizing her for her excesses and exoticism. Even "a horse-drawn billboard"[326] caricaturing her appeared in the streets of Boston, and followed her in many other cities. Bernhardt wanted to return to Europe immediately, but her manager reminded her of her contract, so she stayed.

The bad situation continued. She was denounced by the Catholic archbishop in Montreal, who forbade his congregations from seeing her performances; she received similar treatment from the Episcopal bishop in Chicago. The tour ended in New York in May 1881, after an exhausting trip with many brief stays in Atlanta; New Orleans; Washington, DC; Baltimore; and other cities.

Back in Paris, Bernhardt found that people continued to believe her star had fallen. After waiting in vain for a few weeks for offers from Paris to come in, she embarked on new trips abroad. She traveled again to London, then to Italy, Greece, Switzerland, Belgium, Holland, and Russia. During this period, another cause of worry was added to Bernhardt's life: She fell in love with a Greek man named Aristidis Damala (in Greek: Damalas), eleven years younger than her. Damala was the son of a wealthy Greek shipowner who had moved to France. After he completed school in France, the son went back to Greece in 1878, where he served as a cavalry officer, then returned to France. There he began to work as an actor, but "he also became a gambler, a womanizer, and a drug addict,"[327] Bernhardt's biographer, Elizabeth Silverthorne, says. Bernhardt ignored these and other flaws, and despite her son's objections she married Damala in 1882.

But a "winter" now entered her life—the bad consequences appeared soon: In the fall of 1882, Bernhardt purchased the Ambigu Theater in Paris, where she and Damala performed in a play, *Fédora*. But Damala's performance was so bad that the whole production failed. Damala became angry and abusive. Finally, he left Bernhardt for North Africa, where he enlisted in the army; she was heartbroken.

The next year, the Ambigu Theater was in a bad condition financially. To pay the creditors, Bernhardt sold some of her jewelry. Soon after, Damala returned to Paris and Bernhardt took him back. But he apparently had a serious morphine addiction, was critical and intolerant toward Bernhardt, and became openly involved with a young actress. On top of everything else—he acquired major gambling debts and thought nothing of asking Bernhardt to pay them. She had had enough. She obtained a legal separation from him in 1883, since she was Catholic and divorce wasn't an option.

In 1884 and 1885, Bernhardt collaborated with Jean Richepin, the French playwright, and performed in several of his plays in Paris. But none were successful. Disappointed, she decided to go abroad again in 1886, this time to South America. Her thirteen-month tour of Uruguay, Chile, Peru, Ecuador, and Panama turned out to be arduous, because the traveling conditions were often primitive. The worst disaster happened on her trip back to France. Bernhardt had a bad fall and seriously injured her right knee. She suffered unbearable pain that came and went for the rest of her life. Later, she had to have her right leg amputated above the knee.

In November 1887, Bernhardt appeared in Paris in Victorien Sardou's play *La Tosca,* which he had written for her. But the French press was highly critical, dismissing it as a play "fit only for ignorant Englishmen and American savages."[328] (Thirteen years later, in 1900, the play would be developed into an opera by Giacomo Puccini—*Tosca*—which is still performed worldwide with great success).

A few weeks later, at age twenty-three, Bernhardt's son, Maurice, married a Polish princess. Bernhardt was devastated, not because she disapproved of the bride, but because she feared losing her son's exclusive love. As a consolation, she threw herself into her work; in the spring of 1888, she embarked on a tour that included visits to Italy, Sweden, Norway, Russia, Egypt, and Turkey. Returning to France in March 1889, Bernhardt found Damala seriously ill. She did her best to care for him, but he died a few months later at the age of thirty-four. Now a widow, she returned his body to Greece. Despite her problems with Damala, she never got over the loss of him. She signed legal documents as "Sarah Bernhardt Damala, widow," and whenever she visited Athens, she called on his mother and took flowers to his grave.

In January 1890, Bernhardt played the role of Joan of Arc in *Jeanne d' Arc.* The role required her to fall to her injured knee repeatedly; she experienced excruciating pain, and the knee became so inflamed that her doctor ordered her to stop performing. The play closed for two months.

In 1891, she decided to go on a world tour. This decision ended the bad season that began for Bernhardt in 1875.

# The New Good Season from 1892 On

Bernhardt's good season started with her world tour in 1892–1893. She was a wonderful ambassador for France on this world tour. She went first to Australia, where she was given the red-carpet treatment in Melbourne, Adelaide, and Sydney. She went on to New Zealand, then to Hawaii and Samoa. In the United States, she performed from San Francisco to Brooklyn, then traveled to South America. She ended the tour in Europe, where she played from Russia to Portugal. Triumphantly returning to France in September 1893, Bernhardt was "richer by 3.5 million francs."[329]

The first thing she did with all that money was to build a retreat on a small island in Brittany. A home was constructed that combined comfortable bedrooms with a dining room, salon, and studio. She spent most of her time there, with friends and other guests. The second thing Bernhardt did was to take over the management of the Renaissance Theater in Paris, where—between 1893 and 1898—she successfully appeared in several performances. In the summer seasons of each year, she continued to go to London, while, in 1896, she had a brief tour of the United States.

The good season continued into the next years. In 1899, Bernhardt acquired the Nations Theater in Paris, which she renamed the Théâtre Sarah Bernhardt. She renovated it, creating a luxurious apartment for herself on the premises. Between 1900 and 1904, she performed in many plays in that theater, including *La Dame aux Camelias, Tosca,* and *Phédre;* they were always a huge success. Her performance as Napoleon Bonaparte's son in Edmond Rostand's *L'Aiglon (The Eagle)* was also considered a glorious success. In 1905–1906, Bernhardt had another successful American tour, and, in 1908, she went on her last tour of Europe.

# The New Bad Season from 1909 On

Bernhardt's last tour of Europe ended in 1909. She had two more American tours in 1910 and 1912, but in South America she had a second terrible accident: While performing *Tosca,* she fell on stage and re-injured her right knee. She remained in bed for weeks. After returning to Paris in 1913, she couldn't walk without assistance.

In August 1914, World War I started, and Bernhardt was forced to leave Paris and seek refuge in a villa near Bordeaux. In the meantime, her leg had become worse and had been put in a cast. After the removal of the cast a few months later, in 1915, gangrene was discovered in her knee. The worst moment in Bernhardt's life occurred: The doctors determined that to save her life, they would immediately have to amputate the leg above the knee.

Bernhardt was stoical—she knew she had no choice—but she had a protracted and painful convalescence. A wheelchair was improvised to allow her to get around. It allowed her to perform some plays—in tents, hospitals, and other locations—during the war, and travel to the United States on her last tour in 1916. But further health problems set in. She was found to have kidney problems, and underwent an operation.

In 1918, Bernhardt returned to France; the war had not ended yet. She needed to continue working, since she had no money. Between 1919 and 1921, she appeared in several plays in her wheelchair, but the audiences came to see her only out of pity. At the same time, her financial situation was precarious. Though she had made millions during her career, toward the end of her life "she lived on loans [and] by selling her jewelry."[330] In 1922, Bernhardt suffered worsening kidney problems and soon collapsed. On March 26, 1923, the end came: The greatest actress of the nineteenth century died—in the arms of her son, Maurice.

# Conclusion

Bernhardt's alternations of seasons show that her life's good and bad seasons alternated every 16–17 years in 1859, 1875, 1892, and 1908. These dates are exactly the same as those of Rodin we have seen earlier. Since Rodin belongs to the second course of seasons as we've also seen, that means that Bernhardt also belongs to the second course. It is also confirmed that the alternations of seasons in a second, opposite course are valid not only for men but also for women.

In the next chapter we'll continue and extend our confirmation by seeing how the good and bad seasons alternated in the life of Josephine, Napoleon's I wife.

# Chapter 21
# JOSEPHINE, NAPOLEON'S WIFE

Josephine was born in 1763 in Martinique, then a colony of France. She was a Creole, since both her parents—Joseph and Rose Tascher—were French. Her baptismal name was Marie-Rose, but her parents called her Yeyette. (Later, her first husband Alexandre de Beauharnais called her Rose, but her second husband—Napoleon—changed it to Josephine.) Until 1776, when she was thirteen, Yeyette's childhood in Martinique was a good season for her.

Her father was a successful sugar plantation owner—sugar cane was produced in abundance in Martinique, making the island one of France's most important colonies. Yeyette was happy, enjoying the island's "rare beauty . . . [and] sparkling . . . turquoise ocean."[331] But in 1776, a bad season started for her.

## The Bad Season from 1776 to 1792

In 1776, the British navy blockaded Martinique's harbors and stopped the export of sugar to France. For Yeyette's family—she had two other sisters—this was a catastrophe. The only solution for the girls was to get married. But in 1777, Yeyette was only fourteen. However, a boy four years older, named Alexandre de Beauharnais, was selected by his father as a suitable husband for her. Also a Creole born in Martinique, Alexandre went to France at the age of six, and at eighteen he was an officer in the French army.

But he wasn't the suitable husband: He didn't want to marry Yeyette; he loved another woman—Laure de Girardin, who was already expecting a child. But though he had to get married in order to obtain his mother's inheritance—according to the terms of the will—he couldn't marry Laure since she was the wife of a naval officer. So he compromised with Yeyette. Also, Yeyette was in no hurry to get married, and she didn't want to go to France. But she had no choice. So, late in 1779, she arrived in France accompanied by her father. Though Yeyette, like Alexandre, was unenthusiastic, they married.

Yeyette was now renamed Rose—and soon Rose's marriage turned to tragedy. Alexandre started enjoying himself, spending his newfound inheritance and going out every evening without taking his wife with him. He would return home late at night, drunk, and slept until the afternoon. In 1780—after almost one year of marriage—he left Rose for months. When their first child was born in 1781—a son named Eugene—quarrels erupted between the spouses.

In 1782, the situation worsened. Alexandre abandoned his wife—who was pregnant again—and went to Martinique, with Laure. There he started collecting evidence that would allow him to divorce Rose (something she soon learned about). Later, he sent Rose a letter demanding that she leave his house. When he returned to France in 1783, Rose was forced to leave the house and enter a convent that offered shelter to women suffering from marital problems. Their second child, daughter Hortence, was already born.

Now, the "winter" of this bad season entered Rose's life. Not having any other alternative, Rose decided, in 1784, to seek a legal separation. But she was penniless, so she went to live with her father-in-law. When conditions in that house became unbearable and Rose continued to face tremendous financial problems, she made, in 1788, a painful decision—to return to Martinique with her two children. However, the situation in Martinique was worse. Her father had become a feeble man, and she had to deal with the consequences of Alexandre's attack on her reputation when he was in Martinique collecting evidence against her.

In 1789, the worst came: the French Revolution of July 14 of that year started in Paris, when the crowds stormed the Bastille and obtained governmental power. Soon the revolutionary climate affected Martinique. Battles began between citizens and soldiers and between blacks and whites, while "men were hanged . . . women were kidnapped."[332] Panic-stricken, Rose decided to return to France. After a torturous trip, she and her two children arrived in Paris late in 1789. But the situation there was equally bad: There was no bread or coal, the prices raised dramatically, and there wasn't any money available.

The only way Rose could survive was to do the last thing she could imagine doing: to have affairs with men who could sustain her. As her biographer, Carolly Erickson, says, she entered a "shadow-world at the margin of respectability populated by women whose sexual arrangements and financial survival were intertwined."[333] She was twenty-six.

This situation continued into 1790–1792. But somewhere here, this bad season for Rose would end.

# The Good Season from 1792 to 1809

Late in 1792, the monarchy in France was abolished, and in January of 1793 King Louis XVI was executed. Queen Marie Antoinette followed a few months later. A powerful Committee took the king's place, and almost everybody was suspected as "an enemy of the revolution." Rose was also a suspect, and to avoid arrest, she needed a "certificate of citizenship."[334] Late in 1793, the first sign of the good season that had started for her appeared: Using her acquaintances, she managed to obtain the certificate. She had survived.

Though in April 1794 she was arrested and spent three awful months in prison, soon she was released—the Committee had found nothing against her. In the same year (1794), another major event occurred that drastically improved her life's conditions: While she was in prison, her husband—Alexandre de Beauharnais, then a general in the French army—had been executed as a traitor. Rose now was free to remarry.

The opportunity to remarry arrived soon. In the summer of 1795, Rose met Napoleon Bonaparte, then a brigadier general in the French army. In January 1796, Napoleon proposed to her, and they were married only three months later. She was thirty-three; he was twenty-seven. Her dream had been realized. Now she obtained a new name: Napoleon named her Josephine. Immediately after the marriage, Napoleon left Paris to become chief commander of the army of Italy. Josephine had to stay in Paris. But she felt she didn't need to stay alone: She continued her love affairs as before.

One of her lovers was a rich and influential man, Paul Barras, who helped her financially and introduced her to his wealthy friends. Finally having plenty of money to spend, Josephine shopped and bought the newest fashions, and spent hours making herself attractive, "attending [lots of] receptions and parties . . . [and dancing] until the early hours of the morning."[335] Another man Josephine became involved with was Hippolyte Charles, a lieutenant. He wasn't rich; on the contrary, Josephine often gave *him* money. But she was in love with him—and very happy: He was the only true love in her life until this point.

When Napoleon learned that Josephine was unfaithful, he wrote asking her to come to Milan—and she left Paris for Italy in June 1796. There, the glory awaited her. According to Josephine's biographer, Carolly Erickson, "a parade of Italian notables arrived [at the Palace of Milan, where Napoleon was staying] to be presented to Madame Bonaparte. . . . [They were] counts and countesses, dukes and marquises, . . . who bowed [to Josephine]."[336] In a letter from Milan to her aunt, Josephine praised her husband's devotion, saying he treated her like a goddess.

In full glory, Josephine returned to Paris in December 1797—and she continued to see Hippolyte almost every day, and sometimes she also saw Barras "the same day, before going home"[337] to Napoleon, who in the meantime had returned to Paris. The same situation continued when, in May 1798, Napoleon left for another campaign: to conquer Egypt. At the same time, Josephine realized a dream she'd always had: She had saved so much money that she bought a home of her own, a three-story residence, the château of Malmaison, on the banks of the Seine. By the spring of 1799, Josephine had moved in; Hippolyte stayed there as well.

In October 1799, the crucial moment arrived: Napoleon came back to Paris after almost a year and a half in Egypt. Because of his wife's infidelity, however, he had decided to divorce her. When she went to his house, she was informed that Napoleon had ordered his porter not to let her in. In a state of panic, Josephine pushed the porter aside and rushed up to Napoleon's room. But the door was locked. She cried and begged him to let her in, but in vain. She stayed there until early in the morning. Then, her children Eugene and Hortence, came and knocked on Napoleon's door. Hearing them, he unlocked the door. His face was tearstained. It took only a few moments before Napoleon, Josephine, Eugene, and Hortence—all weeping—"joined in an embrace."[338] Napoleon the Great had forgiven his wife. Josephine's good season had greatly helped this.

From that point on, the culmination of this good season started in Josephine's life—the "summer" of this season entered her life. Early in 1800, Napoleon became France's leading figure—and moved into the Tuileries Palace, with Josephine. There, she stayed in the apartment of Queen Marie Antoinette—and she lived like a queen. She had several personal attendants and a large contingent of servants who ran the household. In 1801, Josephine—now thirty-eight—wrote her mother that Napoleon made her very happy. She "lived amid the grandeur of the palace"[339] and enjoyed her life. Her love affair with Hippolyte was now over, as was her affair with Barras; Napoleon had sent him away.

The above situation continued into the following years 1802–1803. In May 1804, the greatest moment arrived: Napoleon was named Emperor of France. From then on, Josephine was addressed as "Your Imperial Majesty."[340] The coronation of the new emperor was to be held in December 1804. Napoleon had decided—over his brothers' objections—that Josephine would be named and crowned empress along with him. At the coronation ceremony, "she knelt before her husband . . . [and received] the circlet from his hands . . . her tears flowed freely [from her eyes]."[341] An ordinary woman had been named an empress.

From now on, Josephine lived the life of an empress. There were hundreds of balls, open-air festivals, and evenings at the theater and the opera. She spent more and more, sparing no expense on jewelry, art, stylish clothing, and elegant household objects. She continued buying even after her wardrobes were full of the most expensive gowns and other fashionable items. She had also other reasons to be happy as well: In 1805, Napoleon named her son Eugene— then twenty-three—viceroy of Italy. The same year, Napoleon defeated the armies of Britain, Austria, Prussia, and Russia, and became the ruler of Europe. Sharing the grandeur and wealth of her husband, Josephine continued to experience good fortune for several more years.

In 1808, the final great moment of Josephine's good season arrived. She had always feared Napoleon would divorce her if she couldn't give him a son and heir. That fear disappeared in 1808. Napoleon decided that year to take the painful step of divorcing her and ordered that the legal preparations be set in motion. But he soon rescinded the order. His decision had caused him "spasms and … severe stomach pains."[342] Anguished, he rushed to Josephine and admitted he couldn't leave her. In what was one of the high points of Josephine's life, they had a passionate reconciliation. The possibility of divorce seemed now a thing of the past.

As a result, Josephine started now to live the best possible life. She bought everything she could imagine: "plants, furniture . . . vases . . . chandeliers."[343] Her house, the château of Malmaison, "was full of treasures . . . and, in 1809, a new gallery was built to house them."[344] Though she had "more dresses . . . than any woman could possibly wear, she ordered more and more."[345] According- ing to her biographer, Josephine accumulated "nearly a thousand pairs of gloves, 800 pairs of shoes, several thousand pairs of silk stockings . . . [and] hundreds of embroidered chemises, . . . camisoles, . . . [and] nightcaps."[346] To see her guests' reactions to her wealth, she had displayed all her jewels on a large table. There were diamonds, "pearls . . . rubies, sapphires, emeralds, and opals surpassing . . . any other European collection."[347]

But in the same year (1809), this good season in Josephine's life ended. Late in the year 1809, a bad season would begin for Josephine, the last of her life.

# The New Bad Season from 1809 On

On the night of November 30, 1809, Napoleon invited his wife to dinner and gave her devastating news: He had decided he had to "find a wife who could provide [him] an heir to the throne."[348] In fact, he had already found someone: Marie Louise, Archduchess of Austria. Hearing the news, Josephine collapsed on the floor. Aided by a palace prefect, Napoleon carried her to her bedroom. Josephine's second marriage was over.

In December 1809, the legal formalities for the divorce were underway. In a state of melancholy, Josephine went to live at Malmaison, "wearing wide hats to hide her tear-stained face."[349] She was "constantly in tears,"[350] saying she felt as if she was dead. When, in 1810, Napoleon married Marie Louise, Josephine complained to her son that her house resembled a convent.

By February 1811, the economy of France had started to decline sharply. There were starving people and riots everywhere. The unrest entered Josephine's house, too. Her servants deceived her, stealing food, clothes, and objects d'art. Josephine began to suffer from headaches and other health problems. In 1812, Russia declared war on France; Napoleon's campaign against Russia began. But before Christmas of 1812, he was defeated at Moscow, and France's famous Grand Armée had been destroyed. Paris was mourning, and Josephine dressed in black.

By October 1813, the situation worsened: Napoleon was also defeated at Leipzig. Josephine was panic-stricken. Despite the divorce, she continued to love Napoleon. When in March 1814, the Russian and Austrian armies were a few days away from Paris, Josephine was forced to leave Malmaison and go to Navarre. There, she had little money and couldn't find food or coal. On March 31, the end came: The Russians and Austrians entered Paris. Napoleon was forced to resign. Trying suicide, he swallowed poison, but failed. A few days later he was exiled to the island of Elba. Josephine's sorrow was unbearable.

Less than two months later, her health began to deteriorate sharply. She became feverish, and when her children were called to her room on May 29, 1814, they found her unable to speak. An abbé was called to give the sacraments. A few minutes later, the woman who had become wife of an emperor, died. She was only fifty-one.

# Conclusion

Josephine's alternations of seasons show that her life's good and bad seasons alternated every 16–17 years in 1776, 1792, and 1809. These dates are exactly the same as those of Napoleon we have seen earlier. Since Napoleon belongs to the second course of seasons, that means that Josephine also belongs to the second course. We can confirm that the alternations of seasons in a second, opposite course are valid not only for men but also for women.

However, from Josephine's seasons we can also confirm that the alternations of seasons we've seen in this book are not valid only for famous people but they are also valid for ordinary persons. Though some people might not consider Josephine an ordinary person, this is not so. As you have seen in her biography, Josephine was an insignificant woman in the early periods of her life, soon reduced to the role of courtesan, until the age of thirty-eight. Also, though later her husband Napoleon named her an empress for five years, she didn't become a *ruling empress*, but remained as his shadow and at his mercy. When later Napoleon divorced her, at age forty-six, she continued being an insignificant person until her death.

Since Josephine's seasons alternated exactly the same way as that of famous people, we can further confirm that the alternations of seasons are valid for ordinary persons, too.

In the next chapter we continue and extend our confirmation by seeing how the good and bad seasons alternated in the life of famous King Henry VIII of England.

## Chapter 22
# KING HENRY VIII OF ENGLAND

Henry VIII was born in London in 1491; his father was King Henry VII, and his mother was Elizabeth of York. Little is known about his early childhood. From the few facts available, however, we know that from 1496 on—after Henry was five—the season was good for him. As a young boy, Henry attracted much attention and was an active participant in the court festivities. In 1502, he became heir apparent and was named Duke of Cornwall. In 1503—at the age of twelve—he became Prince of Wales. The same year, he was betrothed to Princess Katherine of Aragon. Six years his senior, she was the widow of Henry's brother Arthur, who had died the previous year.

But Henry's greatest moment of this season came in 1509, after his father's death. Henry became King of England, as Henry VIII, at age eighteen. At the same time, he inherited a vast fortune from his father, and he married Katherine of Aragon—after a papal dispensation permitted him to marry his brother's widow.

Of course, Henry was extremely happy. In a letter to the king of Spain—Katherine's father—he wrote: "If I were still free, I would choose her for a wife before all others."[351] And Katherine loved him. "Our time is spent in continuous festival,"[352] she wrote her father. Between 1510–1512, Henry was so busy enjoying his life that he relied exclusively on his ministers—whom he had inherited from his father—to govern the country. An expert dancer, he preferred taking part in court festivities to taking part in politics, while hunting interested him more than the problems of his government.

## The Bad Season from 1512 to 1529

In 1512, a bad season got underway for Henry. He decided to embark on an expedition to conquer Aquitaine, in France. But much to his disappointment, this was an unsuccessful operation; after only four months, the demoralized

English army returned home having achieved nothing. The next year, Henry decided to personally lead his army against France. But though he took the towns of Thérouanne and Tournai, he accomplished very little, as his biographer, Alison Weir, points out: He conquered "two minor towns of little significance"[353] at a cost of nearly $2 million, which was equivalent to $600 million at today's rates.

In the meantime, Henry had begun to be frustrated with his wife, because she hadn't yet given birth to a son to succeed him. In 1515, the situation worsened; she gave birth to a boy, but he survived only a few days. Though they had been married for four years, Henry still did not have a male heir. In 1516, Henry's disappointment deepened: the queen bore a girl, Princess Mary—not a son. (Princess Mary later became Queen of England, as we've seen in another chapter.) From this point on, Henry and Katherine grew apart.

In the spring of 1517, another source of concern was added: an "epidemic of the sweating sickness"[354] broke out in London. Fearful, Henry fled London to escape the epidemic, moving from house to house in the country, where no one was allowed to come near him. That situation lasted throughout 1518. In November of that year, Henry had another disappointment: the Queen had another child, but it was again a daughter and she died within a few days.

In 1520, another failure was added: Henry had always hoped for harmonious relations between England and France. So, in May 1520, he left for France to meet King Francis I to negotiate a peace treaty. But the old rivalry resurfaced when Henry challenged Francis to a wrestling match. To Henry's unbearable chagrin, he was thrown by Francis. As a result, Henry left and the treaty never materialized.

From now on, the situation worsened even more for Henry—the "winter" of this season had entered his life. Between 1521 and 1525, he became more and more preoccupied with the problem of his succession. He had started to realize that Queen Katherine "would never bear him a son."[355] And "he had begun to see his lack of sons as a judgment on him for offending God"[356] because he had married his brother's widow.

Henry's main target that time was to marry a woman who could give him a successor. All other matters came next. He found that woman in 1526. She was Anne Boleyn, who had just returned to England after serving as a maid of honor at the French court. She was twenty-five; he was thirty-five. However, Anne would cause Henry much trouble in the following years. Henry was passionately in love with her. In a letter to her, he wrote: "My heart shall be dedicated to you alone. . . . [I am] your loyal and most ensured servant."[357] But to Henry's great disappointment, Anne refused to become involved with him until he divorced his wife. That meant he had to ask the Pope to annul his marriage—something he realized the Pope would be extremely reluctant to do.

Henry became increasingly anxious—a situation that worsened when the sweating sickness broke out in London again in 1528. Terrified, this time Henry fled to an isolated tower. Fearing that "the plague might be a sign of divine displeasure,"[358] he attended mass almost every day, took communion and confessed, and visited holy sites for the improvement of his soul.

In October 1528, the final blow came. The Pope sent a cardinal to London to discuss the annulment of Henry's marriage. But the bad season couldn't be reversed: Soon it became clear that the Pope was not prepared to take that step. On July 23, 1529—and after several months of discussions—the cardinal referred the case to Rome without reaching a decision. Henry thus couldn't marry Anne Boleyn. The son he hoped she would produce as his heir would never arrive.

# The Good Season from 1529 to 1545

In 1529, however, Henry finally found a solution to his marriage problem. In October of that year, he accused English Cardinal Wolsey of illegal interference in the public affairs and stripped him of his post. The next year, he appointed another cardinal to replace Wolsey: Thomas Cromwell. Early in 1531, Cromwell and all of the clergy recognized Henry as Supreme Head of the Church of England. Henry had now attained such a power that he could do whatever he wanted. In July 1531, he took the decisive step: He ordered the Queen to move to other quarters. Anne Boleyn was installed in the Queen's lodgings—and from then on, she was constantly at Henry's side, acting as a queen.

In 1532, Henry broke with the Pope, while at the same year, a majority of the universities declared in his favor, finding that his marriage was null and void. So, in November 1532, Henry "secretly married Anne."[359] In May 1533, the English Archbishop "pronounced the King's union with [Queen] Katherine null and void, [and] . . . declared that Henry's marriage to Anne Boleyn was valid and lawful."[360] According to Henry's desire, Anne's coronation, which took place at the end of that month, out-rivaled "any of those of her predecessors in splendor."[361]

In September 1533, Anne gave birth to a girl—Princess Elizabeth (who would later become Queen of England, as we've seen). Though Henry was disappointed that he still didn't have a son, he took up with other maids of honor in his court, believing that one of them could produce the male heir he longed for. One of these women was Jane Seymour, twenty-seven years old—and soon, he decided to marry her. Early in 1536, he said that "he had been seduced by witchcraft into . . . [marrying Anne], and for this reason [he] considered . . . [the marriage] null."[362]

In May 1536, he took the final steps to get what he wanted. Anne was accused of seducing various members of the King's government—"including her own brother."[363] After a short trial, she was sentenced to death, and "despite . . . [her] protestations of innocence,"[364] she was executed on May 19, 1536, at the age of thirty-five. During Anne's trial, Henry showed "extravagant joy,"[365] dining in the company of ladies until after midnight and being accompanied by his musicians and other entertainers. One day after Anne's execution, Henry and Jane were formally betrothed, and ten days later they were married.

One of Henry's other passions was acquiring property. He owned "more houses and property than any other English monarch."[366] His property included seventy residences and eighty-five hunting parks and forests, including two now famous parks in London: Hyde Park and Regent Park. Most of his properties came via the dissolution of the monasteries that he ordered in the year Anne was executed: 1536. He then "took possession of monastic lands . . . [that represented] one-fifth of . . . [England's] landed wealth."[367] At the same time, the monasteries' "vast revenues . . . were diverted into . . . [Henry's] treasury . . . [thus financing the] acquisition of new property"[368] for him. "Wagonloads of jewels, removed from crucifixes, relics, [and] shrines,"[369] even found their way into the royal treasury.

In October 1537, the big news arrived for Henry—the "summer" of this good season would follow. Queen Jane gave birth to the long-awaited son. He was Prince Edward, later King of England, as we've seen in Queen Elizabeth's I biography. Henry was ecstatic—though twelve days later, Jane died of puerperal fever.

After Jane's death, Henry was ready to marry another woman. She was Anne of Cleves, daughter of the Duke of Cleves in Düsseldorf, Germany. This time Henry wasn't motivated by the desire for a son, since he already had an heir. Instead, he thought it was wise to form an alliance with the German states. After negotiations that lasted almost two years, Anne of Cleves arrived in London late in 1539, and in January 1540, Henry married her. But soon he changed mind. "She has nothing fair and has very evil smells about her,"[370] Henry complained. So Anne never achieved true carnal copulation, since

Henry "avoided consummating the marriage so that it could be annulled"[371] later. After six months, Henry accomplished what he wanted: in July 1540, the marriage was proclaimed invalid, "on the grounds of the King's lack of consent to it."[372]

In the meantime, Henry had begun having other interests in his life: women. Governing his country had almost no interest to him. One of these women was Katherine Howard, niece of the Duke of Norfolk. She was fifteen, and Henry was forty-nine. In the same month that his marriage to Anne of Cleves was proclaimed invalid, Henry married Katherine Howard. But he soon became displeased with Katherine, too, and the next year (1541), he sought pleasure elsewhere. In February 1542—a year and a half after her marriage—Katherine's end came. She was accused of withholding information of her past from the King, was sentenced to death, and was executed—at age seventeen. Within a week of Katherine's execution, Henry was hosting banquets for his councilors and nobles—and for a number of ladies. (Executions were another of Henry's passions. He ordered executions not only to rid himself of wives he didn't like any more but also to ensure his reigning power. According to one of his early biographers, Henry executed 70,000 people—his cardinal Thomas Cromwell included—though that number may be exaggerated. The fact, however, that he had executed two of his six wives—Anne Boleyn and Katherine Howard—later gave him the title of the "bluebeard"—the legendary French knight with a blue beard, who had killed six of his seven wives, their skeletons later found by his seventh wife in a locked room of his tower.)

In February 1543, he began to show an interest in another woman: Katherine Parr, a well educated woman about thirty. Five months later, she became Henry's sixth and last wife. The next year (1544), Henry experienced the culmination of this season. Imbued with a new zest for life, he led an invasion of France—riding at the head of his army. He first captured Boulogne-sur-Mer; Montreuil followed. He had at last defeated the French. On September 30, 1544, Henry returned to England in triumph.

# The New Bad Season After 1545

But in March 1545, Henry became seriously ill and was feverish for several days. He was depressed and said he had felt much better in France. The malady had attacked his leg; racked with pain, he was confined to a chair much of the time. In the meantime, the war with France continued, but it was frustrating. In July 1545, French ships harassed the south coast of England, and there Henry experienced a terrible blow: The *Mary Rose*—his best ship—sank, and more than 600 men drowned. Henry replaced his general, Norfolk, with Surrey, but in vain. In 1546, Surrey lost St. Etienne, outside Boulonge. If all that wasn't enough, Henry suddenly found that the war had left England financially crippled; his treasury was nearly bankrupt.

In 1546, Henry was ill again, and his legs caused him great pain. He had two invalid chairs made for himself, and could not go up or down stairs. He was in low spirits and spent his time in privacy. He was losing his grasp on affairs, and struggled to maintain his control over the warring factions in his government. In December 1546, he asked his will to be read to him. His face was ashen.

On January 1, 1547, Henry was feverish again; it was obvious he was dying. Three days later, he summoned the Queen to his bedside, and on January 27, he saw his confessor and received Holy Communion. The next day, the wealthiest king of England, who had married six wives and had executed hundreds of people, died—at the age of fifty-five.

# Conclusion

King Henry's VIII alternations of seasons show that his life's good and bad seasons alternated every 16–17 years in the dates 1496, 1512, 1529, and 1545. We see also that Henry VIII lived more than 500 years ago—like Columbus—and if we extend Henry's dates every 16–17 years, we arrive at the year 1990—this way: 1496, 1512, 1529, 1545, 1562, 1578, 1595, 1611, 1628, 1644, 1661, 1677, 1694, 1710, 1727, 1744, 1760, 1776, 1792, 1809, 1825, 1842, 1859, 1875, 1892, 1908, 1925, 1941, 1957, 1974, 1990.

We can again confirm that the alternations of seasons start more than 500 years ago, as we've seen in Columbus's seasons. But while in 1496 a bad season started for Columbus, an opposite good season started the same year for Henry as you've seen in this chapter. This is because Columbus belongs to the first course of seasons while King Henry belongs to the second course. We can confirm that the alternations of seasons that started more than 500 years ago happen in both courses of seasons—the first and the second.

But Henry's VIII biography also confirms how you can benefit when you are in a good season of your life. As you can recall, when Henry was at a bad season, he became totally disappointed because the Pope of Rome didn't allow him to marry Anne Boleyn. But when he entered his following good season, he found a spectacular solution to his problem: He broke with the Pope and became the Supreme Head of the Church of England. That permitted him not only to marry the woman he loved, but also to marry four more women in the following years.

In the next chapter we continue to extend our confirmation by seeing how the good and bad seasons alternated in the life of former US President Jimmy Carter.

Chapter 23
# JIMMY CARTER

As Carter himself has written in his book, *An Outdoor Journal,* his childhood was a happy season. Born in the small farming town of Plains in southwest Georgia, he grew up on an outlying farm near Archery, two and a half miles from Plains. His life there was busy and happy. While "he was responsible . . . for managing [the farm's] commissary in the evenings"[373] (his father's landholdings were among the largest in the community), he also had his own pony, played tennis with his father or joined him on fishing trips, went to the movies, and "spent many boyhood hours in his own tree house."[374].

Sometimes, the family's handyman took him to hunt raccoons, and he spent some nights with his grandmother Carter. He was also deeply attached to his nannies, one of whom he loved especially. School kept him busy, too; at Plains High School, he was one of the best students in his class. Later, at Georgia Southwestern College as well as at Georgia Institute of Technology, he also got good grades, being remembered as a very intelligent student.

But the good season for Carter would end around 1941.

## The Bad Season from 1941 On

As a boy, Carter worshiped his father. When "his father missed a shot when hunting, Jimmy fumbled for excuses on his behalf with the remark: 'They are sure flying high this morning.' "[375] But the situation changed in 1941–1942, when Carter was seventeen or eighteen. In the largely African American community of Archery, all his friends were black. But his father did not allow black visitors to enter through the front door. Jimmy disagreed with his father about this and started rejecting his racial views. He finally decided to leave home: he left for the Naval Academy in Annapolis, Maryland, in the summer of 1943 despite his parents' disapproval. He was not quite nineteen.

The escape brought with it its own problems. At the Naval Academy Carter wasn't a good student. In all his years there, his leadership grades were poor, and like other students, he was subjected to paddling and other forms of hazing—made to do pushups, and so on. He didn't make any close friends. He graduated in 1946 without any top honors. Immediately after his graduation, in the summer of 1946, he married Rosalynn Smith (he was twenty-one, she was eighteen).

During the first two years of his career as a commissioned officer (1946–1948), he faced an especially difficult battle with depression. He was assigned to a decrepit ship and admitted that "had he not been . . . obligated to serve, he would have resigned immediately."[376] Carter was also frustrated for other reasons: In 1948, he was denied the Rhodes Scholarship he had applied for—a rejection that he took hard. Although by the fall of 1948 he was accepted into the navy's submarine corps—an elite service that offered him the opportunity to be home several nights, followed by assignments in Hawaii, San Diego, and back in Connecticut—his life between 1948 and 1952 had unsettling undercurrents. He "began . . . to doubt his ability to become a leader,"[377] his biographer Kenneth E. Morris says. The "winter" of this bad season had entered his life.

Over the Christmas holidays of 1950–1951, he had an argument with his father on the issue of race. His father supported racial segregation, and Carter rejected those views. It was the last and most bitter argument between them. Two years passed without visits or real communication between the two. Early in 1953, his father was diagnosed with cancer, and in July, he died. Over the determined opposition of his wife, Carter resigned his commission in the navy immediately and returned to Plains to take up where his father had left off. He wanted to be his own boss and to create stability in his life.

But the bad season continued: Things were not as he expected. There wasn't enough of an estate from his father for him to inherit. He acquired only his father's peanut warehouse but no house to live in. Furthermore, because of his racial views, he refused to join the white Citizens' Council in Plains, and as a result, he was boycotted by the community. So, he was obliged to move his family into the "government subsidized apartments for the poor."[378] The family now consisted of three children: Jack, born in 1947; James, 1950; and Jeff, 1952. This poverty-level situation lasted for three years: from 1954 to 1956.

Then, however, things began to become surprisingly good: Carter had now—from the warehouse—an income that was almost twice the salary he'd had in the navy, and he was, therefore, comfortable financially for the first time in his life. The bad season of 16–17 years from 1941 to 1957 had at last ended.

# The New Good Season from 1957 On

By 1957, the Carter family no longer had to live in public housing. First, they found a house and rented it, and then, in 1958, the Carter family moved into a new farmhouse near the town. Three years later, they acquired their own home. This was a ranch house near downtown Plains. At the same time, they lived a very satisfying life: They went to dinners and dances, took trips to Atlanta and Florida, or visited restaurants and nightclubs in Albany, and regularly found friends to fish or hunt with.

Also, Carter's desire to be a leader would be fulfilled. By 1960, he was appointed chairman of the Sumter County School Board, and the next year, he was named chairman of its Economic Development Committee. He also became district governor of the Lions Club and, later, chairman of the Club's Council of Governors. In 1962, he surprised even his wife by announcing publicly that "he intended to qualify for election to the state senate"[379]—an election that he finally won after overcoming some hurdles.

During his four years at the state senate (1962–1966), Carter worked very hard, and was respected by many of his colleagues. When he announced his intention to run for governor of Georgia in 1966, he was in a very good position to win. But it was too soon; he lost the election. However, he took the loss as an opportunity to acquire more experience. He began organizing his campaign for the 1970 Georgia gubernatorial election almost immediately.

Money was no longer a problem for Carter—he was now rich, and raising funds for his campaign wasn't difficult. The "summer" of this good season had already started in his life. His warehouse was now a multi-million-dollar business. During his four-year campaign for governor (1966–1970), furthermore, he had as many interests as possible. At the same time, a religious reversal occurred in his life—he "gave his life to God"[380]—a change that enabled him to feel reborn.

In 1970, Carter was elected governor of Georgia by a margin of almost 60 to 40 percent. As he said later, his four years as governor (1971–1974), were among the most satisfying of his life. Never again "would he display so enormous a capacity for work . . . or accomplish so much."[381] He made huge efforts to reorganize the state of Georgia, and he was the first governor of Georgia to reform its judicial system. His life was entirely full.

The crowning moment came at the end of 1974 when Carter announced his candidacy for the presidency, surprising everybody. But this announcement marked the end of this good season of his life.

# The Second Bad Season from 1975 On

Almost immediately, in 1975, serious difficulties started appearing in Carter's life. First, Democratic Party leaders declared their objection to his candidacy. Then, during the primaries the following year, Carter came close to defeat: He lost almost all Western states and two-thirds of the Midwestern states and won only a little more than half of the Eastern states. Carter's candidacy was thus in great danger. Almost all the political commentators predicted he would lose the election.

And when he was finally elected president in November 1976, that fact wasn't a success for him; on the contrary, it marked the beginning of an ordeal instead of a triumph. His victory was by a slim margin of 50.1 percent, a margin that could not produce the necessary mandate to govern successfully. The signs of an impending catastrophe appeared immediately. First, there were the president's relations with Congress. The house speaker started by even objecting to the menu the president offered to congressional leaders at their first meeting.

Almost everything Carter proposed turned to ashes. His comprehensive energy policy floundered in the Senate for months, and when it passed in Congress in 1978, it had so many compromises that the president called it a partial victory. His finance reform and hospital cost containment proposals failed, as did his anti-inflation efforts (inflation rates more than doubled during his presidency). The same happened to his national health care and welfare reforms, as well as to all his domestic reform efforts. Naturally, the president was deeply frustrated by his failures.

Outside the administration the opposition was also fierce, if not fiercer. Labor unions openly defied the president. The 1977–1978 coal strike continued for 109 days and Carter seemed unable to solve the dispute. (Though, in 1978, Carter facilitated a historic peace agreement between Israel and Egypt, which was signed in 1979, that event didn't reverse his bad conditions; they continued more fiercely).

The final blow came in November 1979, when the US embassy in Iran was seized by terrorists who took sixty-two Americans hostage. They also burned Carter in effigy and set US flags on fire "in front of waiting television cameras . . . which every evening brought the . . . images into the nation's living rooms."[382] Carter was unable to end the ordeal. When, in April 1980, he approved a rescue plan, it failed miserably—his bad season didn't help: Two helicopters crashed and dead men were added to the sorrowful situation.

The crisis of the hostages ironically enabled Carter again to be nominated a candidate of his party for the next election in 1980. But the bad season continued: He lost to Ronald Reagan. After leaving the White House early in 1981, Carter was, as his biographer, Kenneth E. Morris, says, "young enough to do something else and poor enough to need to."[383] He started his new life by building furniture for his home, and he felt extremely alone. The "winter" of this bad season had already started.

In the next two years, he built a cabin in the mountains, in which all the furniture was made by him. Soon, he had to sell his peanut warehouse to pay off the debt he incurred during his presidency. In 1983, a growing public animosity toward Carter began to surface that lasted almost seven years. "An awful lot of folks in Georgia are growing deathly tired of Jimmy Carter,"[384] a local newspaper wrote in 1983, while the Washington Post said, in 1984, that public perceptions of Carter were more negative than when he lost his reelection bid.

Also in 1983, his beloved sister, Ruth, died of cancer at the age of fifty-four, and soon his mother, Lillian, died, too. His brother, Billy, died of cancer in 1988, at the age of fifty-one, and in 1989, his other sister, Gloria, was diagnosed with the same form of cancer. Jimmy then started to worry about his own health.

# The New Good Season from 1990 On

Early in 1990, a good season started for Carter, however. The signs appeared immediately. The Washington Post published an article that year titled "Jimmy—Come Back! All Is Forgiven!"[385] At the same time, the Economist asked: "Jimmy Carter for President in 1992?"[386] Meanwhile, a poll discovered that in his home state of Georgia he had a favorable approval rating with 74 percent of his fellow Georgians.

In 1991, Carter inaugurated the Atlanta Project he had inspired in an effort to combat urban poverty in the United States. By 1993, the project had tremendous success: It had raised $32 million in private donations, instead of the $25 million that was the initial goal. By the next year, Carter's return was complete. A Nebraska senator called him the "finest living ex-president,"[387] and when he appeared in bookstores to autograph copies of his book *Turning Point*, lots of people were waiting for him.

On a June Tuesday in 1994, at the age of seventy, Carter was present in a ceremony in Atlanta for the unveiling of a sculpture of himself. Also present were many dignitaries and his former associates. He was "being honored in life by the kind of tribute usually paid only posthumously."[388] The same summer, Carter was again thrust into the international scene. In late June 1994, "he successfully diffused tensions between North and South Korea, bringing both to the negotiating table."[389] In September 1994, "he headed the negotiating team that won a peaceful transfer of power in Haiti and halted the hostile US invasion there."[390]

In mid-1994, Carter's reputation was "skyrocketing,"[391] while by September 1994, a poll found that six in ten Americans had a very positive opinion of him. In October 1994, *Time* magazine featured Carter on its cover. In 2002, Carter's efforts on behalf of global peace were recognized worldwide: He won the ultimate honor, the Nobel Peace Prize. At the same time, many Americans said they would also "welcome Carter's [further] involvement in domestic"[392] as well as international affairs.

# Conclusion

Carter's alternations of seasons show that his life's good and bad seasons alternated every 16–17 years in 1941, 1957, 1974, and 1990. Although these dates are the same as Gorbachev's, their seasons are opposite, as you can see when you compare them. This confirms that since Gorbachev belongs to the first course of seasons, Carter belongs to the second course, as indicated in Chapter 1.

To see what is also confirmed from Carter's seasons we will compare these with the seasons of America's national hero astronaut John Glenn that we'll see in the next chapter.

# Chapter 24
# JOHN GLENN

John Glenn was born in 1921. As he himself says in his memoirs, a boy "could not have had a more idyllic early childhood"[393] than him. In those years he lived in a big house, and "never doubted even once that . . . [he] was loved."[394] Even during the Great Depression of 1929—he then was eight years old—he did not suffer much. His family "grew almost everything in . . . [their] gardens,"[395] so they had enough to eat, and his father sold cars, making them better off than many in their town of New Concord, Ohio.

At the end of the Depression in 1934, his father's new jobs resulted in "another step toward . . . [their] financial recovery."[396] By the age of fourteen, Glenn was earning big money working for his father, while in 1937, he got his driver's license, and his father let him use an old car. In the summer of 1939, he also had a wonderful time: With three other friends, he took a trip from New Concord to New York, where the World's Fair had opened with the theme "The World of Tomorrow."

The highest moment in this good season came in 1941. Glenn had dreamed of becoming a pilot since the age of eight, when he'd had the opportunity to fly in a plane with his father. But the cost of flight training seemed prohibitive, so he had abandoned the idea. But early in 1941, when he was twenty, he saw a notice that the US Department of Commerce was offering free training for pilots. The era that would shape the rest of Glenn's life had started.

This notice, however, signaled the end of the idyllic season for Glenn.

## The Bad Season from 1941 On

When Glenn told his parents that he was entering flight training, they strenuously objected. World War II was escalating in Europe, and the application he'd signed for the free training said that, if necessary, he would be trained for military purposes, too. He, too, was not unaware of the risks. As he says in his book, *A Memory*, "the war news from Europe dampened . . . [his] enthusiasm."[397]

Glenn's enrollment in the army didn't take too much time. He entered flight school only a few days before the Japanese bombed Pearl Harbor—in December

1941. The war in the Pacific had started. Glenn then signed up for the Army Air Corps, saying goodbye to his parents, to his girlfriend, Annie Castor, and to his boyhood. In the next two years, he was first trained as a military pilot, then the war started for him, too: He was sent to the remote Midway and Marshall Islands in the Pacific, fighting the Japanese there, not having any fresh vegetables or meat available for months. He wrote letters to Annie (whom he had married in the meantime, when he returned home for a few days on leave) almost every day, describing how horrible the war was.

After the war ended in 1945, Glenn continued to serve in the army and went with the marines to China. Deployed there in 1946–1947, he found China so different from anything he was accustomed to that he longed for home and Annie, and also experienced weariness and futility, as he says in his book. In 1948, he was in the Pacific again, on Guam, facing the same situation. In the meantime, Annie had given birth to two children (in 1945 and 1947); they knew their father from photographs only.

Though Glenn spent the years 1949 to 1952 at home, he wasn't happy—the "winter" of this bad season had entered his life: He served in the army in assignments he didn't like. In 1953, he was ordered to the Korean War, where his plane was hit twice by the communists, and he miraculously survived. Between 1954 and 1956, Glenn was assigned another extremely risky job—back in the United States—as a test pilot. On this assignment, he came near death at least three times.

Early in 1957, Glenn was transferred to a bureau in Washington, DC. He wasn't happy, of course—that place was for a bureaucrat, he said. When, also early in the same year, he fantasized about crossing the United States in a plane at supersonic speed for the first time, he was greatly disappointed: The navy and Pentagon couldn't be persuaded—his bad season couldn't end yet.

# The Good Season from 1957 On

In July 1957 the navy and the Pentagon suddenly came around and Glenn realized his dream: He crossed the country by plane, from California to New York, at supersonic speed, in three hours and twenty-three minutes. When he landed, he was greeted by reporters and television crews, while a military band marked the event. The next day, the *New York Times* ran a profile of him and Annie. A brilliant season had thus begun for Glenn.

The next year, Glenn took another step forward: He decided he would become an astronaut, in order to go into space. Early in 1959, he volunteered for that purpose. He passed his exams successfully, and during the following two years (1960–1961), he was trained for the great experience, along with six other elite astronauts, waiting for the final go. In February 1962, the big event happened: Glenn became the first American to orbit the earth. After a spectacular trip of three orbits that lasted four hours and fifty-six minutes, he returned to earth when his capsule landed in the cold waters of the Atlantic.

He had no idea of the tumultuous welcome that awaited him. Vice President Lyndon B. Johnson accompanied him back to Cape Canaveral, with thousands of people lining the parade route. President John F. Kennedy presented Glenn with NASA's Distinguished Service Medal, and the whole country watched the events on their television sets. Glenn's good season had helped to make him an American hero.

In 1963, Glenn also entered politics: He developed a growing friendship with Senator Bobby Kennedy and his wife, Ethel, discussing, as Kennedy proposed, a run for the Senate on Glenn's part. The following year, Glenn announced his decision to pursue the nomination for the seat of the Ohio Senate. But because of an accident he'd had, he withdrew after a month. He would try later, however—and would succeed.

The same year Glenn became financially independent: He was appointed vice president of the Royal Crown Cola Company, at a salary of $50,000, which compared favorably with the $15,000 he had earned in the marines. He retired from the marines in 1965—and a new "summer" started in his life. In 1966, he increased his financial independence through a joint venture in four Holiday Inn franchises. He spent the next seven years (1967–1973) in that climate of financial abundance. In 1974, his political ambitions were finally realized. He decided to seek the nomination for the Ohio seat in the US Senate, and he triumphantly won the general election. Glenn had thus arrived: He had become a US senator.

# The New Bad Season from 1975 to 1990

As soon as he took the oath of office in the Senate in January 1975, however, Glenn felt as if he was imprisoned and tortured there, like "Daniel praying in the lions' den,"[398] as he says in his book. The next year, Glenn had his first great disappointment: He was mentioned as a possible vice president for Jimmy Carter, but after a "dull" speech he gave at the convention, Carter picked Walter Mondale.

In 1979, he had another similar disappointment. He'd prepared a speech to give in the Senate on the occasion for the verification of the SALT II treaty.

But when he sent the speech in advance to President Carter, the president phoned him and expressed strong disapproval. "No president before or since had ever talked to me that way,"[399] he says in his memoirs.

The disappointments—and Glenn's bad season—continued, and the "winter" of this season entered his life. In 1982, he decided to seek the Democratic presidential nomination for 1984, announcing his candidacy in April 1983. Mondale was his opponent. But he did poorly in the primaries and withdrew from the race in March 1984. His campaign "was almost $3 million in debt"[400] when he withdrew. When, in 1988, Glenn's name appeared once more as a potential vice president, Michael Dukakis, who was the nominee for president, chose Lloyd Bentsen.

In 1989, came the culmination of this season's problems for Glenn: Press reports questioned his integrity. They accused him of having been involved in the savings and loan industry's crisis that had burst that year. The Senate Ethics Committee initiated investigations and sent him a letter calling him to give his replies to the charges. He fought the case "with every fiber of . . . [his] being,"[401] he says in his book, but he felt that he was at the *lowest point* of his life. The episode "cost him $520,000 in legal fees and great personal anguish."[402]

# The New Good Season from 1990 On

In the summer of 1990, however, the counsel of the Senate's Ethics Committee recommended that Glenn "be eliminated from the investigation."[403] In February 1991, the committee decided that the charges against Glenn "failed to produce a single finding."[404] Glenn was deeply relieved. In 1992, he was re-elected to the Senate by a sound margin; he was the only senator from Ohio to serve four consecutive terms.

In 1995, a different good era began. "What would happen if somebody older went [into space]?"[405] Glenn wondered. Why shouldn't that person be him? So at the end of 1995, he mentioned his interest to NASA's director Dan Goldin. "You're serious about this?"[406] Goldin asked. "Serious as I can be,"[407] Glenn replied. He was then seventy-four. But he was in a good season. In February 1997, Glenn announced his decision to retire from the Senate; he wanted "to serve . . . [his] country in other ways,"[408] he said. "When I leave the Senate, it will not be an end, but a new beginning,"[409] he added.

In January 1998, he learned from Goldin that he had been accepted to go into space again. The idea of "an ancient guy like . . . [him] going into space was exhilarating,"[410] he says in his autobiography. People stopped and wished him good luck; while in Houston, "a forest of red-white-and-blue banners with . . . [his] picture on them,"[411] proclaimed the road "John Glenn Parkway."

On October 29, 1998, the great day arrived—a new "summer" in Glenn's life would follow. Cape Canaveral "hadn't seen reporters and photographers in such numbers since the Apollo moon launch days,"[412] he also says in his autobiography. The crowds on the beaches and along the waterways were huge, too. He "couldn't have been happier,"[413] Glenn said.

After a trip of 134 orbits and 3.6 million miles, the *Discovery* and its crew returned to earth. A great parade followed in New York City, then a tour of Europe and Japan early in 1999. The flight had received international recognition, and this good season continued for Glenn in the next years.

# Conclusion

Glenn's alternations of seasons show that his life's good and bad seasons alternated every 16–17 years in 1941, 1957, 1974, and 1990—as Carter's as seen in the previous chapter. In these same dates Gorbachev, Mandela, the Dalai Lama, Thatcher, Taylor, and Kennedy Onassis's good and bad seasons have also alternated.

But though Glenn's dates are the same to the Dalai Lama's, their seasons are opposite, as you can see when you compare them. That confirms that since the Dalai Lama belongs to the first course of seasons, Glenn belongs to the second course, as indicated in Chapter 1.

We see also that the *last* alternation of seasons in the lives of all prior seven persons happened in 1990. That means that the next turning point of seasons in our lives lies 16–17 years after 1990—in 2007—as indicated in Chapter 1. We can confirm that a new season starts in 2007 that lasts 16–17 years, until 2024, and so on every 16–17 years.

Finally, Glenn's life also confirms that, as indicated in Chapter 2, you should not blame yourself for the fact that you are in a bad season of your life. Recall that when Glenn was at one of his bad seasons, he was accused by the press of having been involved in the savings and loan industry's crisis, and the Senate Ethics Committee sent him a letter calling him to give his replies to the charges. But he was not involved at all in that crisis, so he was acquitted. When he entered his next good season, the Senate's Committee decided that the charges "failed to produce a single finding." Glenn hadn't made any mistake to cause the accusation; it was his bad season that caused this. He couldn't have done anything to avoid the arrival of his bad season; it would have inevitably arrived in any case.

# EPILOGUE

With Glenn's alternations of seasons we fully confirmed our whole discovery. As you have seen, our life's good and bad seasons alternate every 16–17 years at certain dates (1974, 1990, 2007, 2024, and so on). That happens in two opposite courses: the first course and the second course. These alternations have occurred that way for more than 500 years (from 1496 up until now) and continue into the future.

Based on these findings, you can foresee how your own good and bad seasons will be in the future. As explained in Chapter 1, first you have to find which course of seasons you belong to: the first course or the second. For this purpose you have to examine whether, in 2007, a good or bad season started in your life. In doing this, you have to see your life "from above" as a helicopter pilot, in large periods, not day by day.

Recall also that a good season tends to include both inner satisfaction and outer success, while a bad season is a season of anxiety, with failure and disappointment. Also a good season is not always like a paradise, without any concerns or difficulties. Similarly, a bad season is not necessarily a hell; it may contain moments of satisfaction. Recall also that the first part of each good season resembles spring, and the first part of each bad season resembles fall.

Remember also that the specific criteria that characterize a good or bad season usually include factors like money, fame, love, and health. These criteria differ from person to person and can change over time. But usually there is only one main factor that shapes at a given moment the good and bad seasons of a person. For Onassis, for example, only money had any meaning throughout most of his life, as we've seen. But at the end of his life, when he fell seriously ill from an incurable disease, only his health counted.

Recall also that for finding whether your years after 2007 were a good or bad season, you have to see what big events, good or bad, regarding your studies, or health, business, career, love, family, etc., happened—and continued—in your life during 2007, 2008, 2009 and so on up to now. For example, does a period of failures and disappointments or a period of successes and satisfactions characterize your studies, or business, family, love, or health in the above years?

As also explained in Chapter 1, if you find that a good season started in your life in 2007, that means you belong to the first course of seasons; if you find that a bad season started, you belong to the second course of seasons. You are able after that to foresee how your life's good and bad seasons will be in the future. If you belong to the first course of seasons, the years from 2007 to 2024 will be good, while the years from 2024 to 2040 will be bad—and so on every 16–17 years. If you belong to the second course, the years from 2007 to 2024 will be bad, while the years from 2024 to 2040 will be good—and so on every 16–17 years.

Of course, readers who are too young and cannot recall their years before and after 2007, would not be able to find which course they belong. Those readers have to put this book aside and wait for more years to find their course. Specifically: in order to recall your years before and after 2007 you have to have been born before 1990—so that in 2007 your age was at least seventeen. Also, those who will read this book after 2024 (and before 2040) have to have been born before 2007. They will easily see what happened in their lives before and after 2024—their age will be then at least seventeen. Older readers can of course, examine whether a good or bad season started in their life not only in 2007 but also in 1990, or in 1974, too, or even also in 1957.

In any case, I hope my book will give you the means to learn whether the years just ahead are good or bad for you—and how long this season will last—so that you can act accordingly and benefit from the discovery. If you want other people to benefit, too, tell your friends to read this book. You will contribute to the creation of a much better world where, as explained in Chapter 2, superficiality and imprudence will drastically be reduced.

# ENDNOTES

## Chapter 3

**Special author note:** I have taken all the facts and details in this chapter from Gino Pugneti's *Beethoven*, published in Greek by Fytrakis Publications, Great Men of All Seasons series, Athens, 1965. There are also Beethoven's biographies in English, which you can examine to confirm the truth of this chapter's facts, as for example: a) Barry Cooper's *Beethoven*, Oxford Press, 2001, or b) Maynard Solomon's *Beethoven*, Schirmer Books, 2001.

1. Gino Pugneti, *Beethoven* (Athens, Greece: Fytrakis Publications, 1965), 10.
2. Pugneti, *Beethoven,* 16
3. Pugneti, *Beethoven,* 19
4. Pugneti, *Beethoven,* 21
5. Pugneti, *Beethoven,* 44
6. Pugneti, *Beethoven,* 44
7. Pugneti, *Beethoven,* 44
8. Pugneti, *Beethoven,* 109
9. Pugneti, *Beethoven,* 32
10. Pugneti, *Beethoven,* 57
11. Pugneti, *Beethoven,* 57
12. Pugneti, *Beethoven,* 57
13. Pugneti, *Beethoven,* 57
14. Pugneti, *Beethoven,* 57
15. Pugneti, *Beethoven,* 34
16. Pugneti, *Beethoven,* 62
17. Pugneti, *Beethoven,* 64
18. Pugneti, *Beethoven,* 53
19. Pugneti, *Beethoven,* 70
20. Pugneti, *Beethoven,* 72
21. Pugneti, *Beethoven,* 72
22. Pugneti, *Beethoven,* 75
23. Pugneti, *Beethoven,* 75

## Chapter 4

**Special author note:** All the facts and details in this chapter derive from Gino Pugneti's *Verdi*, published in Greek by Fytrakis Publications, *Great Men of All Seasons* series, Athens, 1966. There are also Verdi's biographies in English, as for example: a) Mary Jane Phillips-Matz's *Verdi: A Biography*, Oxford University Press, 1993, or b) William Weaver's *Verdi: A Documentary Study*, W.W. Norton and Company, 1977.

24. Gino Pugneti, *Verdi* (Athens, Greece, Fytrakis Publications, 1966), 10.
25. Pugneti, *Verdi,* 10
26. Pugneti, *Verdi,* 12

27. Pugneti, *Verdi,* 14
28. Pugneti, *Verdi,* 16
29. Pugneti, *Verdi,* 16
30. Pugneti, *Verdi,* 17
31. Pugneti, *Verdi,* 18
32. Pugneti, *Verdi,* 20
33. Pugneti, *Verdi,* 25
34. Pugneti, *Verdi,* 41
35. Pugneti, *Verdi,* 54
36. Pugneti, *Verdi,* 54
37. Pugneti, *Verdi,* 56
38. Pugneti, *Verdi,* 65
39. Pugneti, *Verdi,* 66
40. Pugneti, *Verdi,* 70
41. Pugneti, *Verdi,* 70
42. Pugneti, *Verdi,* 71
43. Pugneti, *Verdi,* 73

# Chapter 5

**Special author note:** My source for all details in Picasso's biography is Lael Westenbaker's (and the editors' of Time-Life Books) *The World of Picasso*, Time-Life Books, Library of Art series, Amsterdam, 1976, European edition. For further reading you can see Patrick O'Brian's *Pablo Ruiz Picasso: A Biography*, Collins, 1976.

44. Lael Westenbaker, *The World of Picasso* (Amsterdam, Holland: Time-Life Books, Library of Art, 1976), 11.
45. Westenbaker, *The World of Picasso,* 54
46. Westenbaker, *The World of Picasso,* 57
47. Westenbaker, *The World of Picasso,* 59
48. Westenbaker, *The World of Picasso,* 85
49. Westenbaker, *The World of Picasso,* 85
50. Westenbaker, *The World of Picasso,* 106
51. Westenbaker, *The World of Picasso,* 107
52. Westenbaker, *The World of Picasso,* 145
53. Westenbaker, *The World of Picasso,* 147

# Chapter 6

**Special author note:** I have based Gorbachev's biography on his *Memoirs* (New York, Doubleday, 1996).

54. Mikhail Gorbachev, *Memoirs* (New York: Doubleday, 1996), 29.
55. Gorbachev, *Memoirs,* 30
56. Gorbachev, *Memoirs,* 46
57. Gorbachev, *Memoirs,* 49
58. Gorbachev, *Memoirs,* 53
59. Gorbachev, *Memoirs,* 82

60. Gorbachev, *Memoirs*, 82
61. Gorbachev, *Memoirs*, 83
62. Gorbachev, *Memoirs*, 95
63. Gorbachev, *Memoirs*, 97
64. Gorbachev, *Memoirs*, 112
65. Gorbachev, *Memoirs*, 115
66. Gorbachev, *Memoirs*, 17
67. Gorbachev, *Memoirs*, xxxiii

# Chapter 7

**Special author note:** I have based all the Dalai Lama's biography of this chapter on his autobiography *Freedom in Exile, the Autobiography of the Dalai Lama*, Harper Perennial, New York, 1990.

68. The Dalai Lama, *Freedom in Exile, the Autobiography of the Dalai Lama* (New York: Harper Perennial, 1990), 12.
69. The Dalai Lama, *Freedom in Exile*, 12
70. The Dalai Lama, *Freedom in Exile*, 27
71. The Dalai Lama, *Freedom in Exile*, 83
72. The Dalai Lama, *Freedom in Exile*, 88
73. The Dalai Lama, *Freedom in Exile*, 112
74. The Dalai Lama, *Freedom in Exile*, 124
75. The Dalai Lama, *Freedom in Exile*, 135
76. The Dalai Lama, *Freedom in Exile*, 2
77. The Dalai Lama, *Freedom in Exile*, 147
78. The Dalai Lama, *Freedom in Exile*, 158
79. The Dalai Lama, *Freedom in Exile*, 167
80. The Dalai Lama, *Freedom in Exile*, 208
81. The Dalai Lama, *Freedom in Exile*, 222
82. The Dalai Lama, *Freedom in Exile*, 230
83. The Dalai Lama, *Freedom in Exile*, 241
84. The Dalai Lama, *Freedom in Exile*, 254

# Chapter 8

**Special author note:** I have taken all facts and details for Thatcher's biography in this chapter from Libby Hughes's *Madam Prime Minister: A Biography of Margaret Thatcher* (An Authors Guild Backinprint.com Edition, Lincoln, NE, 2000).

85. Libby Hughes, *Madam Prime Minister: A Biography of Margaret Thatcher* (Lincoln, NE: An Authors Guild Backinprint.com Edition, 2000), 13.
86. Hughes, *Madam Prime Minister*, 13
87. Hughes, *Madam Prime Minister*, 36
88. Hughes, *Madam Prime Minister*, 37
89. Hughes, *Madam Prime Minister*, 38
90. Hughes, *Madam Prime Minister*, 49
91. Hughes, *Madam Prime Minister*, 51
92. Hughes, *Madam Prime Minister*, 71

93. Hughes, *Madam Prime Minister*, 72
94. Hughes, *Madam Prime Minister*, 72
95. Hughes, *Madam Prime Minister*, 73
96. Hughes, *Madam Prime Minister*, 74
97. Hughes, *Madam Prime Minister*, 92
98. Hughes, *Madam Prime Minister*, 96
99. Hughes, *Madam Prime Minister*, 97
100. Hughes, *Madam Prime Minister*, 100
101. Hughes, *Madam Prime Minister*, 102
102. Hughes, *Madam Prime Minister*, 112
103. Hughes, *Madam Prime Minister*, 118
104. Hughes, *Madam Prime Minister*, 122
105. Hughes, *Madam Prime Minister*, 133
106. Hughes, *Madam Prime Minister*, 134
107. Hughes, *Madam Prime Minister*, 134
108. Hughes, *Madam Prime Minister*, 137-138
109. Hughes, *Madam Prime Minister*, Addendum after page 144

# Chapter 9

**Special author note:** My source for Taylor's biography in this chapter is Larissa Branin's *Liz, the Pictorial Biography of Elizabeth Taylor*, Courage Books, New York, 2000.

110. Larissa Branin, *Liz, the Pictorial Biography of Elizabeth Taylor* (New York: Courage Books, 2000), 29.
111. Branin, *Liz*, 53
112. Branin, *Liz*, 60
113. Branin, *Liz*, 63
114. Branin, *Liz*, 62
115. Branin, *Liz*, 64
116. Branin, *Liz*, 67-68
117. Branin, *Liz*, 78
118. Branin, *Liz*, 80
119. Branin, *Liz*, 85
120. Branin, *Liz*, 83
121. Branin, *Liz*, 91
122. Branin, *Liz*, 73
123. Branin, *Liz*, 93
124. Branin, *Liz*, 95
125. Branin, *Liz*, 102
126. Branin, *Liz*, 105
127. Branin, *Liz*, 106
128. Branin, *Liz*, 105
129. Branin, *Liz*, 109

# Chapter 10

**Special author note:** All facts and details for Jackie's biography derive from Sarah

Bradford's *America's Queen, The Life of Jacqueline Kennedy Onassis*, Penguin Books, New York, 2001.

130. Sarah Bradford, *America's Queen* (New York: Penguin Books, 2001), 1.
131. Bradford, *America's Queen*,13
132. Bradford, *America's Queen*, 31
133. Bradford, *America's Queen*, 38
134. Bradford, *America's Queen*, 59
135. Bradford, *America's Queen*, 117
136. Bradford, *America's Queen*, 120
137. Bradford, *America's Queen*, 129
138. Bradford, *America's Queen*, 130
139. Bradford, *America's Queen*, 140
140. Bradford, *America's Queen*, 149
141. Bradford, *America's Queen*, 194
142. Bradford, *America's Queen*, 231
143. Bradford, *America's Queen*, 302
144. Bradford, *America's Queen*, 315-316
145. Bradford, *America's Queen*, 337
146. Bradford, *America's Queen*, 357
147. Bradford, *America's Queen*, 371
148. Bradford, *America's Queen*, 405
149. Bradford, *America's Queen*, 408
150. Bradford, *America's Queen*, 411
151. Bradford, *America's Queen*, 428
152. Bradford, *America's Queen*, 431

# Chapter 11

**Special author note:** I have based all Columbus's biography of this chapter on Cesare Giardini's *Columbus*, published in Greek by Fytrakis Publications, The Great Men of All Seasons series, Athens, 1965. There are also Columbus's biographies in English, as for example: a) Gianni Granzotto's *Christopher Columbus, The Dream and the Obsession, A Biography,* Olympic Marketing Corporation, 1985, or b) Salvador de Madariaga's *Christopher Columbus*, Greenwood Publishing, 1979.

153. Cesare Giardini, *Columbus* (Athens, Greece: Fytrakis Publications, 1965), 35.
154. Giardini, *Columbus,* 35
155. Giardini, *Columbus,* 35
156. Giardini, *Columbus,* 43
157. Giardini, *Columbus,* 44
158. Giardini, *Columbus,* 44
159. Giardini, *Columbus,* 49
160. Giardini, *Columbus,* 57
161. Giardini, *Columbus,* 63
162. Giardini, *Columbus,* 63
163. Giardini, *Columbus,* 63
164. Giardini, *Columbus,* 65
165. Giardini, *Columbus,* 64

166. Giardini, *Columbus,* 66

# Chapter 12

**Special author note:** My source for all facts and details in Elizabeth's biography in this chapter is Susan Doran's *Queen Elizabeth I,* New York University Press, 2003.

167. Susan Doran, *Queen Elizabeth I* (New York: New York University Press, 2003), 16.
168. Doran, *Queen Elizabeth I,* 25
169. Doran, *Queen Elizabeth I,* 29
170. Doran, *Queen Elizabeth I,* 29
171. Doran, *Queen Elizabeth I,* 44
172. Doran, *Queen Elizabeth I,* 47
173. Doran, *Queen Elizabeth I,* 68-69
174. Doran, *Queen Elizabeth I,* 69
175. Doran, *Queen Elizabeth I,* 77
176. Doran, *Queen Elizabeth I,* 88
177. Doran, *Queen Elizabeth I,* 89
178. Doran, *Queen Elizabeth I,* 90
179. Doran, *Queen Elizabeth I,* 118
180. Doran, *Queen Elizabeth I,* 120
181. Doran, *Queen Elizabeth I,* 120
182. Doran, *Queen Elizabeth I,* 120
183. Doran, *Queen Elizabeth I,* 128
184. Doran, *Queen Elizabeth I,* 128
185. Doran, *Queen Elizabeth I,* 132
186. Doran, *Queen Elizabeth I,* 134
187. Doran, *Queen Elizabeth I,* 134

# Chapter 13

**Special author note:** All the details in this chapter derive from Mario Rivoire's *Napoleon,* published in Greek by Fytrakis Publications, The Great Men of all Seasons series, Athens, 1965. There are also Napoleon's biographies in English, as for example: a) André Castelot's *Napoleon: A Biography,* Rombaldi Publishers, 1971, or b) Frank McLynn's *Napoleon: A Biography,* Arcade Books, 2003.

188. Mario Rivoire, *Napoleon* (Athens, Greece: Fytrakis Publications, 1965), 10.
189. Rivoire, *Napoleon,* 17
190. Rivoire, *Napoleon,* 19
191. Rivoire, *Napoleon,* 19
192. Rivoire, *Napoleon,* 20
193. Rivoire, *Napoleon,* 22
194. Rivoire, *Napoleon,* 22
195. Rivoire, *Napoleon,* 24
196. Rivoire, *Napoleon,* 28
197. Rivoire, *Napoleon,* 32
198. Rivoire, *Napoleon,* 49
199. Rivoire, *Napoleon,* 51

200. Rivoire, *Napoleon*, 57
201. Rivoire, *Napoleon*, 58
202. Rivoire, *Napoleon*, 56
203. Rivoire, *Napoleon*, 60
204. Rivoire, *Napoleon*, 61
205. Rivoire, *Napoleon*, 62
206. Rivoire, *Napoleon*, 67
207. Rivoire, *Napoleon*, 72

# Chapter 14

**Special author note:** I have based all Hugo's good and bad seasons in this chapter on Cesare Giardini's *Hugo*, published in Greek by Fytrakis Publications, The Great Men of All Seasons series, Athens, 1966. There are also Hugo's biographies in English, as for example: a) Matthew Josephson's *Victor Hugo: A Biography of the Great Romantic*, Telegraph Books, 1992, or b) Graham Robb's *Victor Hugo: A Biography*, W. W. Norton & Company, 1999.

208. Cesare Giardini, *Hugo* (Athens, Greece: Fytrakis Publications, 1966), 18.
209. Giardini, *Hugo*, 18
210. Giardini, *Hugo*, 26
211. Giardini, *Hugo*, 26-27
212. Giardini, *Hugo*, 34
213. Giardini, *Hugo*, 40
214. Giardini, *Hugo*, 40
215. Giardini, *Hugo*, 40
216. Giardini, *Hugo*, 40
217. Giardini, *Hugo*, 40
218. Giardini, *Hugo*, 42
219. Giardini, *Hugo*, 47
220. Giardini, *Hugo*, 48
221. Giardini, *Hugo*, 51
222. Giardini, *Hugo*, 51
223. Giardini, *Hugo*, 67
224. Giardini, *Hugo*, 71
225. Giardini, *Hugo*, 75

# Chapter 15

**Special author note:** My source for Rodin's biography is William Harlan Hale's (and the editors' of Time-Life Books) *The World of Rodin*, Library of Art series, Nederland, 1976, European Edition.

226. William Harlan Hale, *The World of Rodin* (Nederland: Time-Life Books, 1976), 47.
227. Hale, *The World of Rodin*, 50
228. Hale, *The World of Rodin*, 51
229. Hale, *The World of Rodin*, 71
230. Hale, *The World of Rodin*, 118
231. Hale, *The World of Rodin*, 122

232. Hale, *The World of Rodin,* 141
233. Hale, *The World of Rodin,* 145
234. Hale, *The World of Rodin,* 167
235. Hale, *The World of Rodin,* 167
236. Hale, *The World of Rodin,* 168
237. Hale, *The World of Rodin,* 172

# Chapter 16

**Special author note:** My main source for Churchill's biography of this chapter is Sebastian Haffner's *Churchill,* Haus Publishing Ltd., London, 2003. Other biographies on Churchill are: a) Stuart Ball's *Winston Churchill,* New York University Press, 2003, or b) James C. Humes's *Winston Churchill,* DK Publishing, 2003.

238. Sebastian Haffner, *Churchill* (London: Haus Publishing Ltd, 2003), 9.
239. Haffner, *Churchill,* 12
240. Haffner, *Churchill,* 13
241. Haffner, *Churchill,* 14
242. Haffner, *Churchill,* 14
243. Haffner, *Churchill,* 16
244. Haffner, *Churchill,* 16
245. Haffner, *Churchill,* 26
246. Haffner, *Churchill,* 27
247. Haffner, *Churchill,* 28
248. Haffner, *Churchill,* 35
249. Haffner, *Churchill,* 34
250. Haffner, *Churchill,* 48
251. Haffner, *Churchill,* 55
252. Haffner, *Churchill,* 57
253. Haffner, *Churchill,* 61
254. Haffner, *Churchill,* 63
255. Haffner, *Churchill,* 76
256. Haffner, *Churchill,* 91
257. Haffner, *Churchill,* 102
258. Haffner, *Churchill,* 134

# Chapter 17

**Special author note:** All the facts and details in Onassis's biography in this chapter derive from N. Fraser, P. Jacobson, M. Ottaway, L. Chester's *Aristotle Onassis,* Lippincott Co., New York, 1977.

259. Nicholas Fraser, Philip Jacobson, Mark Ottaway, and Lewis Chester, *Aristotle Onassis* (New York: Lippincott Co., 1977), 4.
260. Fraser, Jacobson, Ottaway, Chester, *Aristotle Onassis,* 8
261. Fraser, Jacobson, Ottaway, Chester, *Aristotle Onassis,* 16
262. Fraser, Jacobson, Ottaway, Chester, *Aristotle Onassis,* 16
263. Fraser, Jacobson, Ottaway, Chester, *Aristotle Onassis,* 23

264. Fraser, Jacobson, Ottaway, Chester, *Aristotle Onassis,* 41
265. Fraser, Jacobson, Ottaway, Chester, *Aristotle Onassis,* 62
266. Fraser, Jacobson, Ottaway, Chester, *Aristotle Onassis,* 103
267. Fraser, Jacobson, Ottaway, Chester, *Aristotle Onassis,* 110
268. Fraser, Jacobson, Ottaway, Chester, *Aristotle Onassis,* 112
269. Fraser, Jacobson, Ottaway, Chester, *Aristotle Onassis,* 156
270. Fraser, Jacobson, Ottaway, Chester, *Aristotle Onassis,* 183
271. Fraser, Jacobson, Ottaway, Chester, *Aristotle Onassis,* 357

# Chapter 18

**Special author note:** All the facts and details in Mandela's biography derive from Anthony Sampson's *Mandela*, Alfred A. Knopf, New York, September 1999.

272. Anthony Sampson, *Mandela* (New York: Alfred A. Knopf, 1999), 7.
273. Sampson, *Mandela,* 10
274. Sampson, *Mandela,* 29
275. Sampson, *Mandela,* 33
276. Sampson, *Mandela,* 74
277. Sampson, *Mandela,* 82
278. Sampson, *Mandela,* 112
279. Sampson, *Mandela,* 112
280. Sampson, *Mandela,* 170
281. Sampson, *Mandela,* 173
282. Sampson, *Mandela,* 178
283. Sampson, *Mandela,* 198
284. Sampson, *Mandela,* 246
285. Sampson, *Mandela,* 253
286. Sampson, *Mandela,* 339
287. Sampson, *Mandela,* 359
288. Sampson, *Mandela,* 378
289. Sampson, *Mandela,* 447
290. Sampson, *Mandela,* 488
291. Sampson, *Mandela,* 496
292. Sampson, *Mandela,* 541

# Chapter 19

**Special author note:** I have based all Callas' biography in this chapter on Anne Edwards's *Maria Callas,* St. Martin's Griffin, New York, 2003.

293. Anne Edward, *Maria Callas* (New York: St. Martin's Griffin, 2003), 25.
294. Edward, *Maria Callas,* 38
295. Edward, *Maria Callas,* 63
296. Edward, *Maria Callas,* 77
297. Edward, *Maria Callas,* 87
298. Edward, *Maria Callas,* 89
299. Edward, *Maria Callas,* 98
300. Edward, *Maria Callas,* 110
301. Edward, *Maria Callas,* 121

302. Edward, *Maria Callas,* 139
303. Edward, *Maria Callas,* 142
304. Edward, *Maria Callas,* 148
305. Edward, *Maria Callas,* 158
306. Edward, *Maria Callas,* 191
307. Edward, *Maria Callas,* 206
308. Edward, *Maria Callas,* 213
309. Edward, *Maria Callas,* 228
310. Edward, *Maria Callas,* 245
311. Edward, *Maria Callas,* 272
312. Edward, *Maria Callas,* 314
313. Edward, *Maria Callas,* 314
314. Edward, *Maria Callas,* 319

# Chapter 20

**Special author note:** I have based Bernhardt's biography of this chapter on Elizabeth Silverthorne's *Sarah Bernhardt,* Chelsea House, Philadelphia, 2004.

315. Elizabeth Silverthorn, *Sarah Bernhardt* (Philadelphia: Chelsea House, 2004), 24.
316. Silverthorn, *Sarah Bernhardt,* 30
317. Silverthorn, *Sarah Bernhardt,* 37
318. Silverthorn, *Sarah Bernhardt,* 37
319. Silverthorn, *Sarah Bernhardt,* 42
320. Silverthorn, *Sarah Bernhardt,* 42
321. Silverthorn, *Sarah Bernhardt,* 47
322. Silverthorn, *Sarah Bernhardt,* 49
323. Silverthorn, *Sarah Bernhardt,* 55
324. Silverthorn, *Sarah Bernhardt,* 68
325. Silverthorn, *Sarah Bernhardt,* 71
326. Silverthorn, *Sarah Bernhardt,* 82
327. Silverthorn, *Sarah Bernhardt,* 87
328. Silverthorn, *Sarah Bernhardt,* 96
329. Silverthorn, *Sarah Bernhardt,* 103
330. Silverthorn, *Sarah Bernhardt,* 116

# Chapter 21

**Special author note:** My source for Josephine's biography is Carolly Erickson's *Josephine,* St. Martin's Griffin, New York, 1998.

331. Carolly Erickson, *Josephine* (New York: St. Martin's Griffin, 1998), 11.
332. Erickson, *Josephine,* 74
333. Erickson, *Josephine,* 82
334. Erickson, *Josephine,* 96
335. Erickson, *Josephine,* 136-137
336. Erickson, *Josephine,* 147-148
337. Erickson, *Josephine,* 177
338. Erickson, *Josephine,* 196
339. Erickson, *Josephine,* 210

340. Erickson, *Josephine*, 230
341. Erickson, *Josephine*, 239
342. Erickson, *Josephine*, 281
343. Erickson, *Josephine*, 282
344. Erickson, *Josephine*, 282
345. Erickson, *Josephine*, 282
346. Erickson, *Josephine*, 283
347. Erickson, *Josephine*, 283
348. Erickson, *Josephine*, 287
349. Erickson, *Josephine*, 294
350. Erickson, *Josephine*, 295

# Chapter 22

**Special author note:** My source for all Henry VIII's biography in this chapter is Alison Weir's *Henry VIII, The King and His Court*, Balantine Books, New York, November 2002.

351. Alison Weir, *Henry VIII, The King and His Court* (New York: Balantine Books, 2002), 15.
352. Weir, *Henry VIII*, 85
353. Weir, *Henry VIII*, 161
354. Weir, *Henry VIII*, 202
355. Weir, *Henry VIII*, 247
356. Weir, *Henry VIII*, 242
357. Weir, *Henry VIII*, 271
358. Weir, *Henry VIII*, 281
359. Weir, *Henry VIII*, 326
360. Weir, *Henry VIII*, 331
361. Weir, *Henry VIII*, 332
362. Weir, *Henry VIII*, 361–362
363. Weir, *Henry VIII*, 368
364. Weir, *Henry VIII*, 372
365. Weir, *Henry VIII*, 372
366. Weir, *Henry VIII*, 36
367. Weir, *Henry VIII*, 385
368. Weir, *Henry VIII*, 385
369. Weir, *Henry VIII*, 385
370. Weir, *Henry VIII*, 419
371. Weir, *Henry VIII*, 422
372. Weir, *Henry VIII*, 427

# Chapter 23

**Special author note:** All facts and details for Carter's biography in this chapter derive from Kenneth E. Morris's *Jimmy Carter, American Moralist*, University of Georgia Press, Georgia, 1996.

373. Kenneth E. Morris, *Jimmy Carter, American Moralist* (Athens, Georgia: University of Georgia Press, 1996), 49.

374. Morris, *Jimmy Carter,* 50
375. Morris, *Jimmy Carter,* 68
376. Morris, *Jimmy Carter,* 103
377. Morris, *Jimmy Carter,* 106
378. Morris, *Jimmy Carter,* 115
379. Morris, *Jimmy Carter,* 123
380. Morris, *Jimmy Carter,* 157
381. Morris, *Jimmy Carter,* 199
382. Morris, *Jimmy Carter,* 276–277
383. Morris, *Jimmy Carter,* 288
384. Morris, *Jimmy Carter,* 293
385. Morris, *Jimmy Carter,* 305
386. Morris, *Jimmy Carter,* 305
387. Morris, *Jimmy Carter,* 305
388. Morris, *Jimmy Carter,* 289
389. Morris, *Jimmy Carter,* 294
390. Morris, *Jimmy Carter,* 294
391. Morris, *Jimmy Carter,* 308
392. Morris, *Jimmy Carter,* 319

# Chapter 24

**Special author note:** All the facts and details in Glenn's biography derive from his autobiography *A Memoir*, Bantam Books, New York, 1999.

393. John Glenn, *A Memoir* (New York: Bantam Books, 1999), 5.
394. Glenn, *A Memoir,* 5
395. Glenn, *A Memoir,* 17
396. Glenn, *A Memoir,* 27
397. Glenn, *A Memoir,* 50
398. Glenn, *A Memoir,* 333
399. Glenn, *A Memoir,* 342
400. Glenn, *A Memoir,* 351
401. Glenn, *A Memoir,* 356
402. Glenn, *A Memoir,* 356
403. Glenn, *A Memoir,* 356
404. Glenn, *A Memoir,* 356
405. Glenn, *A Memoir,* 359
406. Glenn, *A Memoir,* 360
407. Glenn, *A Memoir,* 360
408. Glenn, *A Memoir,* 363
409. Glenn, *A Memoir,* 363
410. Glenn, *A Memoir,* 379
411. Glenn, *A Memoir,* 385
412. Glenn, *A Memoir,* 388
413. Glenn, *A Memoir,* 391

# BIBLIOGRAPHY

Bradford, Sarah. *America's Queen, The Life of Jackie Kennedy Onassis*. New York: Penguin Books, 2001.

Branin, Larissa. *Liz, the Pictorial Biography of Elizabeth Taylor*. Philadelphia: Courage Books, 2000.

Doran, Susan. *Queen Elizabeth I*. New York: New York University Press, 2003.

Edwards, Anne. *Maria Callas*. New York: St. Martin's Griffin, 2003.

Erickson, Carolly. *Josephine*. New York: St. Martin's Griffin, 1998.

Fraser, N., P. Jacobson, M. Ottaway & L. Chester. *Aristotle Onassis*. New York: Lippincott Co., 1977.

Giardini, Cesare. *Columbus*. Athens, Greece: Fytrakis Publications, 1965.

Giardini, Cesare. *Hugo*. Athens, Greece: Fytrakis Publications, 1966.

Glenn, John. *A Memoir*. New York: Bantam Books, 1999.

Gorbachev, Mikhail. *Memoirs*. New York: Bantam Books, 1997.

Haffner, Sebastian. *Winston Churchill*. London: Haus Publishing Ltd, 2003.

Hale, William Harlan. *The World of Rodin*. Nederland: Time-Life International, 1976.

Hughes, Libby. *Madam Prime Minister*. Lincoln, NE: An Authors Guild Backinprint.com Edition, 2000.

Maurois, André. *Napoleon*. Athens, Greece: Classical Publications, 1966.

Morris, Kenneth. *Jimmy Carter, American Moralist*. Athens, Georgia: University of Georgia Press, 1996.

Pugneti, Gino. *Beethoven*. Athens, Greece: Fytrakis Publications, 1965.

Pugneti, Gino. *Verdi*. Athens, Greece: Fytrakis Publications, 1966.

Rivoire, Mario. *Napoleon*. Athens, Greece: Fytrakis Publications, 1965.

Sampson, Anthony. *Mandela*. New York: Alfred A. Knopf, 1999.

Silverthrone, Elizabeth. *Sarah Bernhardt*. Philadelphia: Chelsea House, 2004.

The Dalai Lama. *Freedom in Exile, the Autobiography of the Dalai Lama*. New York: Harper Perennial, 1990.

Weir, Alison. *Henry VIII, the King and His Court*. New York: Balantine Books, 2002.

Westenbaker, Leal. *The World of Picasso*. Nederland: Time-Life International, 1976.